Gorgeous *for* God

Gorgeous *for* God

Awakening through A Course in Miracles

Lisa Natoli

authorHOUSE®

AuthorHouse™
1663 Liberty Drive
Bloomington, IN 47403
www.authorhouse.com
Phone: 1-800-839-8640

© 2013 by Lisa Natoli. All rights reserved.

No part of this book may be reproduced, stored in a retrieval system, or transmitted by any means without the written permission of the author.

Published by AuthorHouse   03/15/2013

ISBN: 978-1-4817-1183-8 (sc)
ISBN: 978-1-4817-1182-1 (e)

Library of Congress Control Number: 2013901914

Any people depicted in stock imagery provided by Thinkstock are models, and such images are being used for illustrative purposes only.
Certain stock imagery © Thinkstock.

This book is printed on acid-free paper.

The views expressed in this work are solely those of the author and do not necessarily reflect the views of the publisher, and the publisher hereby disclaims any responsibility for them.

"As your awareness increases, you may well develop abilities that seem quite startling to you. Yet nothing you can do can compare even in the slightest with the glorious surprise of remembering Who you are. Let all your learning and all your efforts be directed toward this one great final surprise, and you will not be content to be delayed by the little ones that may come to you on the way."

—A Course in Miracles

Acknowledgments

A very big thank you to Shipley Allinson, the minister at Unity on the River in Amesbury, Massachusetts. You are the Presence of God. I feel like the universe was sending me a message THROUGH YOU that it was time to shift to a new level. You have encouraged me to be more daring, have a bigger vision and get active in service. You have challenged me ("This is not a country club! I am here to make you feel uncomfortable!") and gently pushed me right out of my comfort zone, all while doing it with grace and humor. I AM SO HAPPY AND GRATEFUL that you are in the world BEING Who You Came Here To Be: joyful, generous, funny, and a very powerful activator. You are a center of celebration and transformation!

Another big thanks to my sweetheart Bill Free, who inspires me every day. The Christ in me honors and recognizes the Christ in you. You are such a joy to be around. I love you. Namaste.

All my love and gratitude to Max & Leigha. You guys are the original house of fire!! Rock it out. Big kisses to my best girlfriend Marielle School. Many thanks to my mom Debbie Dougal, my dad Ron Natoli and my darling beautiful sisters Lori and Leslie.

And finally, to all my mighty companions, friends and playmates that have stood by me over the years cheering me on, encouraging me when I wanted to throw in the towel and quit. Thanks for believing in me when I didn't believe in myself. Thanks for seeing in me what I couldn't see in myself! Thank you for your strong support. We walk together, you and I, we found a single purpose that we share.

Foreword to the New Edition

I was introduced to A Course in Miracles in 1999. After quickly flipping through it, I was not interested—at all. It had that "God" word in it. A lot. My business partner (we own a gym) had started practicing the Course and had created a study group at the gym which met for an hour each Sunday morning. After hearing her talk about the Course and then watching her practice it, I became intrigued. I was on my own path of practicing Buddhism, but still experiencing much sadness and depression. I was also about to sell my part of the gym and go to school in Boulder, Colorado to study Structural Integration, and I was full of fear about the changes beginning to take place in my life. I did go to the group and I did begin to study A Course in Miracles but I did not complete the lessons until 2003 and then I did them again in 2006. At that point I believed that I had completed my studies with the Course and it was time to "get on with my life"—which brings me to 2011 and 2012.

After five years of "getting on with my life" MY way, I found that I and my life was a complete mess. I had become estranged from my entire family including a niece who was much like a daughter to me. My partner (we had met in the ACIM study group in 1999) with whom I believed I shared a holy relationship with was asking—no, demanding—that I move out of our home. Her entire family was supporting and encouraging her 100%. I never felt so alone and scared. I decided to dedicate one entire year with no distractions to A Course in Miracles—doing the lessons exactly as they are required. It was literally the only thing I had any faith in at all. Soon after I started this journey my partner asked that we stay together and both of us complete the Course as part of our journey as a couple in a holy relationship. I still believed that God had brought us together and we could turn it from special to holy with the help of the Holy Spirit.

I first heard of Lisa Natoli when my partner mentioned a book that she liked very much. She said that it really spoke to her in a way that other ACIM related books did not. She talked about it constantly and loved how down to earth and "real" it was. I asked her what the title was and she said, "Gorgeous for God." My first thought was, "That's a ridiculous title! It sounds like it's probably more about religion than the Course." She started to read some of the passages from the book to me and I liked what I heard. I especially liked the parts where Lisa talks about drinking alcohol and smoking while studying the Course (sounds familiar) and throwing the Course away multiple times in frustration. I could definitely get on board with that. At that time in my life, I much preferred the "My life is going to shit" stories than the "Everything is awesome" version that some spiritual books offer.

Right away I started to google *Gorgeous for God* and *Lisa Natoli*. I found out that she offered a 40-day Online Program. I signed us up! I thought it would make things so much easier as I was really struggling with the Course. Lisa made it clear it was going to require a commitment and that she was not going to do the work for us—we would have to do it. She said she only worked with people who said "Yes" to doing the work and being willing to change because she found through years of working with people that only the people who said "Yes" got results. We said Yes.

In the first email message, she said, "I'm not a counselor or a therapist or a self-help teacher. We are not going to talk about your problems and we are not going to fix your problems. I am going to help you see you have no problems. The #1 goal I have in mind for anyone who signs up for this program is to start relying on their own inner Guide for answers. I am a temporary guide (40-days) to show you how to start trusting in your own Guide who knows you inside & out and who is with you always. Your Guide knows everything about you: the greater Plan, the Big Picture and your part in it. So I teach God-dependency, not Lisa-dependency, not anything-outside-of-you dependency. You'll start to learn to trust God and your own guidance. Most people are not used to making time to listen to that still small Voice encouraging Voice within them. As you start to live in this way, you will know joy and peace."

My spirit wanted these promises to be true more than anything, but my ego was pissed, but I went forward with it anyways.

For 40 days, Lisa guided me with kindness and love through the secrets and darkness I harbored inside that had kept me paralyzed for years. Each step was difficult and challenging but transforming. Each step was a miracle.

After completing the 40-day Program, I found out she was offering a 5-Day Teachers of God retreat in Maine. I signed us up! I was excited because the retreat would coincide with my completing the 365 lessons in the Course. Everything was going well. I was excited thinking of the peaceful, relaxing week long holiday in Maine at a beautiful location right on the ocean—until I checked my email at a layover in an airport in Washington, DC. Lisa had emailed the group to let us all know about one final detail of the trip. We would all be sharing a bathroom and shower! That was all my ego needed. In my mind I imagined 20 people lined up in the hallway with a towel and a toothbrush waiting to get into one toilet and one shower. I felt the heat rising and a roar in my head—my mind was off and running. To add insult to injury, at the end of the message Lisa wrote, "I guess it will be like summer camp all over again, LOL." I was definitely not LOL! My first thought was, "OH HELL NO! I'm going home. I will turn right around in Portland, Maine and get on the next flight to Memphis, Tennessee."

I can't remember exactly what I wrote to Lisa, but I tried to appear calm. It was something along the lines of: Are there hotels nearby? Lisa answered quickly—yes, some lovely hotels right on the ocean. She even gave me a list! That response didn't go over well with me at all. I thought she would catch on to my anger and annoyance. So, I tried again. I wrote, "I'm not coming. I'm turning around and heading back home." Lisa ALWAYS responds quickly to emails. I waited and checked my email to see how she would respond to that. Nothing. I checked again and again and again. No response. I boarded my flight to Maine. In Portland I checked my email again at baggage claim. Nothing. I wanted her to talk me out of it—at least try and get me to stay. Nothing. Silence. I was stunned. Where was the cheerleader coach I had come to know? To add insult to injury, my partner had decided to stay. I was on my own and I was pissed! I watched as my partner drove off in the rental car. For the first time in the whole process of this journey I didn't know what to do. The best I could come up with is do nothing. I asked for guidance. I decided to sit on my luggage outside the airport until something happened—I didn't know what, but I decided to sit for the whole week if I had to. The weirdest thing happened. I became peaceful. The minute I decided to stop creating fear and just wait for guidance (no matter how long it took) things began to happen rapidly. After about an hour, my partner drove right up to me outside baggage claim as I sat on my luggage waiting. I got up, put my things in the car and away we drove—as if we had planned it this way all along. I had changed my mind. I had come to a state of readiness to accept a miracle.

This would not have happened without Lisa's guidance. From the beginning of the 40-day Program that I started with her she led me to trust my own inner Guide. She would respond to everything I threw at her with patience, love, kindness and compassion. I never felt judged. But when it was time for me to find the answer within myself, she stepped back and let that happen. No matter what I had decided to do that day, whether I had gone back home or not, I know that Lisa would have been there cheering me on—saying, "WOOOHOOO!! Good for you Donna! I LOVE YOU!"

Working with Lisa, reading everything she's written and being with her in person has been transformative because she simply stays true to her one calling and one purpose—to help every person she meets to know "You are love, you are perfect and all you need is within you, already perfect."

Her message is always the same—there's no journey, there's only an awakening.

In gratitude,

Donna Isaac
January 2013

Preface to the New Edition

A lot has changed since I published this book in 2007. I got divorced. I moved back to my home state of New Hampshire. I started eating meat again after being a strict (and very vocal!) vegetarian for 10 years. I was healed of my terrifying fear of money. I fell in love after swearing I'd never get into another relationship ever again. I paid off all my debt. This is all surface stuff. The most important change in the past five years is that I stopped seeking, stopped resisting and began to allow things to be exactly as they are without trying to change anything. It was like my eyes opened to what was always there, but I had been blind to it. Suddenly I saw how perfect life is, in all its ups and downs. Things change, but I don't! I remain forever the same: eternal and changeless as Spirit. There is constancy in the way I see life now. I see God in everyone and everything, even in chaos. After years of fluctuation between light and darkness, there came a moment when there was only light and I knew I was changed forever and there was no going back.

This book is the story of my own spiritual awakening. It is very ordinary. Things happened slowly for me—there were no bells or whistles. No going into the light. I didn't have a near-death experience. Instead, one by one, things that were no longer serving me dissolved and fell away—alcoholism, cigarette-smoking, fear, conflict, doubt. I found that as time went on, the ego-identity that I had built up over the years started to crumble, slowly, very slowly (at times painfully-slow!) and I found myself having almost no interest in the things I used be interested in.

This was a disorienting time for me—the old has fallen away and the new has not yet arrived—and I got through it because of the teachers in my life who told me to trust the empty space. I got through it because of the constant reminders that what I was experiencing—my life falling apart—was NORMAL.

So I share my story because of its simplicity and because it didn't progress in a straight line. My awakening didn't happen all at once.

It was messy and not at all graceful like some of the enlightenment stories I've heard. My moments of clarity didn't stick. The ego continued to lurk around. I thought I must be the slowest learner on the planet. I'm glad I kept going. I'm thankful for all teachers in my life who have shared their own stories which encouraged me to keep trusting when I thought I was failing horribly.

I have heard thousands of stories of people awakening and no two stories are alike. There is no formula. There is no one right path. The end result is that you remember what you are. Some awakenings are dramatic and some happen so slowly that the person doesn't realize their eyes are open until one day they "see" they are completely changed and they don't think the way they used to. Some people have spiritual awakening who weren't even looking for one and who don't believe in God, while others struggle and struggle for years on a spiritual path trying to reach enlightenment, reading every book and taking every workshop and nothing seems to happen. For other people, it's one step forward, and then two steps back—an experience of light, followed by darkness and disorientation and confusion.

What does it mean to awaken from the dream? In my own experience, it is A SHIFT IN PERCEPTION from fear to love. The fear-based self-constructed "I" (that worries, plans, plots, controls, lives in the past, lives in the future) dissolves and becomes the "I" that is Christ. This is the "I" that is used in the greeting "Namaste"—a salutation with hands pressed together as you greet another and bow slightly. It means: I bow to you. That "I" is the Divine in me, honoring and bowing to the Divine in you. The gesture represents that there is a Divine spark in each of us that is located at the heart chakra, and it is an acknowledgment of the soul in one to the soul in another: I bow to you. I honor you. I see you. I love you.

So to be "awake" means to live, move, think and see from the perspective of Spirit, or God or Christ or whatever name you want to call your inner true Self. It's like shifting gears and the false self (ego) dissolves and only I AM remains. So when you say "I", when you speak of yourself, that "I" is the Divine speaking and there is an awareness/acknowledgement that everything is part of you, one with you, Divine like you. There is no separation. You see the world and yourself entirely differently from before. People make a much bigger deal of it than it actually is, as if it's some kind of nirvana and the whole world disappears. This is true in a sense, your whole world WILL disappear, but not in the way you might think. You discover who you really are, and the world as you have made it based on separation ideas ceases to be! The best definition I know of enlightenment is from A Course in Miracles: "Enlightenment is but a recognition, not a change at all. Those who seek the light are merely covering their eyes. The light is in them now."

For me, enlightenment was when I stopped seeking for ways to improve myself. It was when I recognized that my old way of being was not working. I realized the necessity to see myself differently, as loved, loving and lovable, and not try to come up with a new improved identity. For most of my life (after the age of 6 or 7), everything I did was to avoid pain and please other people. I was caught up in striving, achieving, seeking—I was very goal oriented—and I rarely let myself just "be." I did not love myself, so I came up with tactics to try to get other people to love me. My life was driven almost entirely by fear. I was never good enough in my own mind, and one day, I realized: this is just frigging crazy! Am I going to keep living my life this way? That's enlightenment: the moment you snap to your senses and realize you've been sleeping. You've been working a job you hate or you've been staying in a relationship you know isn't working or you haven't been expressing what is true for you. You've been sludging along, going nowhere, and suddenly you realize it. That's enlightenment to me: a Whoa! Moment. On that day, you start making new choices, not because you're trying to get anywhere but because you want to live life authentically, in a way that brings you joy. Enlightenment showed me that it was time to start loving myself and loving my life because no one else was going to do it for me.

I think a lot of the difficulty people have with awakening is because of all the misconceptions of what they think it is, what it's supposed to look like. There is an idea that once you wake up, your life will be one big bliss party with no problems and everyone's happy, and that's the biggest lie that will keep you seeking the pot of gold at the end of the rainbow. As everyone finds out, it's not there. It's an illusion.

I realized: This is it. This moment, right here, today, is my life. This is what it looks like. This is it. That was a turn-around day for me—to see that wherever I am, in whatever conditions seem to be happening around me, wherever my feet are is where the pot of gold is. Not "out there" and not "later" but right here in this spot.

My flash of awareness, my big break-through moment, happened to me when I was running a Bed & Breakfast in Wisconsin and mowing the lawn on a huge John Deere tractor trying to cut the grass but mostly to get rid of the yellow dandelions. It took me a couple of hours, but I did it. I was proud of myself. An hour later I looked out the window and was shocked to see the whole lawn covered in dandelions!!!!

I went outside to get a closer look and that's when I discovered that a dandelion is not a flower, it's a root, a strong big root with many little buds. So when you chop off one of the yellow flowers, there are five more buds just waiting to sprout. The only way to get rid of a dandelion once and for all is to dig out the root. I realized: OH MY GOD, THIS IS THE SOLUTION TO PROBLEMS POPPING UP! You can't just fix one problem! By afternoon there will be five more problems. You must get out of the whole root, which A Course in Miracles says is my desire for conflict.

"Conflict is the root of all evil. Conflict is the inevitable result of self-deception, and self-deception is dishonesty."—A Course in Miracles

It was evident to me that my "root" was still firmly in place in me. I secretly liked conflict. I liked chopping off one problem and having three more unexpectedly pop up by evening. I wasn't really conscious of this at the time, but I know it was so. I still loved defending myself, still liked being the occasional victim, still enjoyed that I didn't have to take full responsibility for my life, and that I got to wait and procrastinate instead of fully living life on purpose for God.

Once I became aware of this, I made a decision: "I am done with conflict. I am going to be happy, no matter what." I felt powerful. I felt strong. Until that is, within a very short time of declaring this, my whole life fell apart. My marriage fell apart. My car died. My hearing aids broke. My computer broke, and both my cats—Sam and Enzo—went missing, never to return. At the time, I felt like: OH MY GOD. ARE YOU KIDDING ME? I cried for months in frustration. I mistakenly thought this journey was supposed to be smooth sailing once you dedicated your life to God, and boy was I wrong.

And then one day, in spring 2010, it struck me that I could, in fact, despite it all, be happy all the time. It occurred to me there is no "good" or "bad"—everything is just happening! I am Spirit! Things fall apart. Things break. Life is shifting all the time. People say and do all sorts of cruel things that make no sense—so what! Does that have to affect my happiness? No. Jesus said, "Forgive them Father for they know not what they do."

Who was I to try to get everything to go my way, according to my version of how I thought it should go?? It's not possible anyways, and a huge waste of time and energy. It dawned on me that I could "grow up" (stop being such a cry baby and put my toys away) and allow everything to be EXACTLY as it is, without me trying to fix, change, control or understand it. I could simply be the Awareness of all that is! I could be Christ witnessing events as Christ witnesses them! I could see life through the eyes of Spirit, allowing myself to be a clear channel through which God could live, move and have His Being! I thought: Now THAT would be a fun way to go through life! I suddenly could see all the possibilities for something new to occur. I could stop blaming other people for my lack of motivation. I could start participating and interacting in new ways. I could shine a light in the place I was standing in, instead of striving to find the light. Nothing external changed, but it was instant of recognition that showed me there is no good or bad, no right or wrong. I saw the complete unreality of this world, that what I think I see is simply my observation and perception of it. When I don't resist, that which I am looking at disappears. Judgment became utterly meaningless once I saw I was looking at my own thought projections.

From that moment on, I've wanted only to use my life to bless, heal and love.

This book describes my awakening, my observations and the things I learned.

You have the power to choose how you feel moment by moment. You begin to see how magnificent your life is, how beautiful, how simple and ordinary and lovely and how much there is to be grateful for.

You don't need to struggle. You don't have to listen to the doubting voice inside you anymore. There is an encouraging voice you will recognize if you are still and listen. Let that inner voice be your guide.

Gorgeous for God can provide the motivation, inspiration and support to help you recognize the light that you are and awaken from the dream, if that's what you want.

Nothing can stop you from finding lasting joy, except your own self-imposed imagined fear, which is a thin veil covering your eyes and blocking the magnificence and magnitude of Who you really are!

The veil has to be lifted and that's what this book is about—simple practical tools to help you see things differently and to remove the blocks and obstacles to the awareness of love's presence, which is your natural inheritance.

I hope you enjoy it.

I bless you. I love you. The Christ in me honors and recognizes the Christ in you.

Lisa Natoli
January 2013

Table of Contents

PREFACE .... **XXXI**
INTRODUCTION .... **XXXV**
Gorgeous Girl 1
ask & receive 9
gorgeous for God 14

New Beginning

PRACTICAL APPLICATION **21**
training your mind in a systematic way 21
recognizing your true identity......................................22
keep doing the lessons..24
set aside time for God 26
try, try again 28
no compromise 29
are you ready for a miracle?..30
admit utter defeat 32
push it..34
face your fears..37
be willing to look foolish 40
one sock method 41
know thyself 43

UNSOLVABLE PROBLEM..**46**
feeling the intensity & futility of separation...............46
complete dependence on God....................................47
something is fundamentally wrong here....................50
rise above the battleground...52
the world i see holds nothing that i want....................53

NEW BEGINNING **56**
every day is a new beginning.......................................56
clear a space 59
vigilance is required..60
let me forget the past today...63
let it change..66

TRANSFORMATION 68
new year's resolutions 68
if the house is on fire, get out 69
when it rains, it pours..71
the little garden 72
the test of truth..72
i need do nothing 75

HAPPINESS 79
happy, joyous, perfect & free...79
joy is my function 80
today we continue with the theme of happiness 87
learn to be a happy learner 90
ten ways to be happy 94
love is contagious 95

HEALING 98
healing is always certain 98
you are not a body 99
shifting your energy/changing your mind..........................101
your cells are being regenerated right now as you read this 105
stop analyzing your problems and be healed....................107

Responsibility

FORGIVENESS..115
what is forgiveness?...115
one good reason to forgive 115
forgiveness does make lovely, but it does not create........117
forgiveness vs. creation...119
great advice: forgive and forget 123

SICKNESS 126
are you sick?..126
the real cause of sickness. 128
sadness is a direct attack on God 130
how can you who are so holy suffer? 133
stem cells and you and dead fishes. 134

DEATH 137
  there is no death 137
  what is the resurrection? 139
  the day after resurrection 142

UNDOING OF FEAR 144
  look at your fears 144
  what frightens you? 147
  the correction of error 148
  conflict must be resolved 149
  the undoing of fear 151
  guaranteed way out of fear forever 154
  emerging from conflict 156

UNDOING OF EGO 160
  best advice ever 160

TAKING YOUR PLACE AS SAVIOR OF THE WORLD 161
  you are getting what you ask for 161
  waking from disaster 163
  how i woke from disaster 167
  there is no world or how i got sober 169
  be catapulted 175
  challenging the current thought system 175
  accepting the atonement 179
  the power of decision is my own 181
  no excuse, sir! 182
  the circle of atonement 184
  anger is never justified 187
  you shall know them by their actions 189

Commitment

GOD 193
  only God's opinion matters 193
  the day is accomplished in God 194
  my goal is God 196
  i give my life to God to guide 200

in God, all things are possible 203
to know your brother is to know God 204

TOTAL DEDICATION = TOTAL POWER **206**
the missing piece of the puzzle 206
the wish for constancy 208
be yourself 210

RELATIONSHIPS **213**
married by accident by the moonies 213
God is my one & only 219
commentary on the state of marriage/divorce 222
wanted: a holy relationship 225
walk away 230
do not tolerate nonsense 233
adamantine particles 236

MIRACLES **238**
every day should be devoted to miracles 238
ask & receive : what do you really want? 239
what would you do if you knew you couldn't fail? 240
step back and let Jesus lead the way 241

PRAYER **243**
how i learned to pray in Venezuela 243
prayer as a daily reminder that God is with me 244

Heaven On Earth

WHAT IS HEAVEN? **249**
the great adventure 249

TIME & SPACE **253**
life is a temporary assignment. 253
a hologram of light reflection 256
the world is redeemed through you 258

A CALL TO SERVICE 260
i am here only to be truly helpful. 260
you can be like God, starting now. 260
i choose the second place to gain the first place 262
Heaven is a decision 263
my happiness—my salvation—comes from me. 268

PEACE 271
is world peace possible? 271
Christmas : peace on earth, goodwill toward men 272
on listening, hearing and being a bombshell 274
express only truth 278

PERFECTION 280
be perfect 280
your determination to be holy 282
look only to what is the same 284
a contemporary Jesus 285
why i am vegetarian 287

GRACE & GRATITUDE 291
what is grace? 291
my way vs. God's way 291
thank God 293

PURPOSE 296
you are the light of the world 296
you are the savior of the world 299
what is charity? 302
what is your mission statement? 305
let me not forget my function 306
it's impossible to serve two masters 309
shine on, bright thing 310
our final happy game on earth 312

When we quit thinking primarily about ourselves and our own self-preservation, we undergo a truly heroic transformation of consciousness."

-Joseph Campbell

Dear Reader,

In November 2004, I created a blog called Gorgeous for God which is based on the teachings of Jesus from *A Course in Miracles*. I wrote every morning in the hope that by giving a little time each day to God, I would become more aware of my own self-imposed fears, limitations, and deepest desires and begin to witness what *A Course in Miracles* offers: an experience of living in a world where there is only love, all the time.

What happened was nothing short of a miracle: I became aware of my own perfection.

I began to realize there is another world all around us, just waiting to be recognized. Walking into Heaven, where miracles are our natural birthright, is as easy as walking from one room to another room. It's that simple since Heaven is right here, right now. All you need do is change your mind and this world of pain and suffering transforms into Heaven before your very eyes.

By watching my own thoughts, actions and reactions, I was able to choose a new way of thinking and behaving. With every passing day, I began to feel happier, energetic, joyful and more peaceful. My relationships became harmonious. Conflict disappeared. I began to think differently about myself and differently about others. Suddenly life was a grand adventure.

In the Teachers Manual of *A Course in Miracles* it says: *"The teachers of God are not perfect or they would not be here. Yet it is their function to become perfect and so they teach perfection over and over, in many, many ways until they have learned it. And then they are seen no more, although their thoughts remain a source of strength and truth forever."*

It says the way to "become perfect" is to "teach perfection over and over" until you learn it. Total perfection became my new goal. I wanted to be as God created me. So I kept a daily blog, charting my own transformation—the mood swings, the highs and the lows, the joy along with the futility, the wonder along with the doubt—as I traveled to the journey's destination which is to "know thyself."

What I know now is that there is no process at all. There is no journey. Only acceptance, recognition and awakening. There is only here & now. You don't need to understand how changing your mind will change the world. You don't need to know the way to Heaven. God knows the way. Most importantly, you don't need to believe in God at all! All you need is a little willingness that your life be radically different, starting today. The rest of the path will open up easily before you as you begin to practice giving, gratitude, and love.

The entire blog is over 2000 pages, which I thought might overwhelm you. So I have chosen the best blog entries based on reader comments and organized it in a form that I pray will be useful to you.

May this book spark a light in your own mind that will inspire you to go beyond all littleness to the magnitude and brilliance in which you were created.

You are the light of the world.

I love you.

Lisa

Preface

On Sunday, my cat Sam brought a bird into my room. The bird was unharmed and alive. Sam, happy as can be, carried him in and put him down on the bed beside me. Sam wanted to play. The bird was FREAKING OUT.

I admit, I was freaking out a little myself.

But then I calmed down and realized, "Okay, I have a situation here."

So I got Sam outside (who was immensely pleased with himself, CRAZY CAT) and then I left the door to the outside open so the bird could fly out. Simple, right?

Wrong.

The bird was so wound up in his own mind that he couldn't see the door was open. He kept crashing around the walls. He was flying around, terrified.

TRAPPED. A PRISONER. IN DANGER.

But the door was wide open and he was free to fly away any time he wanted!

I watched this scene in amazement, thinking: "WOW. THIS IS EXACTLY THE HUMAN CONDITION. We can't see that the door (to another possibility) is always open. We think we are trapped in our jobs, our relationships, our current way of thinking. Meanwhile the door is RIGHT THERE and WIDE OPEN."

The interesting thing for me to see is that the room was calm and quiet and peaceful. Nothing at all was happening. No television. No music. No noise. No cats. There was no threat to the bird. And yet the bird was so wound up in his own mind, that all he could do was crash into walls: blind, deaf, and dumb. He was harming himself. No one was doing anything to him, yet HE PERCEIVED A THREAT.

And yet, he was totally safe the entire time. I watched this scene with compassion. I wished only for that little bird's freedom and happiness.

It's like God with us.

God doesn't make bad things happen. He wills only for our freedom and happiness. Nothing at all is happening in the world. The world is doing nothing. People are doing nothing. We're the ones thrashing around and harming ourselves. The world is quiet and yet we are so wound up in our minds that we perceive a threat and create conflict for ourselves.

While all the time, the door is RIGHT THERE AND WIDE OPEN. You can fly out through it at any time.

Finally after much thrashing, the bird calmed down. He started to survey the surroundings. He took a little hop. Then he took another little hop.

I thought to myself, "Okay if he can just stay calm like this, he will be able to see the open door, and he will be able to HOP HOP HOP to the open door, and then fly out."

What a miracle!

It happened just like that, and the little bird HOPPED then FLEW to his freedom.

It is Lesson 182 from A Course in Miracles: "I will be still an instant and go home" and Lesson 155 "I will step back and let Him lead the way."

Be still. Step back.

You gotta calm down enough to be able to survey your surroundings. Truly. You'll never see the open door while your mind is in a panic.

Be still.

It's the only way. The miracle is happening all the time but you're so preoccupied with things like survival and safety, that you don't see the miracles that are all around you, each and every moment. You don't see the beauty & splendor. You don't see there is another way. You don't see the open door. You don't see the solution. You are too busy worrying about the house going into foreclosure or gas prices going up or trying to figure out how to make your partner love you forever and not leave you. Worrying about what other people think about you.

What if you just simply stopped all your planning and organizing?

What if you stopped all the frantic thrashing? Just for a moment? Stopped worrying, stopped trying to figure life out . . . simply stopped.

You don't even have to believe in God. Just stop.

Be still an instant.

Many people will argue, "But if I stop, my life will fall apart and the bills won't get paid and the house will go into foreclosure." Or they think, "If I stop being funny and cute and sweet, my partner will leave me and find someone else."

Now, think of the bird "trapped" in my room. Did any of his attempts help him? No. It just made the situation worse. Only when he STOPPED could he see the solution . . . A SOLUTION WHICH HAD BEEN THERE ALL ALONG!!

You can be still an instant. Your world won't fall apart. You'll simply see the open door and fly to your freedom. What a miracle.

Introduction

"I saw the angel in the marble and carved until I set him free."
—Michelangelo

You are whole and perfect as God created you. This is your true natural state, right now, today and always. This has never altered, although you have lost awareness of this simple fact. Whatever you think about yourself as a limited human being is false. I love how Michelangelo explained how he created the masterpiece "David" out of stone. He said the masterpiece already existed within the stone and his task was simply to carve away the excess stone to reveal what already existed within. So it is with each of us. The masterpiece exists within you, but you have lost awareness of your own perfection.

Transformation is an UNDOING. The journey is simply to allow the blocks, obstacles, old habits, and excess to be removed so that you become aware of the brilliant light that is within you. This book is about truth. It is about love. It is about God. It is about you.

In order to know God, you must have an experience. It does no good to play make-pretend. In order to know truth, you must witness it with your own eyes. YOU MUST LIVE IT. It's one thing to listen to my stories, it's a whole other ballgame to witness miracles in your own personal life. I want you to have your own experience, and so your willingness and participation is necessary.

Don't just read. I encourage you to begin using the ideas found in this book in your own daily life. Practice and apply.

In order to know happiness, you must become happy. In order to know peace, you must become peaceful. Have you ever noticed how you feel like you have reached nirvana when you are alone? You feel blissful when you are meditating or taking a bath or quietly reading a spiritual book. You feel like you have reached total enlightenment in the comfort of your own home and in your familiar surroundings, but the second you are with another person you feel instantly annoyed? This is the reason why you must begin practicing the ideas you read about or which come to you through meditation or inspiration. This is the reason why you must move beyond your familiar environment. You must include your brother. You must practice forgiveness. You must practice extending love. You must become the demonstration of the ideas you are reading/hearing about.

The journey to enlightenment requires your own active participation. Your understanding is not necessary, but you must LIVE truth to know it.

It's one thing to THINK you are a loving person but do you actually physically extend your hand to help your brother? You must live truth. Do you say to a stranger who is in distress, "Are you okay? Do you need some help?" It's one thing to say to yourself "I am the light of the world" while you are sitting in your living room visualizing a pure white light, it's quite another story to walk into a room and be the brightest happiest person in the place.

It's one thing to chant positive affirmations to yourself in your living room, it's quite another thing to forgive your enemy, love your neighbor and refrain from judgment.

This world is false perception. "You will be bound till all the world is seen by you as blessed, and everyone made free of your mistakes and honored as he is." —A Course in Miracles.

God did not create this meaningless world. I did. Will you forgive me? I thought I could be separate from God. It was a mistake. I am really sorry. Will you help me undo this mess I made called separation? Will you join with me in helping our brothers remember God, by being happy and joyful and healed and whole?

People around you will begin to remember their True Identity as they see your joy, your smiling face and hear your happy laughter. This is what it means to be the Savior of the world. This is what it means to usher in a new world. You become the living, breathing, walking, talking demonstration of the Love of God & Laws of Heaven on earth. As you change your mind, the world changes along with you. How simple! What a miracle!

The scientists have proven that there is no world. Everything is simply energy vibrating on different frequencies. The quantum world is one of endless possibilities. There is no such thing as solid bodies or solid matter. Things only appear solid YET there is no denying the chaos and destruction. We've become lazy and sloppy in our thinking. We are stuck in a groove, a pattern of behavior, that quite frankly—let's be honest here—just keeps getting worse and worse.

Change starts with the simple recognition that there is no solution here in the world. The government does not want peace. Real change comes from individuals who have the courage to rise out of their current condition and be the demonstration of a real solution that works.

What is the solution?

TOTAL GOD DEPENDENCY.

For me it has come about through the daily practice of lessons I have found in a book called *A Course in Miracles*. It does no good to repeat phrases like a parrot and hope that does the trick. You must become the ideas. You must live truth. You must practice. You could chant positive affirmations 1000 times a day, but here's a question for you: are you loving the stranger and forgiving your enemy? The path to perfection is uncompromising. It requires action of mind. I know a lot of people who say they love God, but then they turn around and gossip about their co-worker. That's a dead give away they don't know themselves, nor God, nor their brother. Once you know your true Identity, as the Savior of the world, you will love all things, without exception.

Where do you begin?

Right where you are. Open your eyes. Observe. Be honest. Have a little faith. Be willing to see things differently. Stop trying to make the world a nice place. It's not a nice place. We are not changing the world by trying to change external circumstances. That will never work because the world is simply a reflection of the thoughts you are holding in your mind about yourself. The only way to change the world is to change the way you think about yourself and other people. It is the only way.

I used to think: "The world is not that bad" and "There is a lot of beauty and good here" and "I see only love." That's just delusional thinking. This world is a mess.

AND YET . . . there are extraordinary individuals in the world who want to do good, who want to usher in dramatic change, but who have no idea where to begin. The problems of this world are completely overwhelming and impossible, but in God all things are certain.

Real change begins with me saying "ENOUGH IS ENOUGH." I cannot wait for someone else to take the first step. I must take the first step, with Jesus by my side.

It's time for me to put away my toys. Time to stop playing with fear and limitation. Time to stop gossiping, judging and complaining. It's time for new leadership. The time is now. I'M READY.

Are you ready? Have you had enough of the monotony and routine and chaos?

Are you ready to take your place among the saviors of the world?

People say they can't help themselves. People say they are trying to be good but then they say they can't help themselves from being bad—they label it addiction, instant gratification, pleasure, insanity, not thinking, the devil made me do it, and living in the moment.

I know a lot of people on spiritual paths who say they are still practicing, and doing the best they can. They say they want to be good but then they attack, gossip, defend and make excuses and say "I am only human."

What's the solution?

STOP BEING HUMAN.

Is this possible?

Yes, absolutely.

You can positively demonstrate perfection in a world where people say perfection is not attainable, or worse yet, that it is a lofty arrogant goal. Perfection is totally possible because it is the way you were created by God. Perfection is what you are, in truth, underneath all your false ideas, fears and limitations. Take away everything you learned in the world and you will find grace, innocence, beauty, strength and perfection.

There is no excuse for bad behavior and sloppy thinking.

Forget other people. Ask yourself if YOU are willing to be the light of the world, for the Love of God. You. Not someone else. You. It doesn't matter what anyone else does. What matters is what you do. This is how healing is accomplished.

Jesus said: Go and sin no more.

OBSERVE. What do you see? Conflict everywhere. Be honest.

There is conflict between people. Conflict between nations. Conflict between religions. Conflict between politicians, between scientists, between friends, husbands and wives. There is even conflict between spiritual communities who all believe in One God. Then there is the most puzzling conflict of all: the conflict within yourself. Something is seriously wrong here.

We, who are supposedly highly civilized, and with a great deal of knowledge and compassion and understanding and enlightenment have not been able to resolve the conflict in the world. Everyone talks about peace and yet, no one is seriously willing to drop their own particular beliefs, political opinions, theories, agendas, conclusions, pride, position or power.

Now, forget other people. Are YOU willing to demonstrate peace?

All it takes is one individual to light a bonfire.

Lately I've been OBSERVING what I see, just looking. I am observing myself. I am watching how I treat myself and other people. I am looking at my values, my way of thinking, my thoughts, and my actions. I am getting honest by taking off the rose-colored blinders.

What am I observing? That this world is a place of appalling violence. It's a slaughterhouse. Be honest. Humans have become more self-centered, more violent, more manipulative in order to get ahead, more mischievous, asserting their own independence to do what they want, driven by their own pleasure and needs, pursuing their own desires, their own agenda even if it means stomping on other people to get what they want. Everyone looks out for himself, living in the moment, thinking "What's in it for me?"

What a mess. I accept full responsibility. I have no illusions about it. The conflict is not out there, it's in me. I am both the problem and the solution.

Herein lies my salvation, along with the world's salvation. This is the new beginning. There is no separation. There is only One Mind which is God. I am connected to everyone and everything. I take full responsibility. Things don't change, I change. This is how healing is accomplished.

I dedicate my mind, my life, and this day to God. I am here only to be truly helpful. I dedicate this day to miracles. I make a promise to demonstrate God's Love on earth, today and every day.

Will you join with me?

I ask you to be courageous in your thinking. This world needs new leaders. It needs saviors. It needs light.

It needs a miracle.

It needs you.

Gorgeous Girl

I figured everyone talked to God.

All my life I knew there was a world beyond the one I could see with my eyes. I lived in a world of fantasy and had many conversations with my host of "imaginary" friends. I spent a lot of time alone and felt more comfortable in the presence of these invisible characters than I did with my friends and family.

As a child, I was happy and bright. I was always playing and always laughing. I was never sad. I never cried. I was happy all the time. I remember once overhearing my mother tell her friends, "I am worried about Lisa. She never cries." This was my first memory that being happy all the time was not normal.

My friend's parents were constantly commenting that I smiled and laughed all the time, as if happiness was a weird disease.

Around the 3rd grade, I started to go deaf. I could not hear much of what was being spoken around me. I could not hear bad things. Maybe I tuned them out consciously. I could not hear the cruel things children would say. I could not hear fighting. I could not hear chaos. I lived in my own happy bubble.

Because I couldn't hear, I used to sit at the front of the classroom in school. I loved learning. I loved reading. I loved homework. I got perfect grades. I was happy. But once, one of my closest friends told me that no one liked me. She told me that I might be smart with books but that I was actually really stupid. She said I didn't know anything. She said everyone was laughing at me. She said I was retarded about the things that really mattered: music, boys and sports.

Around this time, I started having experiences at night. I found that I had the ability to travel outside of my body. I used to travel down to the river and into the woods. It was always night time and I was never afraid.

About a year later, I moved to the downstairs bedroom where I began having strange experiences of being "trapped" in my body. I would expand out like a balloon, like elephantitis. My body began to grow like Alice in Wonderland and I would grow as large as the room and then be trapped by the four walls. Often I would stay in this enormous shape all night. I had lost my ability to travel outside of my body. One night my parents found me in my room, talking to my clock radio and ripping off my clothes. I wanted to know where the voices were coming from. Nothing made any sense to me during that time. I felt an intense need to know certain things. Where did I come from? Why am I here? What is Heaven? Why did grandpa die? Where did he go?

One morning I woke up and as I came up the stairs, I found my mother sitting on the couch, terrified. She asked me if I was feeling okay and I said "yes, fine." She asked me if I remembered anything from the previous night and I said "no." She said "you were doing some very strange things, and your father and I are very concerned."

This conversation marked a turning point for me. The voices in my head stopped. The imaginary friends stopped. God stopped. The behaviors and dreams at night came to an abrupt halt.

I became a normal little girl. I continued to get good grades. I was loved by the teachers, but not so well liked by the kids my own age. I felt like an outcast, half the time. All I wanted to do was read, read, read. I loved studying. I loved books. I loved writing in notebooks. I loved being alone. I loved doing cartwheels on the front lawn. I loved riding my bike and feeling completely free.

I wanted to be happy and childlike, but everyone was telling me to be serious and grow up. I was getting constant messages that I needed to change myself to be accepted.

In the 6th grade, I was ridiculed in front of an entire class because I didn't know what the "bases" were. Someone went to the chalkboard to explain. Everyone was making fun of me, asking me questions. Had I ever been kissed? Do I like boys? Why was I studying all the time? Little Miss-Know-It-All. Goody-Two Shoes. Brown-Noser. Teacher's Pet.

I made a conscious decision from that moment to be AVERAGE. I wanted to be liked. I wanted to be loved. I did not want people thinking I was a freak. I didn't want to be better than anyone else. Mostly I wanted to blend in and be invisible. Disappear. I wanted to be accepted, or simply left alone. I did not want to stand out in a bright light. I wanted to be bland gray, where no one paid attention to me.

So I let my grades slide. I played less outside and spent more time inside with other kids listening to loud music that I hated, when really I wanted to be home with a book. I went to sleep-over parties and make-out parties where I would sit in the corner, wishing I was home watching The Love Boat on television. It was like everyone was always waiting for something to happen. My happy world inside my own head was much more thrilling than the spin-the-bottle parties and loud music but I was too afraid of being ridiculed and singled out. It was easier to conform.

So I kept being average. Those middle school years were a nightmare for me.

In the 9th grade, a miracle occurred. A girl named Danna showed up from California. She was smart and beautiful, a shining bright star, and she did not care about blending in. She could not be average if she tried. She got perfect grades. She was creative, happy and always laughing. She wore clothes that were outlandish and bright. AND SHE HAD TONS OF FRIENDS. Everyone loved her. But what I noticed is that none of that mattered to her. She didn't care if anyone liked her. She was simply being herself. This is when the shift began to occur for me, back to my natural original happy state of BEING PERFECT AS GOD CREATED ME.

I started being myself—outgoing, funny, enthusiastic & smart—not caring about anyone's opinion and suddenly I was truly happy again.

Then I went to college in Vermont where the drinking age was still 18. I chose my college based on drinking laws. I got into a lot of trouble those years, searching desperately to have a meaningful experience. Life seemed pointless to me. I was studying so I could get a good job and make good money, so that I could keep working for the rest of my life, with two weeks vacation every year, until retirement, only to then get old and die? This was life? I knew something was fundamentally wrong with this picture.

I tried to look at things logically but nothing made any sense, and so I drank. I wanted to be loved and appreciated and liked but everything seemed transitory and fleeting. I wanted stability and purpose and I kept thinking maybe those things came with the adult job, which would come later after graduation. In the meantime, I stayed out all night drinking, dancing, and sleeping with strangers. I was a train wreck waiting to happen but I didn't know what else to do.

One day during the fall of 1988, I knew something had to change in me. I was a total mess. I was in a completely impossible situation and the only thing I could think of to do was to get on my knees and ask God for help. I needed a miracle and I knew that on my own I was incapable of effecting change. By January 1989 I was in Florida, in a whole new environment.

It was a fresh new start. I got accepted into a university in Boca Raton. I stopped drinking, stopped smoking and joined a gym. I lost weight. I reconnected with my family. I fell in love. I felt a new appreciation for myself. I studied hard and got good grades. I was counting my blessings every day and communicating with God again. I was happy.

But the difficulty, always, is maintaining a continuing relationship with something you cannot see with your eyes. I believed in God, but unfortunately, at that time in my life, I only turned to God when I needed help.

As soon as things started getting good, I would forget to pray. Before long, I was drinking again and smoking and screwing up all my relationships. I was continually worried, depressed and lonely. I'd have brief moments of happiness, followed by bitter disappointment.

Everything just seemed so confusing to me. I didn't know what I wanted in life. I couldn't tell heads from tails. I hurt people who loved me. I was terrified of stability. I didn't want to settle down. I wanted unpredictability. I wanted the bad boy. I screwed up a lot of really great relationships with genuinely good guys. If someone was treating me nicely, I'd inevitably do something to wreck it. I couldn't stand the idea of constant happiness. It all seemed so bland to me: the house, the kids, the American Dream.

I felt I was destined for some larger purpose, but I had no idea what that was or meant.

Then I met a someone new. We moved to Manhattan. I got a job in publishing. I started to feel like I could settle down. Things started to look up, right? Wrong. On the surface, everything appeared good. I was making money. I had an apartment. I had a boyfriend who loved me. It's what everyone wants, right? But something was fundamentally OFF. I couldn't place my finger on it. I thought I should be grateful but instead I was bored. On the surface, I was the picture of success: boyfriend, great job, money, apartment in upscale neighborhood, friends, movies, restaurants . . . but inside I felt like a fraud. I knew that my so-called "successful life" was a house of cards and that if I let down my guard for one second, the whole thing would crumble into a pile of dust.

I became vigilant to be the perfect girlfriend, the perfect employee, the perfect friend. I worked at creating a pretty image, never letting myself relax, not even for one second. I was exhausted trying to keep it all going. And then everything fell apart. My boyfriend left me. We lost the great apartment. I rented a crappy mice-infested apartment in a run-down neighborhood. In order to cope, I drank vodka-tonics every day convincing myself I was sophisticated. I took up smoking and pretended I was glamorous and chic. But the picture was not pretty: I was fat, bored, unhappy, and alcoholic.

Somewhere in this sordid mess I read Marianne Williamson's book *A Return to Love* and that led me to *A Course in Miracles*. I didn't understand a word it said, but deep within me I knew it was the answer to my prayers.

I wanted the message to be true. It said *"Miracles are your natural inheritance."* At first I got little glimpses—small miraculous happenings. I suddenly noticed I rarely got sick anymore. I started to wake up happy on some mornings. I felt hopeful. I came to know moments of total relaxation and peace, and that was the biggest miracle of all.

But I was still drinking every day, still groping around in the dark. It was like a giant rollercoaster. Up, then down. Happy, then sad. Sunshine, followed by darkness.

Then on July 4, 2000, I declared God as my new boss. I didn't even know what I was saying. I was simply frustrated and tired. I knew that if I could wish for anything, have anything, it would be to work for a guy like God. So I stood in my living room in Brooklyn and said: God, if you are there, I want to work for you.

Nothing happened.

I thought maybe I would still keep working in publishing and then devote my free time to God.

Six days later, on July 10, 2000, I, Lisa Natoli, the office darling, the superstar who had been working comfortably for 10 years and who could do no wrong, was fired. Oh boy. I couldn't believe it. I was so shocked by the event that I wasn't even upset. I was thrilled, in fact. God had hired me!

So I lost my job. I was working for God, winging it as I went along. I had no idea what I was doing. How do you work for someone you can't see? I was living off unemployment and doing a whole lot of nothing. I figured something incredible would happen: like angels would appear in the kitchen or a dramatic male Voice would instruct me what to do next. Six months passed. Nothing happened. The unemployment came to an end. I continued to drink every day while reading the Course, surrounded by candles and incense. I kept thinking something would arrive by e-mail or someone would call me. I was growing increasingly impatient with God. Where was He? Where were the miracles *A Course in Miracles* promised? Why was I still depressed? Why was I not having an experience? What was I doing wrong?

I told God to fuck off. I ripped up the Course. I told God that if he wanted me, he would have to come and get me. I was finished with waiting. I gave God a final "HA! HA!" because I figured he'd never find me as I only left my apartment for cigarettes, trips to the liquor store and my Wednesday night Course in Miracles group.

Three days later, a woman named Greta showed up in my life. From the minute she opened her mouth, I knew it was God coming to get me. I knew I would follow her wherever she went. She was joyful and certain and listening to her speak filled me with hope.

I followed her out of the room that evening asking for her e-mail, a phone number, some way I could contact her. She told me about an academy in Wisconsin for teachers of God. She said there was a "Master Teacher" who was dedicated to the certainty that there is no world and that I was invited to come for 30 days.

My immediate (silent) reaction was "no way." In that moment I forgot that I said I would do "anything" to know God and to know myself. Isn't it interesting how we make these huge declarations in a moment of desperation but then back down when we are called upon to act? We say we will give everything, forgive all situations, and love everyone until the moment comes when someone steals your coat, insults you, or asks you for $100 . . . and suddenly there are exceptions to the rule.

And so it was with me. I said I would do anything . . . anything that is except leave New York and move to Wisconsin!

And yet, there was something compelling about Greta. I didn't want to lose her. I e-mailed her daily. She spoke a whole new language as if she was from another world or a distant planet. Over the next several months, more teachers showed up in New York to teach about God, and finally there was word that Master Teacher was making an appearance.

My first encounter with him was in a hotel near 42nd Street where he was giving a talk. He seemed nice enough, like a kindly old man teaching *A Course in Miracles*. I liked what he was saying but I had no intention of giving up my life in New York to move to Wisconsin. That would be too weird for words.

Truth be told: everything was kind of freaking me out. I felt like I was losing a grip on my life, all spatial reference. Who were these people? I felt like I was getting sucked into something I wasn't entirely sure I wanted.

Two days later, on a NYC subway, my head split open and then I heard a loud noise that seemed very distinctly like my heart cracking. My whole body seemed to dissolve and I was sitting in light so bright that suddenly I was sobbing for no reason at all. I saw clearly the moment before conception when I came into this world. I flashed back to a promise I'd made to God that I would fulfill a function in this world to be the demonstration of His Love. I sobbed louder. People were staring. I didn't care. I was so happy. I was laughing and crying at the same time. In that moment I knew everything. It was a glimpse into eternity. It was a step into Heaven.

I knew right then and there my destiny was to be with the Master Teacher. I suddenly knew exactly who HE was and what I needed to do next. He was Jesus Himself. He was me. I saw with clarity in that brilliant single instant that everyone and everything (including the tiniest blade of grass) was me. It was the first time in my life that I had an actual experience of seeing there is nothing outside of me. All those years of "studying" *A Course in Miracles*, and suddenly here I was having an actual experience!

I packed my bags and moved to Wisconsin that very same week. It's unexplainable. There is no common sense in what I did. It defies logic. I look back now and I'm shocked at how swiftly I moved. I didn't even stop to weigh my options. I did not make a single plan for the future. I simply got on the first flight available knowing clear well that my life had just turned a corner.

I knew within an hour of arriving at Endeavor Academy that I would move there. It's not something that makes any logical sense, but it was as if mountains were moved and the sea parted for me. I was lifted and transported to a new bright place and time, where the scenery was entirely different. I got lucky, except that I know luck doesn't have anything to do with it. I asked for a total solution and it was given to me. I found the Master Teacher, along with 250 dedicated teachers of God *who come from all over the world*. Or maybe they found me. It doesn't matter. I'm just totally grateful. That's the important thing. I've moved beyond belief into KNOWING. I don't just "believe" in God anymore. I KNOW HIM. He goes with me wherever I go.

I'm not alone anymore. How awesome.

And neither are you.

ask & receive

This is an astonishing story that showed me to start trusting in the invisible realm. A story that demonstrates that you can ask God for things, and He will answer in physical form.

Here it is:

Years ago I was living in NYC and had a copy of *A Course in Miracles*. This was 1995. This was before Endeavor Academy. This was before I'd heard about the Master Teacher. I didn't know a single other soul who studied the Course, or who even KNEW of the Course for that matter. It was a hidden part of my life because I didn't want people thinking I was some kind of Jesus freak.

But I really wanted to meet other like-minded people who knew about the Course, and who could maybe (perhaps?) help me understand what it meant. I went online and found that there were many groups in Manhattan, but I made a few phone calls and found they were all in people's apartments. This was too strange beyond words for me.

I was no way going into a stranger's apartment in New York City. I had no friends to take with me for safety because *A Course in Miracles* was MY BIG SECRET. I imagined these people who studied the Course as metaphysical types, with candles and incense and crystals. For some reason, I imagined chimes and drums. I didn't want that at all. I wanted help but didn't want to end up in a room with a bunch of crazy people, holding hands and hugging and chanting.

I honestly didn't know what to expect. I didn't want any touchy-feely New Age group. I didn't want that at all. There is nothing worse to me than a group of people sitting around talking about their feelings. I also didn't want to get trapped or manipulated.

I simply wanted to understand what the message said, and to find some normal people who could help me.

So I prayed. I said, "God, I really want to find a group of people who know about *A Course in Miracles* and who can help me. But I don't dare go into a stranger's apartment. Can you help me?"

And that was my request, and then I forgot all about it.

Meanwhile, I was online dating, going out on blind dates with men I'd met through the internet. I laugh at the irony now that I thought it was too weird to go into a stranger's apartment, but not too weird to meet them for a meal! I had a date with a guy who I'd talked to on the phone several times and who seemed really nice. On the same night, I got invited to a party on the Upper West Side, which I declined because of my BIG BLIND DATE. The plan was to meet in Little Italy for an afternoon of fun, sampling all the different cafes, and then we would go out for dinner in the West Village. That was the plan.

Well, BIG BLIND DATE turned into BIG FAT BOMB. This guy was the biggest loser I'd ever met. Horrific. It was like out of a movie. He was divorced and still obsessed with his ex-wife. He was terrifically good looking, but arrogant like I'd never known arrogant before, and creepy. I managed to get through the afternoon, but by the time we got to dinner I'd had enough. He was anxious to get married and he thought I was suitable. He was setting down the terms of how I'd be as his wife, comparing me to his ex-wife at every opportunity. He made it clear he was not comfortable with me having male friends, gay friends or black friends. He continued to talk about his wife, all the while claiming he was over her. He was convinced she'd had an affair based on a Big-Slurpee cup he one day discovered in the passenger side of her car.

He said, "SHE HATES 7-11!!!! Obviously she is having an affair!!!!!"

He began stalking his own wife, listening in on her phone conversations, going through her store receipts. I was sitting across a table from psycho-guy. We had ordered our meal and it had not yet arrived and finally I had enough of the nonsense. I knew I could not sit through one more minute. I stood up and said: "You know what? You're the biggest asshole I've ever met. Goodbye."

And with that I high-heeled it out of the restaurant, which felt really liberating and good.

I wasn't planning on going to the party on the Upper West Side, because of my date, but now the evening was free and it was still early. I hopped on the subway and made my way uptown.

I walked in and was DELIGHTED to find one hundred gorgeous gay men, all being fantastically fabulous. I knew I could relax. It was exactly what I needed at that moment. I got a drink from the bar, snacked on some of the catered food. Gay men throw the best parties! I had a brief conversation with the caterers about the cookies which were ALMOST as good as the coffee cookies I used to eat in Portsmouth, New Hampshire, but I couldn't quite remember the name of the bakery. This detail is important to keep in mind for later.

I spotted a guy sitting by himself on the couch, reading a magazine, looking bored.

I sat next to him and asked him why he was sitting on a couch all by himself while there was a party going on around us.

HERE IS THE REST OF THE CONVERSATION:

Chris: Oh, I'm tired. I don't really want to be here.
Lisa: Can I join you?
Chris: Yea, sure.
Lisa: What are you reading?
C: It's an article on twins.
L: Really? I'm a twin! Her name is Lori.
C: I'm a twin too! She lives in New Hampshire
L: Really?? Oh my God. I'm from New Hampshire. Tilton.
C: I'm from Portsmouth!
L: I lived in Portsmouth! On State Street!
C: Oh my God! I lived on State Street!
L: What??? Where?
C: Above the aromatherapy shop.
L: WHAT? I lived above the aromatherapy shop!
C: Oh my God. With Ceres Bakery around the corner?? Wasn't that the BEST bakery ever??

L: I can't believe you just said that!! I was just over there talking to the caterers, telling them how great it was, but I couldn't remember the name! Yes. Ceres Bakery. I can't believe we lived in the same apartment building. I lived on the top floor.

C: I LIVED ON THE TOP FLOOR!! Oh my God. This is too weird. I lived in the apartment to the right, with all the round windows!

L: THAT WAS MY APARTMENT!! OH MY GOD! OH MY GOD! WE LIVED IN THE SAME APARTMENT!

At this point we were SO EXCITED, like little kids, that people were starting to crowd around to see what was all the commotion.

It turns out that Chris moved into my apartment in Portsmouth, NH when I moved to NYC. He was the next person to move in. I asked him if the stove was clean enough for him because the landlord would not give me back the deposit until it sparkled.

We continued our animated conversation and learned even more fascinating facts: that our birthdays were one month apart from each other and that we lived within three blocks of each other in Park Slope, Brooklyn.

So we took the subway back to Brooklyn that night, talking a mile a minute. We were definitely old friends and had a million things in common (meanwhile I'm thinking, "just my luck, he's gay! We'd be perfect for each other!")

So we got off at our subway stop and I invited him to coffee the next morning at my apartment. I had a beautiful backyard garden and I knew it would be the perfect setting for us to relax.

He walks in the next morning, spots my *Course in Miracles* book on the shelf, and says:

"YOU STUDY THE COURSE?? I STUDY THE COURSE!!"

Now, remember, I did not know of a single soul who'd even HEARD of the Course, let alone "studied" it.

He says: I know this great group that meets on Wednesday night. I'll take you there.

And that is how I found my first *Course in Miracles* teacher and I stayed with that group for three years. A total blessing.

Chris only came to the group that first night, to introduce me, and then he never came back again. We became friends that summer, meeting at my apartment as often as possible and then one day he said he had to go, he'd gotten a job as a flight attendant. He gave away all his belongings, invited everyone to come to his apartment and take whatever they wanted, for free.

And then he gave me his cell number and disappeared.

Literally! It was like God sent him in, specifically, for me and when his assignment was accomplished, he went back to the place where he came from.

You can truly ask for things, directly from God, and the request will be granted in a form you will always recognize. Believe me. It's true.

gorgeous for God

Last night I worked a wedding and at one of my tables was a young girl with anorexia. She was somewhere between the ages of 10-13. At first I thought she was much older by the way she was dressed, but she had a kid's meal ticket which made me look a second time at her. She did seem young but too old to eat a kid's meal (chicken fingers, macaroni & cheese, ketchup, brownie). She seemed like a little young sophisticate. Like a little Lindsay Lohan. I asked her if she wanted a kid's meal or a chicken meal. She said kids.

She didn't touch a single bite. She seemed happy and not focused on the plate of food in front of her. Being pretty and charming was her goal. It was like watching a young actress. As I was clearing the table, her mother asked me to leave the bread basket on the table and whispered into my ear "she doesn't eat" and then the father told the girl to eat a roll and she nibbled a baby bite and put the roll back on the plate, finished. That was her dinner.

That is her life.

This is the lives of millions of young girls who look to the media as their source of truth. They see that the "rich & famous" are all skin & bones, with perfect hair (extensions) and perfect faces (Botox, lip injections) and perfect bodies (liposuction, grueling workouts with personal trainers) and this becomes their goal.

This is the world's idea of perfect and beautiful.

Their Louis Vuitton handbags last longer than their relationships and marriages. There is no integrity or commitment. It has become glamorous to have a million dollar wedding and divorce a year later. It's become chic to wear a size 0.

It's shocking to see a body sucked of energy and life . . . a skeleton sitting in a pretty dress with painted red lips. She's somebody's baby. She's a little girl starving herself.

The whole human condition is completely screwed up. People sedating themselves. Starving themselves. Paying doctors to cut them with knives and suck out body fat. This world is a strange distorted place.

When I first started Gorgeous for God my idea was to "inspire and motivate individuals to be as God created them . . . Perfect." I knew my own life had been transformed by *A Course in Miracles* and I also knew that many people (myself included) were turned away by religion. I had an idea that people would return to God if He became contemporary and practical. Not something based on old outdated rules that old strict men had passed down for centuries.

What could be more exciting than knowing that you could change any aspect of your life simply by changing your mind?

When I returned to my own innocence, it was not just a nice idea in my head, it was a real experience. I would look in the mirror and be blown away by my reflection staring back at me. HOW and WHEN did I get so beautiful? How? When? My whole body was transformed. Literally and Physically.

I never thought I was pretty. Growing up I always compared myself to other people. I compared myself to models in magazines. I compared myself to people in movies and on television. I was never good enough. I was always too fat. I was constantly on a diet. I was always thinking "someday." But there was always someone better than me. "Someday" never seemed to arrive. I kept striving to make my body better.

"If only I was thin and beautiful" was the soundtrack playing in my brain.

If only I was thin and beautiful, I would get the love and attention I desire. If only I was thin and beautiful, people would pay attention to me and listen to what I have to say. If only. If only. If only.

But then I got thin and beautiful, and nothing changed. I didn't get the love I desired. I didn't get the attention I craved. I still felt lonely. I still felt afraid. I still felt worthless.

Around this time is when "Gorgeous for God" popped in my mind. I decided instead of trying to change my body (which I had been trying to do, unsuccessfully, for 30 years) I would simply be Gorgeous every day. I would focus on qualities like INNOCENCE, GRACE, BEAUTY, PATIENCE, HONESTY, GENEROSITY, JOY and HAPPINESS.

Gorgeous for God began, really, because I needed a constant reminder of my own function in the world. It began as 3-simple-words, a phrase in my mind, to help me remember my purpose on earth. I was constantly forgetting that I'm the light of the world. I was forever getting sidetracked, forgetting that I'm here to represent God.

I am here only to be truly helpful. I am here to represent Him who sent me.

I was constantly forgetting all the lessons. I would forget that I am Light, Mind and Spirit. I would value the world and give it meaning. I would judge, defend myself and be fearful. These moments of being a contained limited human being would often extend into days and weeks. This is the real reason I started Gorgeous for God . . . as a way for me TO REMEMBER and NOT FORGET. Every time I would begin to judge something, I would remember: Gorgeous for God.

Every time I would start to gossip, I would remember: Gorgeous for God.

Every time I wanted to hold onto a grievance, I would remember: Gorgeous for God.

Every time I would begin to defend myself, I would remember: Gorgeous for God.

Every sigh and frown was replaced by my own self-imposed constant reminder: Gorgeous for God.

I couldn't get away from it. Every day GORGEOUS FOR GOD was staring me in the face. I definitely didn't feel Gorgeous in the beginning but HERE is a proven method that works: "FAKE IT TILL YOU MAKE IT."

Act gorgeous and you will become gorgeous. Act perfect and you will become perfect. It's no coincidence that things began to change for me. I actually started to look better. I began to feel better. I could feel life creeping back into my body. THE LIGHT DOES THE WORK. It makes you look good.

How do we begin to change the world standard? I have no idea. I suppose it would start with a few good role models. People who would say, "I'm going to be myself" and let this be enough.

It starts with me. To demonstrate that I am good enough. Not later, but now. I am whole and perfect as God created me. There is nothing physical that needs changing or improving.

There is only your own recognition of what is already true. You are perfect.

New Beginning

Practical Application

"You may complain that this course is not sufficiently specific for you to understand and use. Yet perhaps you have not done what it specifically advocates. This is not a course in the play of ideas, but in their practical application."
—A Course in Miracles

training your mind in a systematic way

The number one question that seems to arise among students and teachers of *A Course in Miracles* is "How do I 'DO' the course?"

People say "I don't understand this" and "it's not working" and "miracles are not happening" and "this doesn't make any sense" and the worst of them all: "I already know this."

The answer to seeing miracles every day is practice and repetition.

PRACTICE. PRACTICE. PRACTICE.

REPEAT. REPEAT. REPEAT.

A good analogy would be like reading an exercise book and expecting to see results without actually exercising. Action is required. You will not see results by simply reading an exercise book. You must begin to stretch your muscles.

And so it is with *A Course in Miracles*. You must begin to stretch your mind. You are asked to apply the lessons and not make any exceptions. Jesus asks you to love, give and forgive. He asks you to lay aside your judgments, your grievances, your conflict, and be happy.

"You are merely asked to apply the ideas as you are directed to do. You are not asked to judge them at all. You are asked only to use

them. It is their use that will give them meaning to you, and will show you that they are true."

The easiest/fastest way to see results is to do the Workbook lessons every day and to follow the instructions exactly. These instructions can be found in the Introduction to the Workbook.

A Course in Miracles is a systematic way to train your mind to a new way to think about yourself and everyone and everything in the world. The training period is 365 days. The workbook lessons give very specific instructions to follow. It's a simple program and it works, if you simply do what it says.

It asks that you practice the lessons "with great specificity" and to "be sure that you do not decide for yourself that there are some people, situations or things to which the ideas are inapplicable."

Do one lesson at a time, one day at a time, for one whole year. Don't skip a lesson. Don't stay on one lesson for two days at a time. Don't miss a day. Don't try to understand the lessons: just do them. It will take you 365 days to finish the Workbook and you will be amazed by your own transformation.

Good advice is to be a beginner every day. Just read the lesson, and do what it says. Do not make exceptions.

And that's it. An untrained mind can accomplish nothing. A trained mind can accomplish anything. PRACTICE, REPEAT, and APPLY.

recognizing your true identity

Jesus is a man who came to know his true Identity in God. He is no different than you or me, except that he is uncompromising and makes no exceptions. He is the perfect demonstration of what each of us are meant to become. He wanted only love and so he gave only love. He forgave his enemies. He loved his neighbors. He loved God.

In the bible (in Matthew 22) one of the Pharisees, a lawyer, asks Jesus, "Master, which is the great commandment in the law?

Jesus said unto him, "Thou shall love the Lord thy God with all thy heart, and with all thy soul, and with all thy mind. This is the first and great commandment. And the second is like unto it, Thou shall love thy neighbor as thyself. On these two commandments hang all the law and the prophets."

That's it! How simple!

1. LOVE GOD!
2. LOVE EACH OTHER!

That's it. Love God. Love your brother. How simple!

I made some bookmarks years ago that summarize the practical application of Jesus' message, as a simple reminder for myself. Apparently "LOVE GOD! LOVE ONE ANOTHER!" was too complicated for me to remember. I needed further instruction that I could carry around in my purse as a constant reminder.

Here are the instructions:

I will love.
I will give.
I will comfort.
I will guide.
I will be truly helpful.
I will be joyful.
I will be happy.
I will trust.
I will be honest.
I will be defenseless.
I will be gentle.
I will have patience.
I will be generous.

I will not attack.
I will not defend myself.
I will not judge.
I will not worry.
I will not doubt.
I will not be afraid.
I will not criticize.
I will not correct others.
I will not participate in conflict.
I will not be sad.
I will not sacrifice.
I will not feel guilty.
I will not hold a grievance.
I will not hurt myself or others.

It's straight out of Sermon on the Mount, and if you follow these instructions, your life will be one big miracle. If you have never read Sermon on the Mount, I highly suggest it. It's in Matthew in the bible (Matthew 5-7). Jesus is speaking to you directly when he says, "Let your light so shine before men, that they may see your good works, and glorify your Father which is in Heaven."

keep doing the lessons

There is a quote from Song of Solomon in the bible that I have on my mirror in the bathroom. It says: "You are altogether beautiful, my love, there is no flaw in you."

I see it every morning. When I first posted it on my mirror, nothing could have been further from the truth. I cringed when I read it. I did not believe it at all. It was completely UNTRUE. I was not altogether beautiful. I was downright ugly. I was full of flaws, fat and filled with guilt.

But I read the quote every single day. I opened my mind up to the possibility of seeing myself in a new way. This went on for months, until one day I realized that someone altogether stunning was looking back at me in the mirror. Someone altogether beautiful. It was me. It's an extraordinary moment. I realized that I was getting younger looking, not getting older. Then suddenly I couldn't remember the last time I was sick. I realized I had the energy of a child.

I'd transformed into something altogether beautiful.

There really is value in training your mind in a systematic way. There are tangible physical results. I'd always read stories of other people's enlightenment, but I never imagined it would happen to me. I never really thought I was worthy of a miracle. But I kept saying the lessons every day, reminding myself of ancient new ideas. I am as God created me. My holiness envelops everything I see. I have a function God would have me fulfill. I am altogether beautiful. There is no flaw in me. I am entitled to miracles.

I kept doing the lessons.

I kept doing the lessons.

I kept doing the lessons.

It's like training in a gym to get in shape—it takes time to see results. The "experts" say it takes at least 3 weeks to set a new habit. We are so STUCK in our old ways that it takes time & practice to break out of the mold. You have to keep at it, every day, never ceasing.

I kept doing the lessons.

I kept doing the lessons. I kept doing the lessons.

Then one day—without any fanfare or celebration or fireworks going off—I could see clearly. It was a quiet awakening. One day I was in the dark and the next day I was in the light. It wasn't like going through a tunnel. I didn't have a death experience. It was more like waking up in my bed in the morning—one minute I was sound asleep and the next minute I was wide awake.

A Course in Miracles is true. There is only love. God is real.

This program works IF you work it. All problems are solved. All darkness disappears. Keep doing the lessons.

set aside time for God

There is something very important in Lesson 65 in the workbook of *A Course in Miracles*, in case you missed it:

Try, if possible, to undertake the daily extended practice periods at approximately the same time each day. Try, also, to determine this time in advance, and then adhere to it as closely as possible. The purpose of this is to arrange your day so that you have set apart the time for God, as well as for all the trivial purposes and goals you will pursue. This is part of the long-range disciplinary training your mind needs, so that the Holy Spirit can use it consistently for the purpose He shares with you.

This is one of the most important things in *A Course in Miracles*:

SET ASIDE TIME FOR God.

A lot of people think the miracle of communicating with God will just happen to them "miraculously" but it doesn't work that way: YOU need to make the time and the effort.

Your active participation is necessary.

It is exactly like communicating with your mother or wife or husband or friend. It happens because you make it happen. You may have good intentions, but good intentions are not enough. You must make the time and the effort. Even if your husband/wife/friend/mother come to you first—it makes no difference if your attention and focus are elsewhere. So it is with God. He is attempting to speak to you all day long. But are you listening? Are you focusing? Are you paying attention? Are you being quiet and putting your other tasks aside so that you can hear?

This is why deciding in advance that some time for God is so important.

It says the purpose of this is to arrange your day so that you have:

1. Set apart time for God
2. as well as for all the trivial purposes and goals you will pursue.

I love the early morning hours as my quiet time for prayer and communication with God. I also make sure I have quiet time at the end of the day before I go to bed.

All you have to do is:

1. READ THE LESSON
2. DO WHAT IT SAYS

It's so simple. All your problems will be solved. You will have an experience that transcends this world. You will be told exactly what to do with situations concerning money, health, and relationships. This course is not ethereal or magical or make-pretend. IT IS PRACTICAL.

Prayer solves all problems.

We are learning to communicate with God. We are learning to "see" what the body's eyes will never see, but what is truly there. We are entering into the invisible realm where all things are possible.

All you are asked to do is SET ASIDE SOME TIME FOR God each day.

How simple!

try, try again

The only thing to do is stay on the mark. And when you fall off the mark, get back on it as quickly as you can.

Today is all there is. Whatever mistakes you made yesterday can be corrected right now. Let the past go. Start again.

Whatever is behind you . . . is behind you. What good ever came from thinking about mistakes in the past? What can this possibly accomplish? Today is a new day. Let the past go. Just get back on the mark, now, today.

If you said something hurtful yesterday, use TODAY to offer forgiveness. If your acts were less than Godly yesterday, remember that NOW is a new opportunity. Why spend even a moment feeling bad about what is over and gone?

Today is a new beginning.

So you fall off a horse. So what.

So you make a mistake. So what.

Do you stay on the ground or do you get up? Do you live in the mistake or do you live in the solution? THIS IS A COURSE IN MIND-TRAINING. We are training our minds—in a systematic way—to a new way of thinking. We continually and constantly clean the slate so God can be remembered.

WHAT DO YOU WANT?

Keep this clear in your mind. WHAT DO I WANT? When you forget, remember the question again. WHAT DO I WANT? What is the goal?

Then do what needs to be done . . . today.

no compromise

This is the year of NO COMPROMISE. To do what *A Course in Miracles* asks, exactly. No compromise. No exceptions.

Jesus says:

Be happy. Be a bright light

He says:

If your brother asks you for something, do it.

If someone asks you to walk with them a mile, walk with them two miles.

If someone asks for your coat, give them your cloak also.

What does this mean? It means GIVE TWICE AS MUCH and GO TWICE AS FAR.

Be like Jesus. Be like God. Demonstrate the Laws of Heaven on earth. This year be what you truly are: THE HOLY SON OF GOD HIMSELF.

You are not a body. All attempts to prove you are a body will fail. You are mind, spirit, whole and perfect, unchangeable, and eternal.

Why not start today? What else have you got on your agenda? What have you got to lose? Let the past go. The slate is clean. You can forget everything that came before this day starting NOW. Hit the delete button and let the old story go. It's dust now. From this moment on, you can allow everything to be revealed to you. You can let go of all your judgments. All your plans. All your excuses.

You can declare NOW as the time when you will be totally responsible for the salvation of this world. No more blaming your brother for your problems. No more complaining about circumstances. No more gossiping. No more judgment. This is practical advice that works. Do these things and you will never have another problem ever again.

Be wrong about everything and you will be happy!

are you ready for a miracle?

Do you need a miracle? Do you ever wonder if constant happiness is possible? Would you like to be healed of sickness? Would you like the gift of freedom and peace? How would it feel to be innocent and perfect? Is there something you wish for? Something you want? Something you need?

There comes a time after what seems conceptual when the teaching is brought back to a practical/personal level. This is not a course in intellectual discussion. It's not a course in philosophical ideas. It is *A Course in Miracles*. It is for you. It meets you where you are. Nothing is left out. Nothing is required. You don't even need faith. You don't even need to believe in God.

Your understanding is not necessary. You don't need to know a single thing about religion. You don't need to know a single thing about Jesus. This is about EXPERIENCE: about coming to know Heaven, about coming to know God . . . about coming to know yourself.

I think sometimes, in the teaching—in the transformation—people start to become "spiritual" and "holy" based on ideas of how they think one is supposed to act. OR they hide/stand-on-the-sidelines watching someone else have an experience. OR they start imitating those who inspire them.

But at every level of the journey, you are asked to let go of every single idea—which can seem difficult when you think you know something, or have the solution. You are asked to "not know", and then something new can happen.

Every single instant is over the moment it occurs.

It just changed again.
It just changed again.
It just changed again.
It just changed again.
It just changed again.
It just changed again.
It just changed again.

BREATHE.

Everything is changing so fast. It's changing all the time. Do you have any idea how many new moments are in a day? How many bright opportunities are presented for you?

You bring it right back to the basics, which is *"I don't know what anything is for."*

You can stop sequencing time—RIGHT NOW, RIGHT THIS MINUTE—as you make a decision for peace.

The past is gone. All your failures and failed attempts are in the past. All your misery and loneliness are past. All your sickness is past. All your limitation is past. All your learning is past. Over and gone.

In a new moment, you are born again. Brand new.

You come to a place that is clean of your old ideas. A place of total openness. A place of total willingness. With an open heart and mind.

THE LAND OF NEW POSSIBILITY.

THE LAND OF ANTICIPATION & EXPECTATION.

THE WORLD BEYOND THE WORLD.

You become child-like.

You get all wide-eyed and excited, like a kid in a candy store. You ask for what you want and receive it. You know Santa is coming with a bag full of toys for you.

This is what it means to be in the practice of *A Course in Miracles*.

There's nothing to learn. We are simply remembering our true natural state. It will give you a tremendous amount of energy. It will restore you to a youthful state. Don't be surprised if suddenly you want to race around the front lawn like a 5-year old. This is what a miracle will do for you. It will give you everything.

If you want something, ask for it. You need to have an EXPERIENCE of the power of God within you. What do you want?

This is the moment. Don't be afraid.

Ask.

Jesus says in *A Course in Miracles*, "You don't ask for too much, you ask for far too little."

admit utter defeat

How's it going for you?

Are you happy all the time? Is your health in perfect condition? Are your relationships in harmony? Are you peaceful? Is life an adventure?

Maybe you say you don't want to be happy all the time, and believe a little sadness and conflict is a good thing? Maybe that makes the day a little more exciting? I really don't know what goes on in anyone else's mind. Sometimes I have flashbacks to how it used to be for me—how lonely I was, how much I wanted something to change—but I simply didn't know how to reach out to anyone and ask for help. I didn't know how to make anything radically different in my life. I would tinker with my daily routine and change things a little—you know, I would take a different subway home. I would meet new people and do new things, I would take trips to Vermont and California, I would buy new clothes and change my "look" but ultimately I was still the same. I went as far as to move to a totally different location (New York to Cape Cod) but I quickly found out that changing the external picture changes nothing.

But this STILL didn't stop me from thinking a change of scenery could change my life. I moved back to New York and got a better higher paying job. But things remained the same. It might be hard to believe, but it's true. I still got up in the morning. Still made the coffee. Still took the subway to work. Sure the route was different and the office was different and the people I worked with were different BUT "I" WAS STILL THE SAME.

It was an extremely frustrating time for me.

In me was a memory that life was meant to be joyous and thrilling. Somewhere in me . . . I KNEW that my isolation was of my own making. But I couldn't get out of it.

I tried online dating. I took classes. I read books. I listened to tapes. I accepted invitations from friends. I traveled. I knew something was missing. I met people, and life was still the same. I didn't have the TOOLS for transformation. I kept waiting for something (anything) to happen.

What finally happened? I prayed. It's really that simple. I prayed.

One day I realized I'd tried everything and I gave up. I admitted utter and absolute defeat. It was a devastating moment for me. I cried like a baby. I felt like a complete failure. I felt more alone than ever before in my life. I was powerless. But there I stood—at the point of total desperation, having tried everything and seeing the results were the same . . . and I prayed.

I cried and I prayed. I prayed that things be different for me. I prayed that love come into my life. I prayed for peace of mind. I didn't even believe in God, but apparently that didn't matter or affect the power or prayer because almost immediately my life started to shift.

I saw how much I was responsible for my own state of mind—whether it be depressed or happy. I began to see that in every situation there was another way of looking at things.

And some incredible teachers began appearing in my life and months went by with me standing on the sidelines, as a spectator, listening to them talk about their own experience. They kept trying to encourage me to be more fully active, to participate in my own awakening but in the beginning I was content to listen to their stories and live vicariously through them.

My greatest gift was the transition from sitting on the bench as a spectator to actually playing the game on the field. I needed someone to nudge me off the sideline and hold my hand for a while. I needed a guide to teach me the rules of the game and stand beside me and cheer me on.

push it

I was thinking about Jesus the other day and how he didn't just walk around all smiles and flowers and sunshine. He didn't walk around healing people like he was a magician with a magic wand. He wasn't just this nice happy person. He was the savior. He confronted, challenged and inspired people. He did it with love, but he still pushed people past their comfort zone. He pissed off a lot of people.

He didn't just walk around saying everything is great, everything is good, everything is perfect.

He knew that there was work to do.

I was thinking about great coaches. They go in and push their athletes to be the best. They don't walk in and say, everything is perfect. They know there is work to be done. Great coaches don't accept laziness. They don't accept excuses. A great coach pushes until there is blood, sweat and tears. They push an athlete past the point of pain and physical exhaustion. They push until it hurts. But not because they are being mean. There is a difference between being a bully and being someone who inspires people to greatness.

A great coach knows that beneath a person's excuses and laziness is a strength they don't know exists. A great coach sees potential. He knows that underneath the surface are abilities that can only be brought out by pushing past a certain point.

If you have ever run before, you will know that at the point you start to sweat, something new happens. It actually gets easier. You start to feel stronger. You will never know about this while you are walking or taking a stroll. You will never know how much love is in your heart while you are still attacking your brother, just a little. You must push past a certain point (past the point where you want to give up, past the point where it hurts) and then you find a strength that you didn't know existed.

A great coach doesn't "talk" an ability out of an athlete. They don't sit around having tea, discussing potential. A great coach challenges individuals to go the distance, and not stop halfway. The best athletes are those who have learned to listen and to trust that the coach knows best.

This is Jesus. He confronts, challenges, and inspires. He needs you to trust in his instruction and to do what he says. He knows best.

He doesn't say everything is fine. He says go and sin no more. He tips over the money tables. He says put down your sword. He says forgive your enemy. He says pick up your bed and walk. He says love your neighbor, yourself and God.

He doesn't do the work. You notice? He makes YOU do the work. A great coach does not run laps. He makes others run laps. This is Jesus. He doesn't wrestle the sword from you. He says, if you want to be on my team, there are a few rules. Rule #1: No swords. Rule #2: You have to love yourself and your neighbor. Rule #3: Trust what I say and do it. Rule #4: I'm in charge around here.

Jesus is the greatest coach of all time. He stays with you, guiding you, shining a light, inspiring you, until you are able to heal the sick and raise the dead with no effort at all.

Sometimes (often?) you will feel like you want to give up. Any athlete in training knows how this feels. You think your body won't hold up for even one more minute. You just want to lie on the grass and cry. You want to sleep. You want to quit. Ask any athlete, and they will tell you the road to greatness had many bad days. They will tell you about doubt and pain, and total anger at their coach.

Many coaches are hated, until the athlete recognizes his own inner power, and then the coach is loved and respected. Finally the athlete sees that the coach had his best interest in mind the entire time. It's impossible to see this when a coach is screaming for you to get up when you want to quit.

Most people give up at this point, but if you're smart, you'll realize this kind of instruction is the best gift you will ever receive.

Sometimes the people you hate the most are the ones who bring out the best in you in the end. You should be thanking the ones that challenge you, and who don't accept mediocrity from you. You should be glad to have a few people who tell you to get off your ass and stop being lazy and depressed.

You gotta push though the DISCOMFORT zone. First you have to break out of the comfort zone, then you have to push through the discomfort zone. Keep going. Push it. Push it real good. Don't give up when you feel like a total failure. Don't stop when it looks like nothing is happening. You are in training.

Keep going. You look good.

face your fears

"Do on*e thing every day that scares you."*
—Eleanor Roosevelt

I totally love this quote. It's on a magnet on my refrigerator, and reminds me every day to do one thing that scares me. I love Eleanor Roosevelt. She also said *"You must do the thing you think you cannot do."*

These kinds of words inspire me like no other.

My whole life I've been jumping off bridges and going where no one else dared to go. I've always been spontaneous and reckless. I was the girl who would start the evening in Vermont and wake up in Montreal with no recollection of how I got from Point A to Point B. Of course, back then, I was always drunk. I went where the wind took me. Once I said "the worst thing that could happen is I could get killed and that seems a small price for the fun I'm having." I was young and stupid. When I sobered up, I became more contained and cautious. I began to think about actions and consequences, cause and effect.

Where I finally found freedom is in my total acceptance to make as many mistakes as possible. I learned this in New York in publishing, from my mentor and publisher Rodney Friedman. He is a great man. He taught me to never follow the crowd. Always blaze a path for others to follow. He made hundreds of mistakes, but as a result he had a thousand successes, and was totally respected for being a risk-taker. He left a trail and legacy. While the guys that played it safe (with their expensive looking suits and perfect images) didn't have any successes, just same-old, same-old.

The thing I love about *A Course is Miracles* is that you get to be yourself. You get to make a million mistakes because the correction is always there. There is nothing worse than someone who watches their every step and move trying to be their idea of "perfect" and "holy." Talk about boring.

A Course in Miracles wants you to be your passionate fabulous self. mistakes, flaws, and all. Because only in the mistake is the correction. You can hear this. Come on, *there is nothing to fear.* Just go for it.

In order to go into new territory, of course you are going to make mistakes. You see? The choice is to stay safe (where you watch your every step) and have life be exactly as it has always been (yawn) or you be free and happy and yourself and BREAK NEW GROUND, and not worry about looking like a fool. Because of course you will make mistakes, because that's just how that goes, but in the practice of training your mind you will instantly know what to do to correct the error. AND HERE IS THE MIRACLE: you will know not to do that ever again!!!!

MISTAKE = CORRECTION.

It's like, let's say I force myself to not gossip and be the perfect little angel. I'm constantly watching what I say. But it's forced. Well, one day I gossip. I can't help myself. It's just too darn juicy. Well, I immediately feel the effect of it. It feels horrible to talk behind someone's back. Suddenly I am having an EXPERIENCE of why not to gossip, but that could only come . . . are you ready?? . . . as I gossiped!!!!!!!!

See?

We go head first in. We don't worry if we look stupid. We say things that make us cringe a month later. We don't mind being corrected by other people.

Take it from me, I know. But you will see how much faster this transforms you, rather than trying to have an image of being a good teacher (worker, student, wife, person) who sits in a quiet little corner and says nothing.

We are simply learning to be ourselves. You can choose to stay on safe familiar ground OR you can decide to travel out to the stars.

I used to think I was an utter failure with every mistake. People would criticize me. I would feel bad. I would have to apologize. I'd feel like all my hard work amounted to nothing. I'd feel like an idiot. I'd think of all the wasted time.

But then always the miracle occurred: I emerged stronger and wiser.

All my failures were successes in disguise. There was a brief moment in my life when I didn't want to try anything new because I wanted everyone to think I was wonderful. I didn't want to expose my most inner secret thoughts and desires. I tried to keep my "image" of "holiness" intact. But I was actually boring myself. It's like being one shade of white, when there is a whole palette of colors to choose from. Finally, I just wanted to be authentic and passionate and free.

The best thing anyone ever told me was this: "Lisa, you have no friends."

It was the best thing anyone ever said to me. It was my total release and freedom. At first I was completely insulted because I had tons of friends, but she said, "Don't kid yourself. You have no friends. In a moment of desperation, you will find you are utterly alone and completely abandoned. But here's the thing: you have one 'APPOINTED FRIEND' who goes with you wherever you go and who will never let you down."

And this was my release.

My whole life I wanted everyone to like me. I walked on egg shells to keep my perfect image intact and with one sentence "Lisa, you have no friends" . . . I was free from that prison house.

How can you possibly make a mistake when you keep constant counsel with God? How? It's totally impossible. I let Jesus be my guide in everything that I do. Forward ahead and never look back.

A Course in Miracles says: "*Some of your greatest advances you have judged as failures, and some of your deepest retreats you have evaluated as success.*"

Everything is the OPPOSITE of what I think. Knowing this, I don't judge myself anymore. I don't know what is failure and success. I let God judge for me. I do what *A Course in Miracles* asks me to do, and I trust this is sufficient.

If I am doing what Jesus requests of me, I can't go wrong. He says love your neighbors, love your enemies, and love God. Doing one thing every day that scares me pushes my boundaries and tests my abilities and really . . . what have I got to lose?

Life is much more interesting this way.

be willing to look foolish

I am willing to look foolish. I'm willing to go out on a ledge. FOR MY SAVIOR JESUS CHRIST. I see the necessity for a solid foundation, which is strengthened as I listen and follow instructions. I love bible stories, like Noah with the ark. Noah acted on blind faith and was willing to risk his image in order to follow God's instructions. He most likely appeared as a raving lunatic to the neighbors who were probably telling him he was an idiot to be building an ark in the middle of the desert but Noah did not doubt God's Voice. He did not worry about the neighbor's opinions. He finished building the ark, and the world was flooded.

It's the condition we find ourselves in, entirely. It might not look like a flood (specifically, with water) that's coming, but, beware, this world is going under and sinking fast.

You must be willing to look a little foolish to deny the world and follow Jesus. You must be willing to build an ark, and to go left when everyone is turning right. WHO CARES WHAT THE NEIGHBORS THINK?? When you get direction from God, please go for it.

We, with the help of the Holy Spirit, are building a rock solid foundation on our Lord Jesus Christ and no storm can topple us, no flood can drown us, and we are safe forever.

The saviors of the world.

Meanwhile, the rest of the jesters, the neighbors who called you foolish and told you to get a job and health insurance—are swept away by the flood without a paddle or a life preserver. It all happens in an instant. Don't be blinded. There's no safety in this world. We're all in this together.

Mostly what I'm grateful for is to see how many individuals are coming together, in singular purpose, letting go of all differences, all identity, and coming to a place where GOD'S PLAN is the priority.

It's lovely.

Thank you for your dedication. I love you.

one sock method

A long time ago I heard about a way to motivate yourself to get active. It's called the One Sock Method. It works like a charm every time. If it can work for someone lazy like me, it can work for anyone.

One time, when I was in high school, my dad popped his head into my room (no one dared to actually come into the room because it was so messy, clothes piled everywhere with a path cleared to the bed) and he said "want help cleaning this mess?" and I said "YES" and he said: "let me go get the matches."

Ha Ha.

Very funny.

But the truth is that I was a certified slob. But with The One Sock Method, I changed all that.

Here it is:

When something is overwhelming you, just pick up one sock.

Let's say for example your house is a disaster, there are dishes piled up in the sink, there is laundry to be done, and you have no idea where to begin. Usually the tendency in a situation like this is to feel overwhelmed and do nothing. You go click on the television and either tune out, or feel guilty.

Most people "put off till tomorrow what could be done today." They think they need to wait till they have a huge chunk of free time to do the big tasks.

But a new solution is to pick up one sock rather than beating yourself up for not getting the whole house clean.

ONE SOCK!

The beauty of this solution (in my experience) is that you never just pick up one sock: the miracle is that a small beginning gives you enough of a push or incentive to do more housecleaning (or whatever task is before you).

This applies to anything: you can pick up one dish, or do one lesson, pay one bill, do one sit-up, make one phone call, etc.

If you are working with *A Course in Miracles* (or a recovery program), it works great. Everyone seems to think a lot is required of them: they think they have to be out there saving the world or giving the message away to others who need help. But it's not true or necessary. All that is asked is to do ONE LESSON a day and do it the way it says. HOW SIMPLE!

One lesson is the small beginning that Jesus requires and the power of God takes care of the rest! Which brings us to today's lesson: *I merely follow, for I would not lead.* Lesson 324. All I need to do is read one lesson. How do you save the world? One Lesson at a time. One day at a time. One sock at a time. We are not doing anything. It's God who does the work. He leads. We follow.

How simple.

know thyself

A Course in Miracles teaches only to be yourself.

It doesn't teach anything else. It has 365 lessons all designed to bring you to the final realization that you are whole and perfect as God created you.

If you could remember this today—your perfection, your Identity in God—you wouldn't need any lessons. You wouldn't need a mind-training. Who needs to learn the alphabet when they know it already? Once you know it, you know it for all time.

We don't get stuck in the basic lessons and stop there. We go beyond them. Jesus says in Heaven there is no need for learning. Once you've gone beyond all learning, you have arrived at CREATION. Which means there is a need to first learn the lessons (of forgiveness, of non-judgment) so that we can go beyond them to a place where there is only love.

You learn your ABC's—you learn the basics—and then you move on to more advanced lessons. You don't stay in the first grade forever. You learn to look at the bigger picture and you see how the letters of the alphabet string together to make sentences. They are a complete system that, when learned, work in harmony as a whole. You need to know the entire alphabet. If you skip one letter—let's say you didn't learn "C"—then you will be severely lacking and because of one missed letter, the whole language becomes confused.

You need every letter. Let's say you learned 99% of the alphabet, but missed the "C." Your understanding would be completely confused and limited. I think you will agree there is a world of difference between 99% and 100%. You need every letter.

So it is with the lessons of *A Course in Miracles*—You need them all, and you cannot skip one. They are designed to work together, in harmony, as a whole. If you hold one exception in your mind (a tiny grievance, one person you won't forgive) then the entire miracle is lost to you.

The final teaching for which the Course is based is "to know thyself." You cannot know yourself if there are any exceptions in your life. Either you know everyone as friend or you know no one: sometimes friend, sometimes stranger, sometimes enemy. When you know yourself, all those categories will disappear and everyone will be friend to you. This is what 100% means.

Anyone who has been following this blog for any length of time knows that I change my mind a lot (Jesus says, "You change your mind 10 times an hour, at best.") but the truth is that I remain entirely CONSISTENT in the one thing that matters: my dedication to God and to my brothers.

I remain consistent in the recognition that JOY IS MY JOB. I change my mind about what I should eat, what I should wear, what I should do for money but throughout it all, I'M HAPPY.

That's the difference. There's no emphasis or judgment at all. One day I'm vegan. The next day I want to eat cake. Who cares? I'm happy on both days because *"my part is essential to God's plan for salvation."*

Be yourself. Don't beat yourself up.

The only problem you could ever have is guilt, which arises from separation. In the moment of REMEMBERING YOURSELF you know that you have no problems. You know the separation did not occur. You remember that you are here only for the healing of the world. You remember that nothing you see means anything.

In your forgetting is the remembering.

Just don't let yourself slide too far down into hell. Jesus says once you take the first step into hell, the rest of the steps (the descent into darkness) come quickly. For example, let's say you have a grievance with someone. You're angry. How long are you going to stay angry? How long? O teacher of God. How long? Are you going to stay in hell or are you going to remember that within you is the POWER TO CHANGE YOUR MIND?

You can let other things affect you OR you can remember that you are affected only by your own thoughts. This is the decision. You can be happy or sad. You are the loveliest of all of God's creations. You are the Son He loves. In you is love perfected, fear impossible, and joy established without opposite.

To know yourself means:

To know yourself as LIGHT.

To know yourself as LOVE.

To know yourself as ONE WITH GOD.

Unsolvable Problem

"The mass of men lead lives of quiet desperation."
—Henry David Thoreau

feeling the intensity & futility of separation

Be honest. Who hasn't felt the complete futility of this world? Who talks about it? Why try to cover it up with roses and sunshine and flowers? Why sit around with spiritual people, holding hands and feeling good about life? This world is what hell is. Why not look directly at the devastation and name it as it is. This world is a place of limitation and death. Jesus calls it a *"slaughter house."*

I feel the intensity of all the despair of everyone in the world. I feel the chaos. I feel the destruction. I feel the war. I feel the hopelessness and futility of every person in the whole world.

When I am looking with open eyes, I am reminded of the magnitude of my function. This world is a slaughter house. I caused it. There is work to be done. Sometimes I really feel the total desperation of being trapped in a place of limitation with no way out. LITERALLY. I know what it feels like to have no money. I know what it feels like to be alone. I know what it feels like to be afraid. I know the feeling of wanting to give up, to make different choices, to have different opportunities. I know the boredom. I know the loneliness. I know.

I want only to love and give and be happy and sometimes even that door seems closed. For me, in these moments of frustration and desperation, I let myself feel the totality of the emotion. I let the world come crashing in on me. I let it be total. I don't try to snap out of it. I let myself feel the futility. This is what makes me the savior of the world. I don't try to make the world a nice place. THE WORLD IS NOT A NICE PLACE.

I'm trying to show you that you can leave the world. You don't leave it through death. You leave it through willingness and dedication to leave everything behind. You release the past. You release your thoughts. You release your beliefs. You release your pain. You release your limitations. You release your ideas. And you come with WHOLLY OPEN HANDS unto your Father, who is God.

When you see the magnitude of your own responsibility to change your mind so that the world may change, you will leave all your little meaningless problems behind.

You will take your place among the saviors of the world.

complete dependence on God

Do you have a problem or addiction that is unsolvable? Are you powerless over certain areas in your life? Have you tried solutions only to fail?

You must rise above the battleground. You must rise above your problems. Do not try to fix them. They are unfixable. There is no solution in time-space that will ever work. The miracle introduces a catalyst which breaks up the continuity of your life. It minimizes the need for time.

Each day should be devoted to miracles. The purpose of time is to enable you to learn how to use time constructively. It is thus a teaching device and a means to an end. Time will cease when it is no longer useful in facilitating learning.

"Except ye become as little children" means that unless you fully recognize your complete dependence on God, you cannot know the real power of the Son in his true relationship with the Father.

COMPLETE DEPENDENCE ON GOD.

The miracle shortens time by collapsing it, thus eliminating certain intervals within it. The miracle entails a sudden shift from horizontal to vertical perception. The miracle thus has the unique property of abolishing time to the extent that it renders the interval of time it spans unnecessary.

Jesus knows the whole plan. I don't know anything, but he's walking with me. All I need to do is be still an instant and listen and he will tell me "very specifically" what to do.

Everything changes through my continual dedication. I really have no idea how it works. All I know is that I made a promise to God to be the happy example of His Laws and His Love, on earth, as it is in Heaven. I don't know anything except for my great NEED to leave this world of separation behind. This is not our home and we know it.

If *A Course in Miracles* is true (and it is!) then it means what it says and it's entirely true. If Jesus says, "Greater things will you do" (than healing the sick and raising the dead) and he's talking directly to me, then I trust him. He means what he says. He said I'll do greater things than he did and I believe him.

A Course in Miracles says it takes only ONE teacher of God to save the world. It says it has nothing to do with "doing" things in the world. It says, "YOU NEED DO NOTHING." It has to do with commitment, willingness and trust. Faith the size of a mustard seed. It has to do with remembering the truth.

For every five minutes that I remember God, 1000 years or more are saved. Every minute spent remembering the truth and 1000 minds awaken.

This is what it says, and this is what it means because *A Course in Miracles* is entirely true. There is not one exception in the teaching and it calls for uncompromising dedication. I am asked to be happy and to remember that this world is not my home.

Look at this sentence: *Complete restoration of the Sonship is the only goal of the miracle-minded.*

I love it. I dedicate my mind to remembering the truth, that every single person on the entire planet come to know the peace of God. How marvelous! Complete restoration is accomplished because all minds are joined as One. How simple! I don't need to worry about anything. I'm here only for today. My part is essential to God's Plan for salvation. If I am meant to do something, I will be told specifically what to do (and then the Holy Spirit will go ahead of me and do it for me!)

I can relax.

In Chapter 2, Jesus says, *"You are much too tolerant of mind wandering. Few appreciate the real power of the mind, and no one remains fully aware of it all the time. The mind is very powerful, and never loses its creative force. It never sleeps. Every instant it is creating. It is hard to recognize that thought and belief can literally move mountains."*

A few years ago, before I did ANYTHING, I asked first. Even simple little acts like taking a shower or making a cup of tea. I asked the Holy Spirit everything. I would want to make a phone call or drive to the store or eat something, and I would STOP and ask first. Life was one big miracle back then. I don't know why I stopped with that practice. Suddenly my life was flowing, everything effortless, but then without even realizing it: I stopped praying. I stopped asking. I stopped communicating. I stopped being grateful for every little thing.

Ooops. I thought I knew something. But I don't know anything. There's no one out there to teach. There is only me. There is only Mind. There is only this moment—new & sparkling & clean—in which I release the past.

I RELEASE THE PAST. Now, I let all things be revealed to me.

I'm so tired. I'm tired of this world. I'm tired of all the loneliness, and the sadness, and the death and the poverty, and the limitation, and the constant struggle for survival. This world is not our home.

It's not a real place. Everyone is aging & dying, losing the things they love, fighting, afraid, getting divorced, with some form of sickness or addiction, on some type of medication or drug.

This is NOT God's Will for us.

As I said, if this blog is anything, it's honest.

I prefer to sit in a chair reading *A Course Miracles* from morning to night until I'm inspired or have a revelation rather than to try and push my own agenda of what I think needs to be accomplished. ACTUALLY, I prefer to spend my whole day playing like a little child, and if Jesus needs me to do something, he knows where to find me.

One time, in 2001, I told God to FUCK OFF and he found me within a week, so I'm not really concerned. If He needs me, He will come and get me. He knows I'll do anything. He knows my willingness. He knows where I live. He's got my address and phone number.

I'm asking for a part in this production. It doesn't even have to be the lead, I'm happy to be a supporting actor. I just want a part, any part, I'll take it. Whatever needs to be done, I'll be told. Because this is God we are talking about—all Power in the universe. I trust in Him.

something is fundamentally wrong here

The world is not real. I've said it before and I will most likely say it again. It's a big hoax. Do not be deceived by appearances. It's an illusion.

Have you seen the movie "The Truman Show"? Truman lives in a world of make-pretend—a Hollywood movie set—that he believes is real. Yet there is nothing real about the "world" he lives in. It's a construct made to hide reality. Like Truman, nothing can stop me from finding the truth if that's what I want.

The world is a judgment on myself. It's literally not there at all. In my desire to know the truth, I go beyond the world.

It's a happy dream—like Truman, living in a world that gives an illusion of safety and comfort—but it's not real. The sand is fake. The sun is fake. Day and night are fake. The streets are fake. The stores are fake. All these characters walking around in it, playing a part. They all know me. I'm the "star" of the show. All these people working jobs, going places, saying things, acting out their lines.

Don't be fooled.

It's not about re-arranging things to stay safe (or happy or comfortable) in the world. It's not a real place. It's about getting outside of the construct. It would not make any sense for Truman to go get a better job (or a different wife) because he already recognizes the whole thing is false.

Once Truman sees the cracks, all sorts of characters rush in to hide reality from him. They tell him he's going crazy. They try to get him to settle back down into his "life," to relax, to do something different, to take a vacation, to have a beer. And that's how it is with this world. It's a matrix and you will get all sorts of characters rushing in to tell you it's solid and real.

But Truman knew something was fundamentally wrong, just as I knew something was fundamentally wrong. He suspected there was a whole world of possibilities (on the other side of the bridge), but everyone stopped him from crossing the bridge. They tried to make his life more pleasant, but he recognized he was trapped as a prisoner. From this moment, his only goal was freedom.

Like Truman, the whole world outside the bubble is waiting for his escape. Everyone watching knows he appears trapped, but that the show could end any minute. It's dependent upon Truman. He is trapped only as long as he remains sleeping.

From time to time, someone from the outside gets in to try to tell him the truth, but he's so convinced that his world is real, that at first he doesn't even understand who these new characters are, telling him his world is not real.

Inside, he appears like he is all alone, like everyone is "in" on the joke, and there is no one to help him . . . but in reality everyone is rooting for his escape.

He knows something is fundamentally wrong. Once he starts looking for clues and cracks, he sees them everywhere. Every time he tries to leave, someone stops him. He doesn't know who to trust, but he knows he can't participate in the charade anymore.

rise above the battleground

Once you know you are here for the salvation of the world, you'll never have another problem again. Problems will still arise but you will not be bothered by them. You will let each difficulty be solved by the One who abides with you.

In God, all things are possible.

This world is not real. You can be in it, but not of it.

Sure, you will continue to look upon the images the eyes behold and hear the sounds the ears report BUT you will be completely unaffected. This world is an illusion, folks. It's not a pretty picture, but it's also not real. You can literally ignore the problem, and be about the solution. You can rise above the battleground. From there, up above, you will see all your problems disappear one by one. We are ushering in a new forgiven world.

Please don't waste your time and energy trying to fix this world—it's a place of madness—IT'S NOT FIXABLE. Rather, train your mind to see things differently. BE PART OF THE SOLUTION. Rise above your humanness.

Open your eyes. Open your ears.

This is called HEALING THE SICK AND RAISING THE DEAD.

Don't be blind and deaf to what is happening around you. Don't be sedated by television. Don't believe what you see & hear. Don't fill your body with poison and crap and fake food. Don't attack yourself with thoughts of worry and depression.

Listen. Love. Give. Remember. It's time to wake up. You've been dreaming a dream of destruction. It's over now. Let it dissolve into the nothingness from which it came. This world needs individuals who remember their Identity in God.

This world is not your home . . . and you know it. This is NOT where you belong. You can be happy, all the time, no exception . . . when you give all your problems to God. He'll take care of each and every one of them, so that you are free to be the light of the world.

God needs his teachers. Please do not delay in a world that is not even real. Let Jesus show you how to rise above the battleground. There is a door that leads from the slaughterhouse, and you walk right out of it, into the sunshine.

If you are stuck in a routine, feeling you are down at the bottom of a hole with no ladder, ask for help. There is no need to stay in darkness. Help is all around you.

the world i see holds nothing that i want

I have had terrifying moments of despair, thoughts of suicide. I have destroyed three Course books in fits of rage. I have sat in my car at midnight with the thought that I would drive the car into the river, with me in it. But thankfully, there is reason & logic. I could always see that killing myself would not solve the world's problems, nor my own problems. This recognition always led me back to the bookstore to plop down another $30 for another Course book. I knew somehow that only total 100% responsibility would lead me home. *A Course in Miracles* urges each of us to go the full distance. It is a perfectly orchestrated mind-training program. You begin to see bits of light around the edges that will show you this world is an illusion. You will begin to have experiences that the "guy out there" is only an idea in your mind, and not really solid and not really there at all. You will see that everything is an hallucination. You will see that you made it up.

The world is nothing more than your own state of mind, the outside picture of an inward condition. You must see that the person sitting across from the table talking to you is really you. Your enemy is you. Your neighbor is you. They are characters in a dream, wholly unreal. As you practice, you will see that the world is not solid, not stable and not there at all.

From this point, your escape is guaranteed. Once you know the world is not real, you will see the door and your entire way out, straight into Heaven.

While you still believe the world is real, you will not see the door, although it is literally RIGHT THERE. You hold the key in your hand and yet you will not see it. As long as you think there are people separate from you, you will not understand the necessity for forgiveness. In a very real sense, YOU ARE ROYALLY SCREWED. It's literally being trapped in hell.

You get a glimpse of reality, you've heard there's no world and that love and miracles are your reality but this still may not be your physical experience.

STAND STILL.

It's *A Course in Miracles*.

Keep going. Listen. Trust.

There are two steps:

1. Realize: The world you see is HELL and offers you nothing
2. Realize: There is another world beyond this world that offers you everything.

You cannot stop with the idea that the world is worthless, for unless you see that there is something else to hope for, you will only be depressed. Our emphasis is not on giving up the world, but on exchanging it for what is far more satisfying, filled with joy, and capable of offering you peace.

Whew.

The world I see holds nothing that I want AND beyond this world there is a world I want.

I want the peace of God. I want only to be truly helpful. I want to be happy. I don't want any conflict in any shape or form. LOVE IS WHAT I AM. I want ONLY to see the Holy Spirit's Purpose accomplished that God's Will be done. No more delaying. No more trinkets and toys. There is nothing I want in this world. I've searched my mind. Everything I need and want is in the high frequencies of Heaven.

I see that it's entirely possible to maintain a high vibration of energy, which is love, and call everyone into this space with me. There is no need to enter into conflict. There is no need to go back and forth between the worlds.

Above all else, I want to love.

Above all else, I'm not going back into the battlefield.

New Beginning

"Then, without realizing it, you try to improve yourself at the start of each new day; of course, you achieve quite a lot in the course of time. Anyone can do this, it costs nothing and is certainly very helpful. Whoever doesn't know it must learn and find by experience that a quiet conscience makes one strong."
—Anne Frank

every day is a new beginning.

Every day should be devoted to prayer and to miracles.

Paul in the bible says: DIE DAILY.

Best to get it over with as soon as you wake up. Die upon waking and get it out of the way. This is why I try as much as I can to align my mind to truth as quickly as possible. Usually the second I wake up, my thoughts are already trying to organize and plan based on yesterday and tomorrow. I think about events that are over, e-mails that I sent, letters that I've written, phone calls and conversations, trying to see if I can catch a glimpse, some understanding to what might occur next (today or tomorrow) based on past actions. It's human nature.

But the instruction is: DIE DAILY.

Forget everything that happened yesterday. Forget everything that might happen tomorrow. Forget it all. Be here now.

The Master Teacher says, "You're dying all the time. That is not the problem. Every day and every hour, you're dying. Don't worry about that. The problem is, you keep forgetting to resurrect!"

I love Jesus' directness. YOU MUST BE BORN AGAIN.

What an amazing idea. The scientific practice is to go into higher dimensions of consciousness, and logically and practically, it would be impossible to get into a higher state of being without the you that is you changing. Think about it.

Whenever anything enters into a different energy frequency, vibrating faster or slower, its solid mass changes into something else.

Ice becomes water becomes steam.

Solid becomes liquid and vice versa.

You are currently vibrating at a particular speed. You are. This is scientifically proven. Perhaps you have lots of energy. Perhaps you have very little energy. You know what I am talking about. You know when you are in a rut, when everything seems the same every day. Stale almost. You want something different to occur, but you have no idea how to institute a change. But you can vibrate faster, you can. You already know how to accomplish this: change your routine, change your diet, change your mind, do something different, forgive, release a grievance, take a chance, be courageous.

So the difficulty is not in HOW to change your frequency of energy, that part is easy. The difficulty is fear of transformation, fear of traveling into these higher dimensions of consciousness, fear of entering into the new world. You know that if you change your routine, things will change. You will change. You know this.

So why do we make so little progress in light of what we know about eternal truth? Why do we not change day by day, and week by week, until our friends and family can barely recognize us? Why do we stay in the same old rut, wishing something external would change?

Because there is a price to pay.

The world you currently cling to will fall away. Obviously. If you go into a higher frequency, the lower frequency world will vanish and disappear. Not a trace of it will remain. You think you will lose the things you love, and well, you might. At least in body form.

But what, O teacher of God, do you want?

Here you must be honest and at least ask the question.

You have to bring your whole body and Self with you. You can sit around imagining these changes, thinking about rising up in frequency, but this is not the same as ACTION.

Are you willing to change? How far are you willing to go? Do you just want to change your hairstyle? Or are you willing to go the distance and be totally brand new?

It's like putting a little toe in the water. This is how we come to truth. We put a little toe in, and feel something different and refreshing and cool. Perhaps it makes us afraid. Perhaps it is exhilarating. Whatever the experience is for you, we can all agree putting your little toe in the water is NOT the same as putting your entire body in the lake.

To come into the truth, to experience it in its fullness, to know God as yourself, you must put your whole body in, to have faith, to bring every conscious thought and belief (body, mind and soul), and dive right in. Yes, you will be changed. Yes, it will be shocking at first. Yes, it can be a little scary. But it's a whole new experience, and don't you at least want to give it a try??

You can continue to keep putting your toe in the pools of truth, pretending you are having a full-fledged experience, but you are fooling yourself and merely touching the surface. And you know it.

You must be born again.

How is this accomplished?

By parting with all your prejudices and beliefs and old habits. It means taking the knife to all your character defects: selfishness, pride, vanity, all the little lies you tell yourself and others to make you look good. It means giving up all that holds you in a place of sameness. You know what I am talking about. It will be personal to you. It means shedding the skin and body you currently live in. It means changing direction. It means trying something bold and new.

If you are not prepared to pay the price of becoming new, that's fine and good, but do not expect to receive more than the price you pay. That's all. It's really simple. Give a lot, you get a lot. Give a little, you get a little.

It's a Law. A Universal Law. The Law of God.

You can put your toe in or you can put your entire body in. The choice is yours. You can change a lot or you can change a little.

You can either do a little dusting, some spring cleaning, or you can tear the whole foundation down and rebuild the entire house. The choice is yours.

clear a space

You hear it all the time: a new experience cannot occur until you clear a space. It sounds like a cliché, but it is logical & true. If a house is full of clutter, there is no room for a new piano. You must clear away a space. If you buy a new refrigerator, you must get rid of the old one. It's logical. Everyone knows it's true—but how often do we resist this lesson when it comes to the clutter in our mind?

We keep hatred, grievances, jealousy and limitation . . . all the while trying to move in HUGE new ideas like love, joy and abundance.

These things literally will not fit in your mind while it is cluttered with old ideas.

You—YOU—must move the battered couch out. YOU HAVE TO DO IT. It won't just move by itself. You gotta get a truck and usually the help of some friends. You can't do it alone. I mean . . . you can try . . . but let's see you do it.

You realize the necessity for help. You realize the necessity for action.

So it is with the thoughts in your mind that are cluttering up the space.

I am of the belief that clearing a PHYSICAL SPACE will bring in new experience. I'm convinced. You clean out your closet. You give away old clothes. You throw away furniture that is tattered and torn. You get rid of ideas that are keeping you in the past (photos of your ex, old letters, journals). At a minimum, you put old memories in a box, into storage, to get the past out of the present. You clean out your cupboards of things that are expired and spoiled. You clean the mold out of the bathroom. If you look around you right now, you will notice that everything you see reminds you of something from the past. This should be enough to show you how much you live in memories.

THIS IS THE CLEANING OF YOUR MIND. SAME IDENTICAL THING. Your outer world is a pure reflection of your inner world. Take a look around. What do you see? Is your environment clean or cluttered? This is your mind.

vigilance is required

It really has to be this way, otherwise you will get trapped in your own routine . . . and the result is old age, sickness and death. You have to be constantly vigilant to come into a new moment. Take it from me, I KNOW. There must be a constant dedication to remember the truth.

It is so easy to get trapped into believing in sequential time. You have an idea of how the days are going to proceed, how people will react and because you have the thought already fixed in your mind, it appears to happen. It's so easy to get stuck in the smallness of your own life, with all its little details.

Your mind is part of God's. YOU ARE VERY HOLY. There is a whole universe out there and your mind is connected to it. All you have to do is rise above your problems. Rise above your own thinking. Get out of the muck. Get out of time and space, if only for a minute.

Release the past. Release the future. Release your ideas of the people around you, and find yourself in the shining present with no concept of anything. No memory of anyone. No grievance. No problem.

Just pure awareness of the MOMENT you are in now. Pure recognition that in you is the power to heal the entire world.

In you is every person, place and thing. Sometimes when you think you have a problem that seems unsolvable, many times the problem comes from the race mind. Because remember: all that poverty, sickness, death, war, sadness "out there" in the world is still in your mind. So you will inevitably be affected by all of it. Do not be concerned. In you is the power to heal all of it. Do not dwell on the difficulty. Get your mind out of the muck. Rise above the problem. Know there is no solution to the problem while you are in the frequency upon which the problem first appeared. You must get ABOVE it.

Do not try to fix things. Having a discussion will avail you nothing. Get above it. Get out of it.

Fix your mind on God.

The great Emmet Fox, author of one of the greatest books I have ever read, *The Sermon on the Mount*, says you need a "substitute thought" because if someone tells you "don't think about the Statue of Liberty" then you are immediately thinking about it.

This is the way the mind works. So if someone tells you, "Don't think about your problems" you are immediately thinking about them. You need a substitute thought and the best thought I know is God.

THINK ABOUT GOD

Align your mind with God. Don't worry about anything else. Just think about God.

For every five minutes you do this, hundreds (and thousands) of minds are released from the bondage of their own limitation. ALL BECAUSE OF YOU! This comes directly from *A Course in Miracles*. I am not making this up. This is from Jesus. In you is the power to heal the world.

Here is one example (there are many) from Lesson 106: *"Be still and listen to the truth today. For each five minutes spent in listening, a thousand minds are opened to the truth and they will hear the holy Word you hear. And when the hour is past, you will again release a thousand more who pause to ask that truth be given them, along with you."*

Now do you see how salvation rests on you?

In you is the power to help everyone.

These are desperate times. Yesterday two people drove up to the place I live (which looks like a motel, but which is really church housing for ministers). To make a very long story short, the woman was homeless and needs a place to stay. She has no money, tons of health problems, can't drive a car, has Attention Deficit Disorder, is about to go in for surgery, has no health insurance, no friends, and the list went on and on. I listened and we prayed. I made a bunch of phone calls to various social service agencies and found a few options for her. In the meantime, the man will allow her to live with him for a few more days. We talked about gratitude. We talked about newness. We talked about releasing the past and future and putting our lives in God's Hand.

But the truth of the matter? This world is a very dark place. I truly forget the level of despair that occurs in this world. Listening to them, it brought me back to my own place of GRATITUDE. I was reminded of the necessity to get out of my own limited thinking because this world needs help. My little world and problems become so miniscule and meaningless once I open up my mind to the vastness of the universe.

This world is literally smaller than a speck of dust, and yet it is given to you to offer hope to the lonely, desperate and afraid. It's a paradox that will make you happy once you stop trying to figure it out.

TODAY'S ACTION: I will remember my gratitude. I will count my blessings and think about God. Today I will re-devote my mind to healing and the salvation of the world.

let me forget the past today

Today's lesson—IF ANYONE ACTUALLY DECIDED TO DO IT—would be the end of all therapy, all grievances, all depression, and all anger. If one person decided to do today's lesson, completely, all their problems would be solved forever.

Here it is:

"Let me forget my brother's past today."

Plain and simple. If you do this lesson and really mean it, you will be free. Let me forget my brother's past today.

Totally. Completely. Absolutely. And forever.

"Let me forget my brother's past today."

Be like Drew Barrymore in the movie *50 First Dates*, and develop total memory loss about everything that happened in your entire life.

New Beginning

I used to be in the 12-step program—for alcohol issues, codependency and food issues—and while it is a good program for getting over addictions, I do strongly believe there must be a point you go past the program. You must say "I AM FINISHED WITH LOOKING AT THE PAST." The program says you must always acknowledge that you are an addict, otherwise you will relapse. I totally disagree with this kind of thinking. I'm not an addict anymore. I'm the light of the world.

I declare it, and it's true.

In the 4th Step, it asks you to write down all your grievances. It asks you to put them on paper, including the person's name, what they did, how it affected you and what is your part. The goal of this exercise is to help you see your own self-responsibility.

Now, that's all fine and good, and it's a great practice, but I had notebooks filled with grievances of what other people did to me. I had it all down there on paper, constantly pulling up the past and remembering what someone did to me. I even wrote a list of horrible things someone said to me recently so that I don't forget. I have it tucked away in my calendar right this minute. I wrote the list because I have a tendency to look past all appearances and see only the light that lies beyond, but in this particular situation I felt that I was BLINDED (time and time again) by what this one person was saying to me. It was like a vicious cycle I kept getting trapped in.

Today's lesson says, *"Let me forget my brother's past today."*

It means rip up the list. It means rip up the notebook. It means forget everything that happened yesterday, a week ago, a year ago, ten years ago. It means FORGET EVERYTHING THAT HAS EVER HAPPENED TO YOU.

I don't really want to do this. Let's be honest with each other here. I want to protect myself and not get hurt anymore. I want to remember the horrible things that were said to me so that I don't repeat the same mistakes all over again.

But along comes Jesus and says, *"Forget your brother's past today."*

This is a hard lesson.

It also says, "My brother is my savior." How can my brother possibly be my savior when he says mean things to me? When he attacks me and doesn't honor me as the Son of God?

We are going deep into the core of truth today.

Sometimes in this Course you hit a sore spot. You come to a specific place where you must admit there is still fear & hatred in your heart.

Just when you think the clean-up is done and your mind is SPOTLESS, you see out of the corner of your eye there is a patch of mold growing there.

If you don't clean it up straight away, it takes a life of its own and before you know it, everything is covered in mold, and spreading like wild fire.

Best to catch it when it is still contained to one small corner.

Jesus says (in the Introduction to the workbook):

Some of the ideas the workbook presents you will find hard to believe and others may seem to be quite startling . . . Remember only this: you need not believe the ideas, you need not accept them, and you need not even welcome them. Some of them you may actively resist. None of this will matter or decrease their efficacy. You are merely asked to apply the lessons as you are directed to do. You are not asked to judge them at all. You are asked only to use them. It is their use that will give them meaning to you, and will show you that they are true. Do not allow yourself to make exceptions in applying the ideas the workbook contains, and whatever your reactions to the ideas may be, use them. Nothing more than that is required.

Just do the lesson. Just do what it says.

Forget your brother's past today.

Rip up the list of grievances. Forgive and forget.

let it change

The Master Teacher was saying yesterday when you go into new frequencies of energy, there will always be a little confusion at first. It might be a bit of a bumpy ride. He said the body might have some difficulty adjusting to the new place you find yourself in. He said, "Don't worry about it. Just let it change."

Let things fall apart. Don't try to hold it together. Don't try to locate yourself. Let everything be new. Let it change.

I'm always wanting to try to fix things, but what if this is true?? What if the old world I was living in is gone?? What if I did just catapult into a new time and place, from one frequency of energy to another frequency of energy . . . but because my eyesight still shows me the same images from yesterday and the day before, I still think I'm in the old location.

But what if everything is all brand new? What if I don't hold anything together? What if the past really is gone? What if I don't know where my income comes from? If I don't know who my friends are? If I don't know my daily routine? What if instead of trying to fix or organize everything, I allow everything to change?

Sometimes I like to experiment with this idea and not call or write anyone. It's like being an alien who lands from outer space and doesn't know anything. I love the movie *Holy Man* (with Eddie Murphy). He lands on a highway and immediately things begin to happen. Suddenly he has a place to live and food to eat, without planning. He actually doesn't have any needs. He is a simple man with no attachments, no belongings. He's PRESENT in every situation. I love this idea. He begins to affect everyone around him because he doesn't know the rules and laws of the world.

Today, I give myself to the Holy Spirit for His Purpose. It is my gift to Him.

I go where He would have me go, and do what He would have me do, and say what He would have me say. It is my gift to Him. Today, I rest in perfect certainty knowing that every need is taken care of.

Herein lies my joy.

Transformation

"Just do it."
—Nike slogan

new year's resolutions

New Years. That special time of year when you loudly proclaim "This year will be different!" It is a time of hope and anticipation when you desire to usher in a new experience for yourself.

In years past I always made resolutions to lose weight, be more organized and to try something new. All my resolutions ran along these lines. I always wanted to be different, better, from the way that I was. A NEW AND IMPROVED VERSION OF MYSELF. The truth is that I hated myself and New Years always gave me a glimmer of hope that "this year I'll be different."

I would always think: "I'm going to be fantastically alive this year. I'm going to lose weight, start jogging, and be like those girls in the movies who have it all."

And famous last words: "THIS TIME IT WILL BE DIFFERENT!"

I thought that if I was thinner, more adventurous, more glamorous, and had all my debts paid off . . . I would be happy. If only I had the right skin, the right hair, the right clothes, the right job, the right relationship . . . then life would be different, better somehow.

But then I got the job, lost the weight, paid off my bills, and to my ultimate surprise: I was still miserable. I was still drinking vodka every day to drown my boredom. And that's when I started to see that changing external circumstances will NOT make you happy. Trying to force a change in your external world will not change the inner landscape. Trust me. I've tried it a million times. It doesn't work.

You must go inside. You must get to the root of the problem—which is your own thinking.

How did it finally work for me? How did JOY finally become my one consistent emotion? I GAVE UP. I admitted defeated. I declared myself an utter and complete failure. My whole life, my mantra was "I can do it. I can do it. I can do it" and for the most part, I could do anything. But all my accomplishments felt hollow. I would feel joy and satisfaction for five minutes (or a day or even a week) before I was back to feeling that empty pit in my heart, mind & soul. I was constantly seeking and searching. For what? I had no idea. All I knew is that something fundamental was missing in my life and I was constantly trying to fill the emptiness with food, activities, cigarettes, chaos and drama.

So what did I learn? I CAN'T DO ANYTHING. Alone, I am nothing.

So, my new mantra is "I can't do it. I can't do it. I can't do it."

BUT GOD CAN IF I LET HIM. I want to teach. I want to travel. I want to be active. I want to inspire and motivate individuals to be as God created them . . . perfect. I want to be a shining bright light in this world, representing our Father's Love, His Grace, His Joy, His Peace, His Happiness, His Eternal Changelessness.

On earth, as it is in Heaven.

I can't do it. I can't do it. I can't do it. But God will if I let Him.

Amen.

if the house is on fire, get out

Beyond my desire to alter my body association is a deeper need to usher in a new forgiven world. I let Jesus remind me constantly that I am the light of the world. I am Spirit. Salvation is my only function here.

I like to play and as a teacher of God I keep things light & simple, but I never forget the magnitude of my function. This world will change though me.

Forgiveness, joy and laughter increase frequencies of energy. This world is not a real place. It's a dream. It appears solid, but it's not there at all. It appears as changing energy, shifting, moving, transforming. You seem to start out as dark solid mass but then the energy starts to move and flow and you begin to realize that you can shift anything, travel anywhere, do all things. If you've ever done 50 jumping-jacks real quick, you know that you instantly feel vibrant—it's because you just shifted the energy. If a friend invites you to go someplace that makes you happy (like Starbucks) you instantly feel alive and excited. This is energy moving. Suddenly you are out of the slump.

Energy moving feels good.

There once was a time I was very dense and solid—physically—it took all my energy just to get out of a chair and be active. It was a struggle to get out bed in the morning. I would lounge around all weekend and at night—reading, eating, drinking vodka tonics—and I would justify that this was what I wanted to do but really it was because the energy wasn't moving very fast. I was like in a sea of molasses. Thank God I had a job to get me out of the house every day. But when I wasn't working, I was very slow and lethargic.

Today I am much lighter. I move from one event to another with no effort. I have a lot of energy. Things just roll off me. I don't hold on to grievances. I don't stay in darkness, not even for one second. There have been times when it is like I "open a door" on darkness but I don't stay in it. If there are people in that darkness, I get them out like a fireman gets people out of a fire. I don't close my eyes on ugliness nor do I ignore chaos, but I also don't linger in dark situations. I get people to safety and then I dispel the darkness, like a fireman puts out a fire.

AND THEN I GET THE HELL OUT!

When a house is burning down, you wouldn't stay in it . . . so why would you stay in darkness? Why would you hold onto a grievance? Why would you stay mad for even 2 minutes? Why would you let yourself sink into sadness? THE HOUSE IS BURNING DOWN! GET OUT!

The slightest frown, the merest sigh are little flames that indicate a full-blown fire is about to occur. It's better to put out a flame while it is still small & manageable, and contained in one area. If you are not careful, the flames (the darkness) will spread and destroy everything.

I'm a volunteer. I do it because I love it. I do it because there's a need. I do it to be helpful. I wait patiently until a call comes in, and then I respond.

I stay calm. I stay focused. I do what needs to be done.

It's an honor.

The best plan of action is PREVENTION where a fire (or darkness) doesn't start at all. Don't play with matches and you won't get hurt. Don't play with sadness, worry, anger or hate and there won't be darkness.

when it rains, it pours

Here's what I've learned: you cannot shift energy a little. It either shifts entirely OR not at all. I'm in a totally new place in my life. I had TWO SLOW weeks at the hotel a few weeks back and mistakenly thought it was the trend for July and that is the reason I picked up the housekeeping job. BUT BOOM! Suddenly I'm on the schedule six days a week at the hotel PLUS the housekeeping job. Isn't it always like that? You shift the energy slightly—you think you are in control—but the energy takes on a life of its own. It's impossible to shift energy a little. You cannot control it. If you make a decision to change your life, and then you take an ACTION to alter one thing, the energy takes on a momentum all its own. You cannot contain it. You cannot keep it in a nicely wrapped package. For a while, it may look a little chaotic as things are changing. It's just energy moving. It's nothing to be afraid about. Just go with the flow. Allow events to take you where they will lead. It's impossible to stop energy once it is moving. You ride it out, like a wave on the ocean. You can either enjoy the thrill of the ride—see it as a brand new adventure—OR be terrified about it. These are the choices.

the little garden

You know what I really love?

That where the intensity is . . . is where the most healing occurs. It's not about being in a relationship (or having an experience) that is all flowers and sunshine and butterflies and rainbows . . . it is about feeling the intensity and the passion and the rage and the frustration and watching it transform to love.

This is where the journey becomes an adventure. It's marvelous. You stand still and the barren desert becomes a garden. Have you ever stood still with your enemy and watched him transform into a friend before your very eyes? If you are married, you probably know what I am talking about.

It is the most spectacular thing the body's eyes will ever show you. You just stand still and the scene changes before your eyes. *A Course in Miracles* says, *"The most sacred spot on earth is where an ancient hatred becomes a present love."*

It's totally true, and it's marvelous to witness.

the test of truth

A Course in Miracles teaches how to escape from everything you have taught yourself in the past, by showing you only what you are NOW.

Nothing—and I do mean NOTHING—you have ever learned can help you understand the present, or teach you how to undo the past. This is the beauty of the mind training. You realize in every moment that you don't know a damn thing. Success is the realization that you don't understand anything AND YOU DON'T TRY TO UNDERSTAND. You let everything be exactly as it is without trying to change a single detail. This is where it gets fun. You release every idea, every habit, every ritual, every intention, and you just let it all go.

Analyzing the darkness will not help you at all. You must rise above the problem in order to find the solution. Trying to study darkness to get to the light doesn't make any sense. It's not reasonable. It's not logical.

You simply have to get out of the darkness. It's a waste of time, power, and energy to use creative visualization to turn the light switch on with your mind, when you can just as easily walk across the room and flick on the switch yourself. It's a miracle! The light was all around you while you sat in darkness, attempting mindless magic and abusing the Power of God.

If you want or need something, go get it. Stop trying to wish things into your life. Stop testing God. If you want your problems solved, there is a solution. You must decide you want the peace of God. You must decide you want to be healed. The miracle happens with your participation.

It requires action. Are you willing to give and forgive? Are you willing to see things differently? Everything is transformed as you change your perception about the situation.

There is ONE TEST, as sure as God, by which to recognize if your learning is complete. Here it is, from *A Course in Miracles*:

If you are wholly free of fear of any kind, and if all those you meet or who even think of you share in your perfect peace, then you can be sure that you have learned God's lesson, and not your own. Unless all this is true, there are dark lessons in your mind that hurt and hinder you, and everyone around you.

You were created holy. This course does not make you holy. The lessons do not make you holy. Doing the lessons, however, will bring your holiness into your awareness.

You don't have to do anything. You don't have to analyze your mistakes. You don't have to bring the ego to God which is but to bring error to truth. You simply let error be undone in you by standing in the light of truth—which is to remember that you are whole and perfect.

Let the Holy Spirit be the only Guide you would follow. He knows the way and leads gladly. With Him beside you, you cannot fail.

Let the Holy Spirit make every decision for you. You need only ask of Him what needs to be done, and then he will do it for you, through you.

Your readiness to see differently reawakens the ability to communicate with the invisible realm and to see with Christ vision. It is the reawakening of knowledge.

Now, we are remembering to love.

Now, we are learning to listen.

Now, we are remembering to pray.

Now, we are remembering that help is all around us.

Now, we trust.

Why would you struggle frantically when God is standing right beside you, waiting to lead you away from every problem you think you have? You need only say "Decide for me" and it is done.

You become a little innocent child, full of wonder and full of grace.

Life becomes effortless, lit by miracles every step of the way.

i need do nothing

I am so happy by what is happening to me. A total surrender. Faith restored. Everything up to this point has been PRACTICE and REHEARSAL: learning my lines, going over the script, making sure the costume fits . . . but now the curtain is about to rise. It's Showtime.

And the beautiful part is that I have nothing to do with it. I'm not even needed at all. My understanding is not necessary. I've been practicing and rehearsing, all these years, but now my part is finished. I don't have to do anything.

I was simply cleaning the altar (without even realizing it). Allowing obstacles to be removed. Getting myself out of the way.

I see that Gorgeous for God was only for me. It was my path. Two years of writing to get ME to see what this message really says. It's icing on the cake that other people are here to party and celebrate with me. Thank you. What a gift. It was never about teaching to other people! It was all an attempt for the Holy Spirit to get MY attention. No one else. It was for me. I wrote because of my own deep need to learn.

Yes, I've made tremendous mistakes along the way. Oh God. Those early blog posts I cringe at. How embarrassing. I would love to delete them all but that was all just part of it. A total willingness to expose myself—my dreams, my hopes, my wishes, my desires, my fears—that I might learn.

It was messy, but excavation/renovation is always messy.

Mostly what is surprising me with these chapters is how much the phrase "DO NOT INTERFERE" is used. It's all about TRUST in the Holy Spirit. Surrender. Willingness. Faith.

DO NOT INTERFERE.

Get out of the way and let the Holy Spirit take charge of everything. Ask him everything. Release every plan. Do not plan for your own safety. Do not decide what your needs are. Give over every aspect of yourself, that GOD'S WILL BE ACCOMPLISHED.

Has any other plan ever worked? Ask yourself this honestly.

I'm looking at the state of this world and seeing that nothing really works with total success. My plans are not working. The government's plans are not working. Attempts to solve world hunger are not working. The weather is getting worse. Everyone is in debt. I read an article the other day that more young people are getting cancer and no one knows what to do about it. The divorce rate is sky high. Everyone is scared.

The only thing I am finding that really works, all the time, no exceptions, guaranteed success, is getting aligned with God.

I want to do what Jesus asks, without compromise. Give myself over to the Holy Spirit—ENTIRELY—that His Purpose and Plan be accomplished.

I don't know what it will look like, but I know it's better than the world's way of problem-solving.

In Chapter 16, it says about the Holy Spirit: *He will not desert you, but be sure you do not desert Him. You are not sure that He will do His part, because you have never yet done yours completely.*

WHAMMO!

"YOU ARE NOT SURE THAT HE WILL DO HIS PART, BECAUSE YOU HAVE NEVER YET DONE YOURS COMPLETELY."

I love it. There is nothing better than being put on the hot seat, when you can't blame anyone else. He's talking to me. Directly to me. Not someone else. Me.

And this, more hand-slapping:

Lisa, you are the learner; He the teacher. Do not confuse your role with His, for this will never bring peace to anyone.

Keep one thought in mind and do not lose sight of it, however tempted you may be to judge any situation, and to determine your response by judging it. Focus your mind only on this:

I am not alone, and I would not intrude the past upon my Guest.

I have invited Him, and He is here.

I need do nothing except not to interfere.

I love the section "I Need Do Nothing" from Chapter 18:

"THERE IS ONE THING THAT YOU HAVE NEVER DONE; YOU HAVE NOT UTTERLY FORGOTTEN THE BODY."

It has perhaps faded at times from your sight, but it has not yet disappeared completely. You are not asked to let this happen for more than an instant, yet it is in this instant that the miracle of Atonement happens. Afterwards you will see the body again, but never quite the same. And every instant that you spend without awareness of it gives you a different view of it when you return.

At no single instant does the body exist at all.

This course does not attempt to teach more than you learned in time, but it does aim at saving time. You may be attempting to follow a very long road to the goal you have accepted. It is extremely difficult to reach Atonement by fighting against sin. Enormous effort is expended in the attempt to make holy what is hated and despised.

Nor is a lifetime of contemplation and long periods of meditation aimed at detachment from the body necessary. All such attempts will ultimately succeed because of their purpose. Yet, the means are tedious and very time consuming, for all of them look to the future for release from a state of unworthiness and inadequacy.

Your way will be different, not in purpose but in means.

A holy relationship is a way of saving time. One instant spent together with your brother restores the universe to both of you. YOU ARE PREPARED.

NOW YOU NEED REMEMBER YOU NEED DO NOTHING.

It would be far more profitable now merely to concentrate on this than to consider what you should do. When peace comes at last to those who wrestle with temptation and fight against the giving in to sin; when the light comes at last into the mind given to contemplation; or when the goal is finally achieved by anyone, it always comes with just one happy realization:

I NEED DO NOTHING.

Save time for me (Jesus) by only this one preparation, and practice doing nothing else.

"I need do nothing" is a statement of allegiance, a truly undivided loyalty, believe it for just one instant, and you will accomplish more than is given to a century of contemplation, or of struggle against temptation.

To do anything involves the body. And if you recognize you need do nothing, you have withdrawn the body's value from your mind. Here is the quick and open door through which you slip past centuries of effort, and escape from time.

I need do nothing.

Happiness

"The most revolutionary act one can commit in this world is to be happy."
—Patch Adams

happy, joyous, perfect & free

If you say it's not possible for you to be joyous all the time, to never be depressed, to never be sick, and to never be guilty, then you are listening to the small voice in you that is determined to keep you limited.

Do not be deceived. God's Will for you is perfect happiness. In Him, all things are possible.

If you think you will never find love, you are listening to the tyrant that lives in you. It sounds like your voice. It seems to speak from past experience. It sounds gentle. It seems certain in its words. It promises greener pastures. It promises a possibility of love, losing weight, getting better, meeting more people, doing exciting things, making more money, feeling more secure, feeling more peace . . . but do you notice you never seem to arrive at total contentment?

DO YOU NOTICE?

You're never just happy with what you have, or with what you get. You always want more. Even when you get the mansion and the riches, there is still that DRIVE for more, more, more. Welcome to the human condition.

It's like the dog with the treat attached to a stick in front of it. The dog keeps thinking with every forward movement he will get his snack, but every time he moves forward the snack moves forward also and is always out of reach. The goal is never accomplished UNTIL FINALLY the dog sees the game for what it is, sees the complete impossibility and then has a spastic fit and breaks loose from the stick.

I see it with my cats all the time. They are no dummies. They see immediately when they are being played with, and they do not tolerate it. They get themselves out of whatever tangle I wrap them in (string, ribbon, haha, it's really funny to watch) in about two seconds.

They have done experiments with mice in mazes with cheese where they will put the cheese in a certain location until the mouse figures out where the cheese is, and then they move the cheese but the mouse keeps going back to the original location day after day after day after day even though there is no cheese there anymore. It doesn't try another route. It figures because there was cheese there once before, there will be cheese there once again despite that it never happens.

And that's the human condition.

Here is the "definition of insanity": Doing the same thing over and over and expecting a different result.

Finally, you must come to your senses and realize there is no cheese at the road you are currently traveling on. How many attempts have you made that have failed, with you thinking "this time it will be different." It's very simple. There's no cheese. They moved it. You must change your direction. You must take a new route. It's not complicated. If you want something different to happen, you must do something different.

joy is my function

I am so in love with Lesson 100 in *A Course in Miracles*, I may have to marry it.

Lesson 100 tells me everything I need to know:

1. My part is essential to God's plan for salvation.
2. God's Will for me is perfect happiness.

3. My joy must be complete to let His plan be understood to those to whom He sends to me.
4. I am indeed essential to God's plan.
5. Without my joy, His joy is incomplete.
6. Without my smile, the world cannot be saved.
7. While I am sad, the light that God Himself appointed as the means to save the world is dim and lusterless, and no one laughs because all laughter but echoes mine.
8. My joy on earth calls to all minds to let their sorrows go, and stand beside me in God's plan.

It says in Lesson 100: *We will not let ourselves be sad today. For if we do, we fail to take the part that is essential to God's plan, as well as to our vision.*

I love it. I love it. I love it. I hear wedding bells. I love it so much.

REALIZE YOUR PART IS TO BE HAPPY.

REALIZE YOUR PART IS TO BE HAPPY.

REALIZE YOUR PART IS TO BE HAPPY.

REALIZE YOUR PART IS TO BE HAPPY.

JOY IS YOUR FUNCTION HERE. It is your function that you find it here, and that you find it now. For this you came. Let this one be the day that you succeed!

Isn't this great news? Today is the day you shall succeed! Today! Rejoice! Be happy! Today is the day! Your joy, laughter, smile and happiness is the way all the world's sorrow and despair and problems disappear into the nothingness from which they came.

Salvation is NOT serious business.

I remember that I used to be really happy and someone would say, "You are responsible for that guy's pain over there" as if I was supposed to take on his pain and make it my own.

As if saviorship required conflict.

But now I know the truth: Happiness is the way you deal with the world's pain. Conflict solves nothing. Joy heals everything. Laughter heals every problem. Love heals all pain.

My experience lately is that I finally see the OVERNESS of this place. I have no idea if you know what I am talking about. But I see that IT IS ACCOMPLISHED. *A Course in Miracles* is true because it has worked for me, and that's how I know it will work for you. It is accomplished. This world was over a very long time ago. I don't know if you can understand this conceptually or logically, but your mind hears it and knows what I am talking about.

THIS WORLD WAS OVER A VERY LONG TIME AGO.

Everything you seem to look upon are simply memories and remnants of ideas that are literally no longer here. This is the reason why you can be happy. TODAY!

It will do you no good to wait until the world appears happy and healed. There is no world. You are looking upon ideas in your own mind. This world is not real. This is the reason you can be happy and be unconcerned with everything.

From the Teachers Manual in the section "How Many Teachers of God Are Needed to Save the World?" Jesus says, "God's teachers choose to look on dreams a while. It is a conscious choice. For they have learned that all choices are made consciously, with full awareness of their consequences."

It reminds me of a line from the movie *Bourne Supremacy* about Jason Bourne and the other guys trained in the program: "They don't do anything random."

I love that. As a teacher of God, you don't do anything random anymore. You do everything consciously and with full awareness that YOU ARE RESPONSIBLE FOR THE WORLD YOU SEE.

The reason I am happy all the time is *BECAUSE* I know I am responsible for the world's pain. My happiness is a conscious choice. I am not oblivious to the world's pain. My happiness is not random. I am happy because I have an agreement with Jesus. I do what *A Course in Miracles* asks of me. I follow its instructions and I do what it says.

It says "lay aside all judgment" and every grievance.

It says be happy.

It says love, give and forgive.

It says constancy of joy.

This means NO FLUCTUATION.

No compromise.

The only way it is possible to stay consistently happy is to know God. Once you know God, nothing will bother you.

You are either entirely in Heaven (and happy) or you think the world is a real place and you are in hell (and conflict). There is no in-between and no meeting place between these two states. You are in Heaven or you are in hell.

The beautiful part is that there is a systematic way to train your mind to be in Heaven, all the time, with no worries and no cares, only perfect peace. It's called *A Course in Miracles*.

Everything you look upon is an idea in your own mind. There is nothing there. No one is doing anything to you. This is the coolest practice I know.

I look upon a person. Am I really seeing the person? Or am I seeing my idea of the person based on an old past reference?

If you came with NO REFERENCE, how could anything bother you? Think about it. If you literally released the past, you wouldn't know anybody. You would let all things be revealed to you.

I do this in my marriage every day. I wake up and NOT KNOW my husband. I let every day be revealed to me brand new. This takes practice, because I have an idea of how he will be. But that is just pure murder to put him in a box, based on a past reference.

It's the coolest thing. You wake up in the morning and you don't know anything. It's total liberation to free yourself from the past. You let everything go.

It takes practice to not sequence time. To not know who your friends are. To not know what the day will bring.

More from the Teachers Manual: *AWARENESS OF DREAMING IS THE REAL FUNCTION OF GOD'S TEACHERS.*

Isn't this amazing? *Awareness of dreaming is the real function of God's teachers.*

They watch the dream figures come and go, shift and change, suffer and die. Yet they are not deceived by what they see. They recognize that to behold a dream figure as sick and separate is no more real than to regard it as healthy and beautiful.

And that's why you can let today be all that there is. This is the reason you can be happy.

I love it so much. The journey is NOT about using creative visualization or intentions to manifest worldly things. Using the power of your mind to make a more comfortable world for yourself is child's play.

This journey is about realizing your Identity in God.

I used to struggle for a long time thinking I must be doing something wrong because I never had a lot of money. I kept praying for a "miracle" of money, not realizing that I was praying for an illusion to be true. Now I see the total perfection of everything that has happened in my life. Money or no money makes no difference. It's green paper. It only buys you the "illusion" of safety. Think about it. Most people spend the majority of their time worrying about how to sustain themselves and survive. I have friends who make $100,000 and they still worry all the time: about getting sick, about losing their jobs, about retirement. There is no stability in the world. Anything can happen in an instant AND DOES. Companies close their doors, banks raise their interest rates, people get divorced, stock markets crash, and nations go to war. The rug can be pulled out from under you at any moment.

I depend on God, not on money or things for my happiness.

Jesus wants you to build your foundation on ROCK, not in quick sand. Let yourself be sustained by the Love of God. Then even the most raging storm will not topple you over. You'll be safe forever.

A Course in Miracles wants you to go the full distance and claim your full inheritance, not just a little piece of it in terms of a million dollars. A million dollars and a mansion are nothing compared to your full inheritance. You are being offered full release from every illusion, all sickness, all fear, all limitation. You are being restored to your awareness of your own perfection and your natural ability to create with God.

Jesus teaches that you be happy no matter what is happening.

You be happy whether you are rich or poor, sick or well.

You be happy because God loves you, and because I love you.

You be happy when things appear to be going wrong.

You be happy when things appear to be going right.

Be happy.

Everything that you need to achieve the goal you are searching for can be found today, right here, right now. *A Course in Miracles* is nothing more than a reminder to change your mind.

When you dream about more money, more things, more comfort, more security, just be reasonable and recognize how much of your thinking is based on a past idea, which has nothing to do with present reality. Realize how much of your learning is based on past memories and perception: on things you've read, seen or heard.

Look at a cup. Do you see a cup, or are you merely reviewing your past experiences of picking up a cup, being thirsty, drinking from a cup, feeling the rim of a cup against your lips, having breakfast and so on? What do you know about this cup except what you learned from the past? You would have no idea what this cup is, except for your past learning. Do you, then, really see it?

This is Lesson #7.

Do you, then, really see it?

Do you, then, really see anything???

This is where my joy comes from. I don't know anything. I come into the day and I let all things be revealed to me. I ask the Holy Spirit, each and every moment:

What would you have me do?

What would you have me say?

Where would you have me go?

I love it. I love it. I love it. Help is given to me. I am never alone.

This world is over. You can be happy. If you have no idea what I am talking about, you can absolutely write to me or better yet: you can buy *A Course in Miracles* and begin to practice. If you already own the book and are not having experiences of total happiness, look at it again.

If you came into this day with no idea about anything, you would be happy. Plain and simple.

God is here. There is only love. You stand in Heaven, thinking you are in hell. There is no world.

All your problems have been solved. That's it. You are God's Son. You are the light God appointed to save the world.

Just as your light increases every light that shines in Heaven, so your joy on earth calls to all minds to let their sorrow go and take their place beside you in God's plan.

today we continue with the theme of happiness

God's Will for you is perfect happiness. This is not simply a nice idea. Every day, each minute, every moment should fill you with joy. Is this your reality?

Today's idea—Lesson 102—says: *You do not want to suffer. You may think it buys you something, and may still believe a little that it buys you what you want. Yet this belief is surely shaken now, at least enough to let you question it, and to suspect it really makes no sense.*

As a teacher of *A Course in Miracles*, I am constantly looking for PRACTICAL ways to express and apply this message in daily life. I love to see a miracle in action. This is not about philosophical speculation or discussion. It is about having an EXPERIENCE of a direct encounter with God.

People ask: "How can I be happy when I have so many problems?"

People love to analyze and observe. They love to get together and talk about problems and solutions. They love process.

If there is one thing that remains a mystery to most people is the IMMEDIACY of a miracle. It doesn't take time to change your mind. It doesn't take a group discussion. You simply decide in this moment that you will be a happy person from now on.

Happy all the time?

How?

This makes zero sense to most people, and YET God's Will for you is perfect happiness.

Right here. Right now.

My joy comes from the thrill of watching my thoughts and realizing they create worlds and matter. It's a happy game. I am not bound by anything. I am free. I love knowing I can travel out beyond the stars, through time and space, backward, forward, to the past, to the future, and to Heaven.

Wouldn't you be happy if you knew you could change your mind and watch pain, misery, depression and sickness disappear in an instant? Would there be any cause at all for suffering then?

A Course in Miracles is always practical. Is there some area of your life that needs fixing or improving? Do you suffer from an unsolvable problem? An addiction? Guilt? Do you spend most of your day worrying?

Whatever problem you seem to face today, start with that idea. Don't try to push it away. Just hold that thought in your mind. Think specifically about a problem that is bothering you.

Now, realize:

This thought reflects a goal that is preventing me from accepting my only function.

Think:

This is a past idea.

If you look honestly, you will recognize that whatever thought you are thinking has nothing to do with the present moment. You will realize you are preoccupied with past thoughts and future ideas.

True happiness comes by being in the present moment. Totally focused. For me, I count my blessings. I make a gratitude list. I look around and see what is directly in front of me.

If you knew today was all there is, you would probably have a different perspective about life You probably would not be concerned about what other people are doing or saying. You probably wouldn't gossip or complain on your last day. Most likely, you would do what you love. At a minimum, you would become completely aware of sights and sounds. I've seen people on their deathbeds who come fully alive in the last few hours. They realize they don't have to worry about anything anymore, and peace comes at last.

Wouldn't it be great to live every day like this, without having to die?

How would you spend your last day?

Would you spend it grieving over mistakes? Would you beat yourself up over regrets, over things left unsaid or undone?

OR

Would you spend it in joy? Calling your friends. Going to a movie. Dancing. Playing. Rejoicing. Being happy.

This is how you stay happy. You come squarely into the present moment. You focus. You come into the NOW. You remember God. You remember all the things you are grateful for.

learn to be a happy learner

I was asked to write an article called "10 ways to _____." Blank blank blank.

I was given the luxury of filling in the blanks. I can write anything I want. 10 ways to please your lover. 10 ways to have a perfect marriage. 10 ways to accomplish world peace. 10 ways to a better beach body by summer. Etc.

I've decided to write an article called "10 WAYS TO BE HAPPY." The reason is because Jesus says, *"The Holy Spirit needs a happy learner in whom His mission can be happily accomplished. You who are steadfastly devoted to misery must first recognize you are miserable and not happy."*

This amazes me. It reads like an employment ad in the newspaper. *"The Holy Spirit needs a happy learner."* It's a job qualification. He needs a happy learner. Being happy is NOT an end goal. It's a qualification.

Knowing yourself is the goal. The salvation of the world is the goal. God is the goal. Happiness is the job requirement. The Holy Spirit needs a happy learner . . . *and you who are steadfastly devoted to misery must first recognize you are miserable and not happy.*

I love it.

I get the impression that many good Course students and teachers mistakenly think that being happy is part of the TRANSFORMATION. Part of the prize at the end of the journey. But that's not what this says. It says *"the Holy Spirit needs a happy learner in whom His mission can be happily accomplished."*

Let me give you an example. My dad is a land surveyor. He makes maps. Making maps is a prerequisite to being a surveyor. It's a job qualification. Certainly he can improve his technique as the years go by but he's not wandering around in the dark uncertain about his map-making abilities. HE KNOWS HOW TO MAKE MAPS. He's not thinking "maybe someday when I'm transformed I'll know how to measure land." No. Making maps and measuring land is not an end goal. It's not a miracle. It's part of the job.

He learned to make maps and measure land in order to call himself a surveyor. You learn to be happy in order to call yourself a teacher of God.

When I first started out in NYC back in the 90's, I needed a job and typing was a very important job qualification. I remember many times I couldn't even get through the front door to the interview because I flunked the typing test. So what did I do? You think I gave up? No. You think I prayed for transformation? No. You think I bemoaned my situation? No. You think I begged God for a miracle? No. I practiced typing. I bought a book and I practiced until I was able to type 80 words a minute, and then getting a job was the simplest thing in the world.

I knew flat out I needed to know how to type. It was right there in BOLD LETTERS. It wasn't an issue of praying for a miracle. I needed to type so I learned how to type.

This says: *"The Holy Spirit needs a happy learner in whom His mission can be happily accomplished."*

LOOKING FOR A FEW GOOD TEACHERS. NEEDS HAPPY LEARNER. APPLY WITHIN.

I know people that have been waiting for years to be transformed from sad to happy. They have been waiting for the "light" to do its job. Or for God to do the work.

But to me, being a Teacher of God is MY job and being happy is my responsibility. Just like I needed to learn how to type, I needed to learn how to be happy

I don't always feel happy, but I've got the employee manual and it says: BE HAPPY.

At the hotel where I work now I was told I have to show up in a tuxedo, so I show up in a tuxedo. I don't show up in jeans and a t-shirt. I do what I'm asked to do.

As a teacher of God, I am asked to show up with smiles and laughter and offer forgiveness, so that's what I do.

Being a teacher of God is a function I've accepted. Being happy is the job. I love it. It's exactly what I've always wanted to do, and like any job it has good days and bad days. I'm still required to show up. I'm required to be responsible. I'm asked to offer a solution to those who still walk in darkness.

This manual, from Jesus, asks that I demonstrate God's Love on earth. I don't question it. I just do it. It says in "What is the Resurrection?" that *"God's teachers have the goal of wakening the minds of those asleep, and seeing there the vision of Christ's face to take the place of what they dream."*

I have the goal of bringing the vision of Christ to everyone who sleeps! What an honor! My job is to be a bright reflection of the Laws of Heaven. I have nothing else to do except demonstrate that God's Will for each and every one of us is perfect happiness.

HA. How cool is this for a job?

There is a sign at the hotel where I work, near the time clock where employees punch in, and it says all the words we are FORBIDDEN to say to guests. We must never say:

- no
- I'm busy
- I don't know
- in a minute

So in this employee manual I've got called *A Course in Miracles*, it says in Lesson 167: *All sorrow, loss, anxiety, suffering and pain, even a little sigh of weariness, a slight discomfort or the merest frown, acknowledge death. And thus deny you live.*

So there it is. Spelled out in BLACK & WHITE. It's like the sign near the employee time clock. THINGS YOU MUST NEVER DO IN FRONT OF YOUR BROTHER OR YOURSELF:

- have a slight discomfort
- a little sigh of weariness
- or the merest frown.

No sorrow, loss, anxiety, sadness, suffering or pain.

It says: *BE HAPPY.*

It says: *You should begin with telling yourself: I am the light of the world. That is my only function. That is why I am here.*

Say that out loud to yourself, and really let it sink in: *I am the light of the world. That is my only function. That is why I am here.*

This employee manual called *A Course in Miracles* tells me exactly who I am, what to do and what NOT to do. It's completely unambiguous and clear. It spells out the instructions in simple practical terms, a step-by-step guide, and all it asks is that I do what it says!

In the ten years I worked in NYC in publishing, there were moments when I didn't feel like working. There were times when I felt overwhelmed. There were times I felt inadequate, not capable, completely in over my head. There were times I felt like quitting.

There were days when I called in sick. But mostly I simply put on a happy face. I got to work on time. I gave it my best. I felt proud of my work. I didn't sit around pouting or sighing. I didn't sit around waiting for something to happen. I showed up and I let the work be revealed to me. I did what was asked of me. When I needed help, I asked for it. When I had a question, I found an answer.

And by showing up every day, I began to feel confidence in myself and in my work. I began to shine brighter. In the beginning I had a tendency to hide behind my desk, but by the end I was out there in the open sunlight—confident of my abilities.

And that's what *A Course in Miracles* is. We step into the job. We learn as we go along. We get better as we practice & apply the lessons.

The Holy Spirit needs a happy learner and in the next day or two I'm going to write a list: Ten Ways To Be Happy.

ten ways to be happy

1. Let every day be a new beginning.
2. Let the past go.
3. Forgive and forget.
4. Do what you love.
5. Know that you are never alone. God goes with you wherever you go.
6. Shine bright.
7. Be helpful.
8. Pray
9. Know your own immeasurable worth.
10. Ask and receive. Jesus says, "You don't ask for too much, you ask for far too little." God longs to give you everything. His Will for you is perfect happiness.

Bonus #11: Get a cat.

love is contagious

I am the light of the world. This is one of my favorite lessons from *A Course in Miracles*.

I reflect a light that shines from within. I am a bright star. My only purpose is to SHINE BRIGHT. When you think like this, nothing can touch you or wreck your day. Nothing can bother you. Think about it. What if you went to work today, having made a decision that you would be happy and bright all day long? What would your day be like? What would other people's reaction be to you?

I, personally, love it when there is a happy person in the room.

It brightens up everything. I used to work with a guy named Yves and we had to be to work at 5:00AM in the morning (in the hotel/restaurant business) and he was always happy. It didn't matter what was happening around him. Usually there would also be five other servers around—who were sullen, tired, bored and unhappy—and then there was Yves.

Energetically, you can tell a happy person a mile away. They don't stand against a wall sulking. They usually have their head held high. Mostly they are moving and active. They smile when they see you coming.

Now, the thing with Yves is he MADE A DECISION to be happy. Why do I say "made a decision"? Because at the time I met him, the love of his life was dying of AIDS.

It was a very bad time. Robert couldn't get out of bed. He lost half his body weight. He was weak and frail and afraid.

But somehow, the AIDS sentence made them both stronger, with more of a determination to live each day as if it was the last. This was not a mental game they played. Each day was possibly his last day on earth. The doctors said Robert could pass away at any time. There was no telling when.

And here is the curious thing: love healed him.

Over the course of the summer I knew them, Robert slowly started getting better and then suddenly he was out of bed, and then he was perfectly fine to do all the things he was used to doing. Before long, he was even MORE active than before he'd been diagnosed with AIDS. He laughed all the time. He was like a little precocious boy, playing all the time. He started setting up groups and organizations in Cape Cod, then in Vermont (where they moved), and then the next thing you know he's working with the U.S. Government—traveling all over the country helping other people.

Love healed him.

The summer of love was 1996. That was over 10 years ago, and he's still more active than ever.

What do I think happened? I, personally, think love is contagious.

It heals all things.

I know that the LOVE AND HAPPINESS AND JOY that was in Yves extended to everyone. It affected everyone. If you were in the same room (or probably even the same state), the love that was coming out of Yves would eventually make its way into your cellular system. This is what I believe. Love got into Rob's cells—and since love is the highest vibration there is, it killed the AIDS cells. I know that love healed me. There is no question in my mind where the light was coming from. It was coming from Yves. Before that summer, I was depressed all the time. I drank every day. I wished I was dead. It was a very bad time. But that summer, hanging around with Yves, healed me.

The light in him was coming from God—and it was always there—regardless of his actions, but if he hadn't been extending it, making a conscious decision to let it flow through him—he would have been like every other human being—sullen, tired, bored—leaning up against the wall, waiting for life to begin.

But instead, he was a direct channel for communication. He let love flow through him to others. He KNEW that he had the POWER to affect people. He knew the power of love. He was not doing it to get anything. He simply had a choice: be happy or be miserable.

He chose to be happy.

Thus, he became a FORCE. Wherever he went, people lit up at the sight of his presence coming toward them. After a while, I noticed that Robert was having the same effect on people. People would light up when they saw him enter a room. This was my very first encounter with realizing I could make a conscious decision to be happy which would make me a presence, a force, a light in the darkness.

I could become the brightest person in every room.

It's a decision. You're not just born that way (or actually, you are born that way, but then you are conditioned to cry & sulk and be sullen, waiting around for life to begin). I can choose to let the LIGHT shine through me.

The light of the world brings peace to every mind through my forgiveness. I am the means God has appointed for the salvation of the world.

Healing

"All healing is release from the past."
—A Course in Miracles

healing is always certain

I am not a body and I'm not just saying this as an empty platitude, like a parrot repeating a learned phrase.

I'm actually not a body.

I am spirit.

I can energize myself in 1/2 a second by thinking about God. I can go with no sleep and still work all day. Nothing affects me, except my thoughts. The body is nothing. One of the managers at the hotel where I work described me as a "horse" which I took as a total compliment.

You are a force. You are energy vibrating. You have all Power. You can do anything you decide you want to do. Today.

Someone called me recently with a request to have her cancer healed, and this I know to be true:

1. God heals.
2. There is nothing to heal. You are whole and perfect.

The only thing that needs healing are your thoughts about yourself. My advice is to do whatever it is you think you cannot do because of your sickness, and do it today. If you did not have cancer, what would you do? If you did not have a limitation, what would you do? Do it today. Send a signal to your body that nothing can stop you. Do not wait for healing, because the healing has already been accomplished. There is no such thing as sickness. You might think you see lingering symptoms but, in fact, you can do anything you want to do today. The doctors will tell you otherwise. They will say you need radiation. They will say they need to run tests.

But you are whole and perfect. You could go for a walk. Today. You could go for a swim. Today. You could send love letters. Today. You could call a friend. Today. You could read a lesson. Today. You could go to the movies. Today. You could help someone in need. Today. Most people wait around to "get better" to start living. But what are you waiting for? There is nothing stopping you from being totally alive, today, except your own thoughts about your own limitation. The body is nothing.

IT IS NOTHING.

I cannot stress this enough. It does nothing. It is nothing. The thing that is allowing your legs and hands to move is the spirit within you and that is not broken. Spirit is not in need of healing. It is whole and perfect. It does not know of your ideas of limitation. It knows no boundaries. It does not know about aging. You could be 70 and win fitness contests. You do not have to accept ideas of "slowing down" and "getting sick." These are lies. I just read an article that older women run faster than younger women in marathons. There is no stopping you from doing anything you want, once you put your mind in charge.

What is IT that would make you feel totally alive?

What are you waiting for?

What is holding you back?

you are not a body

There is still a lot of confusion about what it means to be *"not a body."*

Many people still seem to have difficulty realizing it is not there at all. Why? Because it appears solid. It is part of your experience in the physical world. We are not attempting to escape from it. We are simply instructing the part of your mind that already knows this is true. YOU ARE NOT A BODY.

You are so much more.

We've been through this already, but it needs further clarification. Without the spirit/mind, what does the body do? Just look at it logically, without any spiritual concepts. Look at it like a scientist. What does the body do when there is no spirit in it?

WHAT DOES IT DO?

It does nothing. It doesn't move. It doesn't blink. It doesn't breathe. It grows stiff and cold. It starts to rot like old garbage. Where is the life-force? What is the thing that animated the body?

How could it be that one day the body was moving/walking/talking/laughing and then the next day it was a heap of skeleton & bones, ready to be laid aside?

Who is the "person" who was in that body? Now that it's just a corpse lying there, is that your beloved? Or are they somewhere else? Where did they go? Are we even talking about male/female anymore? Look at it. The scientists call it energy and they say that since energy never dies it simply moves into other matter. Some people say the spirit goes to Heaven. Some people say it goes to hell. Some people say it's reincarnated.

No one really knows. It doesn't matter. All I want to show is the reasonable logical conclusion that YOU ARE NOT YOUR BODY.

YOU ARE NOT A BODY.

If you are trying to change your body, you are attempting to change nothing. It's the mind that needs changing. There is no point trying to escape from the body or from disassociating yourself from it. It is your experience in the physical world. It is the vehicle that transports you from Point A to Point B. It's like a car. It's not who you are, but it becomes a useful tool.

All that is occurring is we are beginning to get closer to the Source of our own reality. We are beginning to recognize our Identity.

The body is not who you are. So many people think it is. They feel bad that it is not younger/fitter/more beautiful. The body is not who you are. It represents ONLY the thoughts you think about yourself in your own mind.

If you hate yourself or are fearful, the body has no other choice but to get sick and fat. You might as well hear it. You are doing this to yourself.

Everything that seems to happen to you is by your own decision. You get what you asked for. I know this seems impossible—who would ask for sickness? Who would ask for weight problems?—but it's true.

You simply need to begin associating with the part of you that is real and never dies and be only that.

You are not a body. You are a mind. Wholly mind. One Mind. Spirit. Light. THIS IS THE REASON WHY YOU ARE PERFECT. Your body is not perfect. YOU are perfect. Your body is nothing.

shifting your energy/changing your mind

It's the wildest thing. I can be in the worst mood ever, with no energy whatsoever, and the second I change my attitude I'm a totally different person. Usually there is so much energy that it causes me to leap out of my chair.

I love what Carlos Castaneda says about the "assemblage point." He says that every individual is a bundle of energy configuration and where that energy comes together is called the assemblage point. It is mostly fixed in the same location on each of us, behind the left shoulder (though not "on" the body, because it's just energy) and that is why we see what appears to be a similar world, but for each of us that point is just slightly different, and that is the reason why private worlds differ.

Castaneda says that it is possible to move the assemblage point by shifting it, through your own determination and will (or with the help of a master, teacher, or warrior) and you will literally be in a different world. The sorcerers were capable of shifting the point so much that they would transport themselves into worlds beyond this world.

He also talks about something called "stalking" where you shift the assemblage point and hold it there to become something else altogether. You can become old or young, male or female, like royalty or like a homeless person. You study the characteristics of whatever you want to become (actually you are studying the energy) and then it's just a matter of practice.

So when I wake up in the morning in those strange energy fields where I feel like I can't get out of bed, and all is hopeless, I shift my energy by the simple movement of pulling in my stomach and standing up straight. I am immediately helpful and gorgeous with one simple, single movement! Watch a pet wake up. They always stretch. Always. Watch them. They know how to shift energy. They go from sound asleep to alert & awake by the simple act of stretching.

It's a miracle! It gets easier and easier, doesn't it?

Words cannot express my appreciation for all of you that show up here every day. Thank you. Thank you for your encouragement and support, as we stand together as the teachers of God. What a privilege! What a blessing that we have found each other at the end of this ancient journey! We are together, at last.

I never know what I'm going to write here every day. I just show up and whatever comes out is what comes out. I never plan for it.

Which is the entire teaching of *A Course in Miracles*: Just show up. Don't plan.

I used to teach a class in NYC on Sunday nights in the East Village and there were a couple times when no one showed up. I'd arrive early at 6:45, put the chairs in order, get ready, sit patiently, and the clock would strike 7:00 and not a body in the room. The first time it happened I felt like a complete failure. I felt that since no one showed up, I should go home.

And just as I was preparing to leave, there was a voice in my head that reminded me it only takes One teacher of God to save the world. What does it matter if it does not seem like there are "bodies" in the room?? It's all just going to be me anyway, expressing my gratitude and thanks and certainty that there is no world and that God's Love goes with us always.

I remembered that I made a PROMISE and a COMMITMENT to teach *A Course in Miracles* in the East Village on a Sunday night at 7:00pm.

I remembered that there is only one mind, and that I'm only teaching myself so that I can learn it, and that for every five minutes spent listening to the truth, 1000 minds wake up.

In that instant I was filled with joy. I knew I was not alone. I knew, in fact, the room was FILLED to the brim with all my friends and mighty companions and Jesus and God and the Holy Spirit, and angels, and lovers and strangers and children.

I began to teach. Out loud. To seemingly no one. I was dramatic and expressive, telling funny stories the way I do, leaning in to make a point, waving my hands, really feeling the total passion of expressing a message of hope. Inevitably, someone, would show up. Always. And almost every time they said it was a miracle to have found me.

So the point is, just show up, even if it looks like no one else is there and you feel like you are all alone.

You are not alone.

You are always only giving to yourself.

The miracle happens to YOU as you begin expressing the truth and extending the love you feel even when it looks like no one is paying attention. You simply speak the words so that you can learn them. The miracle always blesses you.

I have a friend who was very overweight and said he could not stop eating like an out-of-control glutton when he was alone at home. He was really asking for help. He would eat like a gentleman out in public, with fork and knife, small portions, but when he was home alone he would eat all his meals standing up, with his hands, with a big spoon out of the pan, etc. and I said, "Would you eat like that if you had guests??"

He seemed a little shocked and said, "NO, certainly not!'

I asked, "What would you do if you had guests?"

He said, "Well, I'd set the table. I'd pour water. I'd eat from a plate. I'd use a fork."

"Well," I said, "Your Guest is with you. He's with you always. So keep that in mind next time you are shoveling something out of a pan standing over the stove. Your guest is sitting at the table, waiting for you to join him."

From that day on, everything changed for my friend. He went on to lose over 200 pounds. Everything changed for me that day also because I reminded myself of what I'd forgotten. My guest is with me. I'm never alone. Every time I speak something, or write something, I take it to heart. I'm being watched and protected and loved. It's quite a gift.

your cells are being regenerated right now as you read this

Everything is changing all the time. THERE. It just changed again.

Oops. It just changed again.

Here we go. It just changed again. It's changing all the time.

Time is not linear, nor sequential. There is a whole universe out there. They used to think the earth was flat until they realized that it was round.

You think you live in a particular year. You think you have a past behind you and a future ahead of you. But it's not true. Time is not passing. It's going on all the time, here and now. God is.

So if everything is constantly changing, and the cells in your body are constantly being rejuvenated, and you have a new skeleton every three months, a new liver, a new heart, a new brain . . . then why do we still have the same memory patterns? Why do we age? Why do we get sick?

This is from Deepak Chopra in his book *Quantum Healing*, pg 48-49:

"Ninety-eight percent of the atoms in your body were not there a year ago. The skeleton that seems so solid was not there three months ago. The configuration of the bone cells remain somewhat constant, but atoms of all kinds pass freely back and forth through the cell walls, and by that means you acquire a new skeleton every three month.

"The skin is new every month. You have a new stomach lining every four days, with the actual surface cells that contact food being renewed every five minutes. The cells in the liver turn over very slowly, but new atoms still flow through them, like water in a river course, making a new liver every six weeks. Even within the brain, whose cells are not

replaced once they die, the content of carbon nitrogen, oxygen, and so on is totally different today from a year ago."

That's Deepak Chopra. I love him.

The only reason sickness is possible is because you have a cellular memory in you that people get sick. When you were a little kid, you saw that people get old and then they die and everyone around them cries in sadness. You saw that death is something to fear. This memory is stored in you.

For me, having a perfect mind/perfect body has nothing to do with the body. I simply come into the NOW. I let myself be brand new. I release the past. I release the future. I come into a space where I recognize myself as SPIRIT and as LIGHT. The ME that is ME cannot get sick. The YOU that is YOU cannot get sick. It cannot die. It's eternally creative.

While you think you are in a body, the YOU that is YOU is perfect and whole. It's ONE with all things. There is no distance or space between bodies. There is only mind. What do you think happens when you think of people living in other locations? You actually bring a person into your awareness. You can see them in your mind. You have conversations with them in your mind. You think you are daydreaming. What if you knew you actually traveled to that person? You think you live in memories, but when your mind travels to an idea, a place or a person YOU ACTUALLY TRAVEL THERE.

We have too much faith in the body. We doubt that what is in the mind is as real as what is physically in front of us. We've been taught to only trust what is solid.

If you came into a NOW reference, with no link of memory as to who you are or what your body is capable (or not capable) of, you would come into a whole new bright energy field. You would be completely energized. This occurs in an instant. It happens as soon as you remember that you are spirit and light.

This is joining your will with God's Will.

Happiness and peace are inevitable the moment you shut off your own internal dialogue and stop the "play" button on your own repetitive story.

You come into a bright new re-association of yourself, in which your mind and body spring into light—and this light purifies and releases all the old memory cells contained deep within you.

You literally are brand new.

Make a decision to not know anything. Decide today that you will let all things be revealed to you and I guarantee you will be amazed by the loveliness you see.

stop analyzing your problems and be healed

The best part that I love about *A Course in Miracles* is that the past is always gone. Whatever ideas I held about myself yesterday are yesterday's news. Today is a brand new day, a new beginning.

I am constantly receiving new instructions, but in order to receive I must be receptive and have a space ready and open and clear. It's impossible for a new thought system to occupy the same place where there is an old thought system. You need to get rid of the old before you bring in the new. You clear a space. You can't fit two of anything in the same location. It's physically impossible. Try it with bodies. It can't be done. You are always going to be in a slightly different space than anyone else, at any given moment.

You can't have a hate thought and a love thought in the same place. You must choose. YOU ARE THE DECIDER. There is no one out there doing anything to you. There is nothing happening to you except what you have chosen and elected. This is a dream of your own making.

A Course in Miracles is about CONSISTENCY. It is about choosing a new way to think about yourself. It requires you to be ruthless and fearless.

YOU DECIDE ON THE TIME FACTOR OF WHEN THIS ALL OCCURS.

Never underestimate the density of your own cellular memories of time and space. You are a solid body undergoing a physical transformation. Of course it's going to be messy at times. Of course it is going to be painful. That is not your concern. Finally, we stop trying to suppress the pain with food or drugs or medication. We stop trying to make ourselves more comfortable. Finally we decide we are going to face our fear and pain straight on. We are going to battle the devil which are only our own ideas about ourselves. Finally, we stop naming things and remember that we are simply allowing old cells/old memories to be replaced with new cells/new thoughts.

It's going to be a little painful, and it's going to hurt a little, but then it will be over.

Most people live a lifetime suppressing pain rather than have a moment of total terror in facing the demon. Most people's solution is to run to the doctor or pharmacy and try to fix a problem by taking a pill and suppressing the problem rather than looking at it straight on, with open eyes.

Is there really anything to fear? What are you afraid of? Do bad things actually happen to you or is it merely anticipation of bad things? Most people are afraid of things that never come to pass. They spend all their time worrying about nothing, and all this worrying and fear makes a body sick and weak and tired.

Why would you do that to yourself?

Our bodies are filled with instructions about our hatred and self-worth. We have years and years and years of telling ourselves how worthless we are. As a result, our cells are old and tired. No wonder we age. We are beaten down by false ideas about ourselves as bodies.

You are not a body, and yet every cell in your body has been programmed with particular memories that are individual to YOU. Think about all the instructions you have given yourself—I am male, I am white, I am good, I am bad, I am married, I am single, I am female, I am black, I am Jewish, I need, I want, I am.

Where are the true ideas?

Do you wake up in the morning and instruct yourself that you are THE LIGHT OF THE WORLD?

Do you remind yourself all day long of your total perfection?

You are whole and perfect as God created you. This is a fact.

Right here, right now.

We need to start reprogramming our cells, reprogramming our minds. We need to excavate old ideas and the only way to do that is to blast guilt, misery, depression and doubt with new bright ideas. HOSE DOWN THE DARKNESS WITH THE LIGHT OF HEAVEN.

Looking at the dark will avail you nothing. Analyzing the darkness will never work. You must turn on the light.

As you practice ideas of truth, your mind changes. But because the body appears as solid it appears to lag behind the mind. So while the mind races ahead with fresh new ideas & exciting inspiring thoughts the body appears to be stuck in the old space. It looks like nothing is happening. Things appear as they have always been even though you "feel" different. This process can be uncomfortable. It can take on feelings of loneliness, futility, depression, laziness, anxiety & discomfort. You know you are destined for greater experiences, yet you seem paralyzed. Then suddenly, one day, as if by miracle, the body starts to move. You start to have more energy.

I was told by a great teacher that the VIBRATION of the sound of your own voice is important in this process. She said "it was the sound of your own voice that taught you the falsity of separation. So it is going to have to be the sound of YOUR OWN VOICE that teaches you the truth. You must sound these ideas from the Lessons of *A Course in Miracles*."

She said this is the reason why understanding is NOT necessary. She said as you SPEAK the lessons, the vibration of the sound of your voice changes you on a cellular level. It's like electricity. You don't need to understand how it works. When the vibration is sent out by switching on a light, the work is accomplished and the light goes on. This is a natural process of energy and vibration. When you pick up the phone and dial you don't need to understand how airwaves work. All you need is the action of picking up the phone and dialing.

So it is with any awakening process. You don't have to understand how it works. You simply send out the vibration. You speak the lesson. Speak it out loud. This is the process of sending a vibration from your mind down to the cellular level of the physical body. You may think you are teaching other people. But in fact, you are simply sending the new signal to yourself. It's quite extraordinary. The more you teach it, the more you speak the lessons out loud, the faster the cells change, and the more you transform. *A Course in Miracles* says, "*to teach is to demonstrate.*" Trust me. It's a miracle. It's physical transformation. I encourage you to try it for yourself.

DO TRY THIS AT HOME:

Read the lessons out loud. I dare you to tell someone they are the light of the world. I DARE YOU. Walk up to someone you know (or don't know!) and tell them you appreciate them. If you want an even faster awakening, start telling people you love them. THIS IS THE FAST ROUTE. Start telling yourself you love yourself. Say the word

God out loud. Do not attempt to understand what is happening. Do not try to figure it out. Your understanding is not necessary.

Here is a test. Say this out loud and with conviction:

I LOVE YOU. NOTHING I SEE MEANS ANYTHING. GOD IS MY SOURCE. GOD IS MY STRENGTH. THANK YOU. BLESS YOU. I AM NOT A BODY. I AM FREE. I WILL THERE BE LIGHT. I AM NEVER UPSET FOR THE REASON I THINK. I LOVE YOU. MY HOLINESS BLESSES THE WORLD. GOD GOES WITH ME WHEREVER I GO. I AM SUSTAINED BY THE LOVE OF GOD. FORGIVENESS OFFERS EVERYTHING I WANT. THERE IS NO DEATH. GOD IS LOVE, AND THEREFORE SO AM I.

Are you able to say these things out loud? It is my experience, you will resist these ideas. If you can say these statements out loud, you will be changed automatically. The healing begins simply as you sound the words. It's like talking on your cell phone or using the internet: you don't have to understand how the process works, you just know that it does. How much time do you spend instructing yourself that you PURE LIGHT and TOTAL PERFECTION? Think about how much time you spent telling yourself that you are a body—24 hours a day, for 20 or 30 years or 50 years. Think about it. All day long you have thoughts about your own identity and how to sustain yourself in the world to keep yourself safe and comfortable. This is the real reason the body gets sick—the mind has been poisoned with false ideas.

You start injecting true thoughts into your mind, and you do it all day long, because there is work to be done. All day long you keep blasting yourself with thoughts like *"I am the light of the world"* and *"Nothing I see means anything."*

The frequency of a thought of God is stronger than the frequency of your ideas of time & space and sickness, and so the God thought blasts all false ideas right out of your mind and body and this is how healing occurs.

You keep feeding yourself light all day long. You keep feeding yourself the lessons of *A Course in Miracles*. Your understanding is not required. You simply have to sound the lessons. Say them. Think them. Do them. Send them down into your body. Do not worry how this is accomplished. Just do the lesson as it instructs.

And you will see that suddenly you feel lighter and happier, and you will want to keep sending new ideas down into your cells and blast the crap cells out.

I love you.

Responsibility

Forgiveness

"Forgiveness is the key to happiness."
—A Course in Miracles

what is forgiveness?

Forgiveness recognizes what you thought your brother did to you has not occurred.

ASTONISHING.

Forgiveness recognizes what you thought your brother did to you has not occurred. It's a reminder that what you thought happened did not occur at all. Literally. There is nothing to forgive. Everything is still as it always was in the beginning. Nothing has changed. Nothing has been altered. Appearances can deceive, but they do nothing. Nothing has happened at all.

Forgiveness is the answer to your search for peace. Here is the key to meaning in a world that seems to make no sense. Here is the way to safety in apparent dangers that appear to threaten you at every turn, and bring uncertainty to all your hopes of ever finding quietness and peace. Here are all questions answered; here the end of uncertainty ensured at last.

Sounds good to me.

one good reason to forgive

1. You'll awaken from the dream.

It's better than winning the lottery. *Forgiveness offers you everything. Do you want peace? Forgiveness offers it. Do you want happiness, a quiet mind, a certainty of purpose, and a sense of beauty that transcends the world? Do you want care and safety, and the warmth of sure protection always? Do you want a quietness that cannot be disturbed, a gentleness that never can be hurt, a deep abiding comfort, and a rest so perfect it can never be upset?*

All this forgiveness offers you, and more.

I love Workbook lesson 192: *I have a function God would have me fill.* It reminds me that creation cannot be conceived of in the world, you have to get to Heaven first in order to begin creating, and the only way this is possible is complete forgiveness in this world.

This lesson is the one that gave me a practical reason to forgive. Until I got to this lesson, I couldn't really see the benefit of letting go of grievances other than I might be a little more peaceful, and at the time, that just wasn't enough of an incentive for me.

But when I got to Lesson 192, Jesus tells me point-blank that I would be stuck in a human condition, with all its limitations, until I forgive everything including myself. THEN, once that had been accomplished, life would get really interesting (at last!) because I would spring into Heaven, which is here (it's just a higher level of consciousness) and my mind would be in a whole new place capable of new ideas. I would be at the level of pure creation. Miracles would occur naturally. There would be abundance all around me. The body would be healed.

Forgiveness cleans the slate, and in this clean and empty space God can now replace the senseless symbols that were written there before.

Forgiveness wipes the slate clean. It literally vacuums out every old conflict, grievance, hurt and in that place God will place new ideas of grace, joy, and innocence.

So a miracle will be that your ideas of your unhappy childhood or devastating relationship will be washed clean and in that place you will begin to remember only the good things that occurred. Your childhood will suddenly be transformed into a happy one. Your love relationships, which were once devastating and a cause of anger, suddenly will be remembered as happy.

I have a function God would have me fill.

And that function is forgiveness.

Therefore hold no one prisoner. Release instead of bind, for thus are you made free. The way is simple. Every time you feel a stab of anger, realize you hold a sword above your head. And it will fall or be averted as you choose to be condemned or free. Thus does each one who seems to tempt you to be angry represent your savior from the prison house of death. And so you owe him thanks instead of pain.

My function is to forgive, and that leads me out of the world entirely.

My function is to be happy. It is here life gets interesting because I'm not in the world anymore, I'm in Heaven where miracles occur naturally. It's just a lot more fun and creative once you get yourself out of the world.

And how is it accomplished?

Through your own forgiveness.

This course is always practical.

forgiveness does make lovely, but it does not create

The above sentence is from *A Course in Miracles*. It's one of my favorite lines. When I read it, a light bulb went off in my head. It reminds me of the necessity to GO BEYOND forgiveness. While I am still in a condition of grievances/forgiveness, I am in a time-space location. Look at it. We've only scratched the surface. There is a whole universe out there. Miracles begin occurring naturally as you express only love.

At the very height of perfect forgiveness you are still trapped in a human condition. Forgiveness is NOT the highest goal. Forgiveness is a door that we go beyond. You reach this place, and you make a decision that you will love everyone and everything, every situation, every event AS GOD DOES. There are no more distinctions. What is left to forgive?

From here, you travel swiftly.

Nothing rattles your cage. You don't care what anyone does. You see that your only function is salvation. What could POSSIBLY upset you when you know that happiness is God's Will for you?

I see that a lot of people are still trying to "wake up." I shall never understand this. YOU WAKE UP NOW BY DECISION AND CHOICE. It is not a process. Enlightenment does not take time UNLESS you still cherish the idea of process and then of course your mind will come up with all sorts of people, places, events that need to be forgiven and healed. In this case, enlightenment will take forever.

But when you have had enough of the drama, jealousy, and chaos, you will see how easy it is to let it go.

You stop dragging in your old story to display to other people. You stop analyzing. You stop trying to understand. You stop making mental lists of things that need to be healed and forgiven in you. You stop looking at your childhood hurts. You stop trying to "get it." There is nothing to get. You are whole and perfect as God created you.

Let's suppose you move to a brand new location where no one knows you as depressed, lazy, irresponsible, a thief, a liar, an addict, or a gambler. You move somewhere where no one knows you. The landscape is entirely untouched by your old story. You are given a brand new opportunity for invention. So what do you do? Do you tell people you have cancer in the first ten minutes of meeting them? Or do you decide that you have been given a new opportunity to not be a victim anymore? To be vibrantly alive and happy. The power of decision IS the miracle. You choose to stop telling people you are sick. You choose to stop telling them you are depressed and limited and poor. You decide that in the new location you will inspire people and bring them hope.

This is what it means to be reborn.

You hear this, and then immediately you are off on "yea, but . . ."

YEA BUT WHAT?

CREATION is your reality.

Staying in a place of forgiveness can make you have a nice human life, full of roses and kisses and happy friends . . . but when you look it, you will see how very limited this is. CREATION IS BEING OFFERED.

Healing the sick and raising dead.

Open your eyes today and look upon a happy world of safety and of peace.

We move beyond forgiveness. We move beyond looking at our grievances and seeing what still needs to be healed. We stop looking at the past. We let it go. WHEN YOU LET IT GO, IT'S GONE. You can't even remember it. It's dust back there.

Think about it. Someone shows up and asks if you want to go on the most fantastic adventure of your life. If you decide to go, THEN YOU GO. You can't stay in your current condition AND go on an adventure. You choose. An adventure is an adventure. It's not make-pretend. You actually go and have new experiences. Cool things happen. You have new stories to tell. You close the travel brochure, you pack your bags and you GO.

forgiveness vs. creation

I am in love with Jesus. I love how there is no religion involved in forgiveness. It's pure common sense. I'm going to keep going with this idea because it's the clearest cut example of why we should not hold on to a single grievance, ever.

Again. Here is the sentence:

Forgiveness does make lovely, but it does not create.

Here is the whole paragraph:

Yet even forgiveness is not the end. Forgiveness does make lovely, but it does not create. It is the source of healing, but it is the messenger of love and not its Source. Here you are led, that God Himself can take the final step unhindered, for here does nothing interfere with love, letting it be itself. A step beyond this holy place of forgiveness, a step further inward but the one you cannot take, transports you to something completely different. Here is the Source of light; nothing perceived, forgiven nor transformed. But merely known.

Can you hear this?

Can you see what this says?

It's unbelievable. Forgiveness is not the end. You will still be trapped in time as long as you are saying you are sorry. Telling someone you are sorry, or forgiving them, or forgiving yourself DOES MAKE LOVELY . . . but it does not create.

You must get BEYOND forgiveness. You must get to the place where you say "I am going to look with Christ vision from now on. I am going to look beyond every appearance of bodies and see only what is eternal and true. I will not let my eyes play dirty tricks on me anymore. I will see God in everyone."

Things still happen to me, and I still say I'm sorry but I don't waste even a half-a-second hanging onto the grievance. I am willing to be wrong. Heck, I LIKE to be wrong! It's faster that way. There's nothing to explain. There's no conversation about "who did what." There's no story. It's END OF STORY/END OF CONVERSATION.

Try it. You'll see. If someone has done something to you, angered you, hurt you, humiliated you, gossiped about you, try taking responsibility for the situation. Try it. It's amazing. There will be no story.

Remember: there are only two emotions, love and fear. And what is not love is a call for love. That simplifies it. If someone is calling you an idiot, they are in fear.

If someone is attacking you, they don't need further attack . . . they need love. They need appreciation. They need recognition. They do NOT need you telling them they are wrong. Give them some love. Don't wait for them to say they are sorry because you will be waiting a very long time.

Why?

Because everything stands still until YOU change YOUR mind. Nothing changes until YOU change. That's the way it works. You step back and the light steps forward. When you decide you no longer want to participate in the conflict, you will do anything to get out of it. Including being wrong.

Try it.

Don't you want to arrive at the place where miracles are occurring?? Don't you want to be creating with God?

I mean, being in the world is so boring. Someone does something, you have to have a conversation about it, you talk to your friends about it, you stew about it for a few days, and maybe someone says they are sorry or they send a gift or a card, and you kiss and make up . . . until the whole boring cycle starts again.

In Heaven, it's one miracle after another. You think something and then it manifests. There are no problems. No worries. No cares. No sickness. No limitation. You ask and receive.

But here's the thing: you can't get to Heaven holding a grievance. Sorry, folks. It doesn't work that way. You cannot enter the kingdom without your brother. You either hold his hand in gratitude and enter the kingdom together OR you are trapped here alone in a very cold place.

The decision is yours. Stop trying to figure out your problems. Just let them go. If someone is hurting you or upsetting you, you have a decision to make:

1. Are you going to hang on to the grievance, try to figure out the problem, be right, and stay in hell?

OR

2. Are you going to remember how much forgiveness offers you so you can spring into Heaven where everything is easy and effortless?

Which choice is it going to be for you? Heaven or hell?

The choice is yours.

Jesus says in *A Course in Miracles*, *"If miracles are not happening, something has gone wrong."*

If miracles are not happening, you are being a limited human being. If your life is not effortless, happy, and lit by miracles, you simply need to change your mind. It's that easy. It's not difficult. Be here only for today, as a bright demonstration of the Laws of God. Be yourself. Be helpful. Give. Love. Go beyond forgiveness.

Forgiveness does make lovely, but it does not create.

Let God take the final step unhindered. He will take the final step, but YOU have to prepare yourself for it. You can't enter Heaven holding on to anything. A step beyond forgiveness *transports you to something completely different. Here is the source of light; nothing perceived, forgiven nor transformed. But merely known.*

Don't you want to know what this place is like? Can you imagine standing in a place where there is no perception? Can you imagine? A place where nothing is forgiven nor transformed? But merely known?

I don't know about you but when I read this paragraph (in Chapter 18), I reaffirmed my commitment to God. My dedication is to let all grievances go, no matter what it takes, so that I can get to the place of CREATION. That's where the adventure really is. Creating with God. Miracles everywhere.

A step beyond this holy place of forgiveness, a step further inward but the one you cannot take, transports you to something completely different.

I want to be transported. Wanna come with me?

great advice: forgive and forget

Today I claim the gifts God is waiting to give to me.

Why wait another day to find the treasures that God offers you? Why wait another day in conflict? Why hold a grievance? Why blame your lover, your family, your spouse, your children, your boss, or your neighbor?

Why?

That makes no sense.

Forgiveness is your function as the light of the world. You have no other function. It is the only function God gave you. This is the ONLY way you can take your rightful place among the saviors of the world. This is the ONLY way you can find peace of mind.

Do you want to be right or do you want to be happy?

YOU DECIDE.

It is a decision you must make.

You can be happy all the time, if you choose.

How is this accomplished?

1. drop the grievance
2. do something nice

The more I look at it, the more I see this is a course that a five-year old could learn. Lots of times people will say "I know that already. It's not working for me."

Well, I say . . . give it another try.

People who are training to be great athletes or musicians or craftsmen, don't give up the first try, or the second try, or even the tenth try, proclaiming that the technique is not working. They try and try again. They practice until they are perfect. They keep picking up the ball. They make mistakes, they fall down . . . AND THEY GET UP . . . and they try again.

It's the same with forgiveness. If you think it didn't work the first time, try it again. If it fails a second time, try it again.

Jesus says in the bible you must forgive seventy times seven times. That's 490 times. So, are you giving up after the 20th attempt? Or are you in a constant condition of practicing 490 times?

You are the savior of the world. You don't give up after the first attempt. You keep practicing. You keep practicing. You keep practicing.

Today is a brand new day with endless opportunities to get up and try again. You can call your "enemy" and say something nice. You can ask for forgiveness. You can write a letter. You can offer to be helpful. You can choose to forget hurtful incidents, by leaving them in the past.

Forgive and forget. It's great advice.

You are the light of the world. That is your only function. That is the reason why you are here.

Sickness

are you sick?

If you are sick and want to know how to never be sick again, read Chapter 8 in *A Course in Miracles*. It's got everything you need to know.

It says, *"A sick body does not make any sense"* and *"sickness is a way of demonstrating that you can be hurt. It is a witness to your frailty, your vulnerability, and your extreme need to depend on external guidance."*

The surprising thing about these early chapters of *A Course in Miracles* is how much Jesus is asking us to teach others. To allow our bodies to be an empty vessel for the Holy Spirit.

The entire "training period" of *A Course in Miracles* is only to remove the blocks that are in us so that the Holy Spirit can use our bodies to extend His Mind through us. That we may demonstrate the Love and Laws of God on earth, as it is in Heaven.

We are not even needed in the process, except to be WILLING to allow this to occur, so that our bodies can be a clean pure communication channel. It's kind of amazing. I need do nothing. Except get out of the way. The Holy Spirit will do everything else BUT HE IS LIMITED IF I STILL BRING IN MY OWN IDEAS.

In the 50 Miracle Principles it says, *Miracles are everyone's right, but purification is necessary first.* Now I see what this means. To totally allow every block to be removed in me, a total surrender to God, to be completely purified of all my past ideas, washed clean of all limiting beliefs. Then my body is used for communication purposes to reach others.

It's amazing how much of the text says you need to teach this message, to demonstrate it, to be the message and the messenger.

It says it over and over and over. You can't learn it until you begin to teach it. *Knowledge is not the motivation for learning this course. Peace is.*

How amazing. We are not learning it to know something. We are learning it to be at peace. To be happy. To be free. We don't even need to memorize the words. We don't need to study them. We don't need to understand them. We simply need to give some time to the Holy Spirit so that he can remove the blocks to the awareness of love's presence. That's why it's a miracle! We need do nothing!

It's also got some very uncompromising sentences in here:

If God's Will for you is complete peace and joy, unless you experience only this you must be refusing to acknowledge His Will. His Will does not vacillate, being changeless forever. When you are not at peace it can only be because you do not believe you are in Him. Yet He is all in all. His peace is complete, and you must be included in it.

Do you see that? If you are not joyful, you are refusing to acknowledge God's Will. How simple! How uncompromising! If you are not joyous, you are sleeping. You are in a nightmare. You are in a death sequence. In that moment of depression, sadness, loneliness or anxiety you have forgotten who you are! That's all! In a moment of remembering that JESUS WALKS WITH YOU, you will become happy again. When you remember you are the light of the world and that God is with you, you will be doing cartwheels.

Another good sentence: *No one who does not accept his function can understand what it is, and no one can accept his function unless he knows what he is.*

You see? You have to know yourself. It's the only goal of the curriculum. Know yourself and you are free. Know that you are light. Know that you are eternal. Know that you can't die. Know that you are what love is. Know yourself.

To fulfill the Will of God perfectly is the only joy and peace that can be fully known, because it is the only function that can be fully experienced.

This is so totally true. I'm only happy when I'm letting the Holy Spirit work through me. I'm happy when I'm helping others. I'm happy when I'm giving. I'm happy when I'm making someone laugh. I'm happy when I join someone, letting all our differences go.

It's our final happy game on earth.

You should be having fun! You're not meant to be sick *(a sick body does not make any sense.)* Is this your reality? If not, read Chapter 8. You were created by God, as whole and perfect. This is your natural state and this should be your experience. Not as an "idea" or a "concept" but as a reality.

As you enter into new frequencies of energy, the body can sometimes appear to be sick but if you don't call it sickness, it will vanish before your eyes and you will actually be in a brighter space then before the "sickness." You will feel lighter and clearer, with more clarity and happiness. You'll be totally amazed, like wow, I feel like a brand new person.

BECAUSE YOU ARE A BRAND NEW PERSON!

Remember, this is PHYSICAL resurrection. Your body is included in the transformation. You go from being dense solid mass to light and as the shift occurs, your body might go through some physical stuff. Don't be concerned. Be grateful. Thank God.

the real cause of sickness.

When you do not value yourself you become sick.

Wellness has nothing to do with proper nutrition or exercise. When you learn to value yourself as God values you, sickness becomes impossible.

You probably know of someone who doesn't drink or smoke, who exercises regularly, takes vitamins, eats a perfectly healthy diet and yet they still manage to get cancer and die. Then there are those who break every health rule in the book and they live to be 100. Doesn't this make you pause and wonder what causes sickness?

Jesus in *A Course in Miracles* is very direct. He says, *When you do not value yourself you become sick, but my value of you can heal you.*

You get sick because you do not value yourself. Plain and simple. This is the real cause of sickness. If you think you are unworthy, shameful, guilty and unlovable, you will eventually become sick. It does not matter how much you take care of the body.

What does Jesus and God think about you? That you are wholly lovable and loving, creative and perfect. *This is the way you should think about yourself.* Your worth is not established by anything you say or do. Your worth is established by God.

Wouldn't it be great to have a perfect body? Wouldn't it be wonderful to feel alive and full of energy? God's value of you can heal you. Are you ready to let go of your limited self-perception of yourself and allow a new experience to transform your life? The results of changing your mind to think like God will heal you.

The body's only true usefulness is to express the Love of God to others.

I really love *A Course in Miracles*. Listen to this:

Remember that it does not matter where in the Sonship God is accepted. He is always accepted for all, and when your mind receives Him the remembrance of Him awakens throughout the Sonship. HEAL YOUR BROTHERS SIMPLY BY ACCEPTING GOD FOR THEM. *Your minds are not separate, and God has only one channel for healing because He has but one Son.*

This is what it means to the be savior of the world. You accept total responsibility for everyone and everything, healing all, simply by remembering God, our Father.

How simple! You heal the world by remembering your True Identity in God!

Here is Jesus speaking to you: *Sickness is a way of demonstrating that you can be hurt*

How about that? You get sick because you think of yourself as frail and vulnerable. You think you can be hurt. You associate yourself with your body. This is the real cause of sickness. You think you are unworthy, shameful, guilty, unlovable. You think these things and you get sick. You do not value yourself.

"BUT GOD'S VALUE OF YOU CAN HEAL YOU."

Here is a description about you. It is the way you should begin thinking about yourself:

"Child of God, you were created to create the good, the beautiful and the holy. Do not forget this. The Love of God, for a little while, must still be expressed through one body to another, because vision is still so dim. You can use the body best to help you enlarge your perception so you can achieve real vision, of which the physical eye is incapable. Learning to do this is the body's only true usefulness."

Your worth is not established by anything you say or do. Your worth is established by God. Period. There is no room for argument or discussion here. You are whole and perfect. It doesn't matter what you think. God established your worth. He created you perfect. Everything else is your own nightmare.

sadness is a direct attack on God

When you are depressed, you are literally attacking God. You are not being neutral. You are making a conscious decision to attack.

Why is this? Because you've been told the truth. You've been told what to do. You've been told who your Father is. You've been told your Identity as the Light of the world. You've been told that happiness is your natural state.

YOU'VE BEEN TOLD.

You can't play dumb anymore. You can't play the "poor-me-boo-hoo" game because now you know. You can't cry in your corner and think everyone is against you anymore, because now you know you're doing it to yourself.

YOU'VE BEEN TOLD.

You know that everything is you, even if you don't entirely believe it, there is a part in your mind that has been instructed.

There is only ONE way out of sadness and that is to change your mind. Please don't wait for external circumstances to change, because it will never happen. You will be waiting for a thousand years for someone outside of yourself to make you happy while you hold the whole world in chains. Please wake up. Change occurs FIRST in your mind—right here, right now—and THEN external circumstances change. It's the way it works.

You are responsible for what you see. No one is doing anything to you. God is not punishing you. It's all you, making a decision for happiness or sadness. That's why at this level conflict seems even more acute than before. BECAUSE NOW YOU KNOW. When you attack someone else, there is a part of your mind that knows you are attacking yourself and God. When you sit and cry, you know that you are lingering in time and Jesus says, *"Delay in time is tragic."*

You've been told that *"sickness is a defense against the truth."* IT'S A DEFENSE. It's not neutral. It's a wall you put up to keep God out. You've been told that *"a little sigh of weariness, a slight discomfort, the merest frown"* are death. DEATH. *Death is a thought that takes on many forms, often unrecognized. It may appear as sadness, fear, anxiety or doubt; as anger, faithlessness and lack of trust, concern for bodies, and envy.*

Please stop for a minute and ask yourself, are you participating in any of these emotions?

SADNESS

FEAR

ANXIETY

DOUBT

ANGER

FAITHLESSNESS

LACK OF TRUST

CONCERN FOR BODIES

ENVY

A LITTLE SIGH OF WEARINESS

A SLIGHT DISCOMFORT

THE MEREST FROWN

Ask yourself. Because if you're doing any of the above, you are killing yourself. You are attacking God and yourself and every one around you. You are keeping everyone in hell while God speaks to you of Heaven. He is with you. You are literally standing in front of the Creator of all Creation, Who offers you every gift in the universe, and you are poisoning yourself with sadness. Please stop doing that to yourself. Please. It's time we came to our senses. Time to wake up. Time to put our toys away. Time to stop dying.

how can you who are so holy suffer?

This is a REALLY good question to keep in mind, especially when things start to go "wrong." How can you who are so holy suffer? Life is one big adventure. There's no such thing as good or bad. Wrong or right. There is only awake or sleeping. There is no need to be depressed for even one second.

Did you know it takes more energy to be depressed than to be happy? That's right. Because your NATURAL state is happiness—so in order to be sad you must OPPOSE your natural state . . . and . . . in order to achieve this you must use the power of God. That's the reason why in a depressed state you have no energy for anything else. You just used all your power to dig yourself a hole. Now you simply want to sleep and slouch and crawl under the covers and sit in front of the television all day. Think about it! You just used all your energy to be depressed!

Be careful!

Once you are in a sad/depressed state, it can be very difficult to pull yourself out. It's easier to stay happy than it is to pull a black cloud over yourself and then have to get yourself out of the deep pit you dug for yourself.

It's easier to NOT take the first step into hell than it is to get yourself out of hell. Do you know what I mean? It's easier to decide to not pull the trigger than it is to try to get yourself out of jail. It's easier to keep your mouth shut than it is to try to clean up a whole mess that gossip creates. It's easier to stay healthy than it is to try and get well. Do you see the difference? All actions have consequences and YOU are the determiner of what happens to you.

You can choose to be happy. You can choose to stand on holy ground while the rest of the world of chaos swirls around you. You can choose to not participate in conflict. There is always another alternative for you to choose.

You can choose to see yourself as needed for salvation. Now we are in MIND-TRAINING, seeing everything in a new way. In the world we are taught that creative abilities are used for art, painting, drawing, writing, sculpting, making music, etc.

But you are using your creative abilities every single minute of the day. Did you know it's a creative act to make a cup of tea? To write a letter, put a stamp on an envelope, drive to the post office and drop it in the mail. To cook a meal. To tell someone you love them. That is a very high form of creative expression. It's not something else. Every movement is energy. Every decision either inspires you or fatigues you. Up to this moment, you simply have not been aware.

Your natural state is one of extension. In order to cave in on yourself and shut yourself off from the world, you are actually using your creative abilities to put yourself in that state. Kind of screwed up, huh? You are taking all your God-given power and using it to slouch in a chair.

Now, we are training our minds in a systematic way to be conscious of our actions and thoughts.

stem cells and you and dead fishes.

The scientists have proven that you can take a perfect specialized cell (a stem cell) and put that cell into a sick adult and that one little healthy cell will create a perfect liver, heal the sickness, cast out the old cells and energize and make vibrant the old body. ONE LITTLE CELL!

And this is exactly what one perfect thought does in the body—it casts out all negative thought!! It drives away all sickness. It blasts out old dead cells. ONE PERFECT THOUGHT OF GOD, INSERTED INTO THE BODY, WILL HEAL YOU PERFECTLY!!!!

You are the physician. You are the patient. You decide you want to be healed, and then you insert a perfect thought into your body and let the healing take place. Your understanding is not necessary. Do you have to understand how a stem cell works in a human body? Do you have to understand how electricity works to turn on the light? NO. But there is an action required. You have to insert the new cell into the old body or you have to walk across the room and switch on the light switch.

And so it is with this. You must begin to remember God when everything around you is falling apart. You must bring in the LIGHT when there is darkness all around you.

Don't try to analyze the darkness. Do not try to fix the problem. JUST BRING IN THE LIGHT. Forget about the problem and think about a lesson from *A Course in Miracles*. THIS WILL HEAL YOU. AUTOMATICALLY AND WITHOUT YOUR UNDERSTANDING OF HOW IT WAS ACCOMPLISHED.

Just do the lesson. Just do what it says. Just read it.

You will be amazed at how radically different your life will become with a little willingness and a little practice.

How often do you practice ideas of truth? How much do you remember God? How often do you remember your function of forgiveness and happiness? 5 minutes every hour? 10 minutes? Morning and night? 45 minutes out of every hour?

OR

Every second of every minute of every day???

The mind-training of *A Course in Miracles* is just that: A MIND TRAINING. You begin to train your mind in a systematic way by watching your thoughts and changing them as they pop into your awareness.

You catch a guilt thought or you have a moment of doubt and the mind-training allows you to catch the thought while you are thinking it, and replace it with a new thought like "God loves me".

Someone says something mean to you, and you begin to feel upset and you catch yourself again and insert a new bright thought like: "I AM THE LIGHT OF THE WORLD!"

All day long, in every situation, you keep catching old dead thoughts (doubt, sadness, worry, jealousy, anger, depression) and casting them out. You keep your body & mind vibrating with new ideas. IT'S MARVELOUS. You keep bringing in the light.

The best part of all is that you don't have to analyze anything at all!! Do you analyze a dead fish???? Why would you?? The moment you see it clearly for what it is—a dead fish—you toss it away!! You don't keep it, hoping it will come alive. You don't study it for weeks on end. You don't bring it to your therapist in hopes of understanding it. You instantly know it as a dead fish. You immediately have a reaction like "GROSS!!" and then you toss it away. You want to get it out of your hands and life as quickly as possible. So it is with all your thoughts. You have a moment of doubt or fear and you go "GROSS!!!!!!!" and you toss it away!!

See how simple this becomes! See the happy game we play!

We are just catching old dead thoughts and throwing them away! We don't keep them and study them in hopes of understanding ourselves better. We recognize fear thoughts are dead and serve no purpose! We throw them away! We don't want deadness and sickness in our bodies anymore. We cast it out!

I find that even my posture straightens when I practice in this way. I instantly come alive. All thoughts of worry disappear, and I get instantly happy.

Death

"A warrior considers himself already dead, so there is nothing to lose. The worst has already happened to him, therefore he's clear and calm."
—Carlos Castaneda

there is no death

Let's review this again. You think death is of the body, but *death is a thought that takes on many forms, often unrecognized.*

Here are the times when you are dead:

When you are:

1. sad
2. fearful
3. anxious
4. doubtful
5. angry
6. in pain
7. suffering
8. bored
9. tired
10. sick
11. worrying
12. envious
13. jealous

You think death is of the body. You do not realize that you are already dead, in what appears to be a body walking around.

You are dead until you change your mind and renounce all forms of death (see list).

Death is the alarm to which you give response of any kind that is not perfect joy. It is the one idea which underlies all feelings that are not supremely happy.

HERE IS DEATH:

1. a little sigh of weariness.
2. a slight discomfort.
3. the merest frown.

Can you see how uncompromising this course really is? It asks that you be happy. It asks you to wipe that frown off your face (one of my earliest teachings as a child).

Are you dead or alive? All you have to do is look at your emotional state to answer this question.

Death is the thought that you are separate from God. It is the belief that conditions change, emotions alternate because of causes you cannot control, that you did not make and you can never change. It is insanity to believe these things.

Death is the fixed belief that something is happening outside of you that is caused by external factors, other than yourself.

Our life is not as we imagine it.

Today we will not accept death in any form. We will not let ourselves be sad. We will be happy and at peace. We strive to keep God's Holy Home today (and always) as He established it, and wills it to be forever and forever.

Today we are aware of the need to keep the altar clean. We will not let darkness intrude upon our minds. We will not sleep. We will not let our mind wander away from the fact that we are One with every thing.

GOD IS THE SOURCE OF ALL CREATION.

He created all things eternal. There is no death. As we were, so are we now and will forever be.

A sleeping mind must waken, as it sees its own perfection mirroring the Lord of life so perfectly it fades into what is reflected there. And NOW it is no more a mere reflection. It becomes the thing reflected, and the light which makes the reflection possible. No vision now is needed. For the wakened mind is one that knows its Source, its Self, Its Holiness.

Amen.

what is the resurrection?

Very simply, the resurrection is the overcoming or the surmounting of death. It is a reawakening or a rebirth; a change of mind about the meaning of the world.

What does this mean to you?

It means that you can make a decision to stop telling your old story. You can take the needle off the record AND THROW THE RECORD AWAY. You can take the crown of thorns off your head and be reborn, brand new. No sin, no history, no past mistakes to correct, nothing that needs fixing. You come into the new moment—which is now—healed, whole, perfect and innocent.

In practical terms it means you stop calling yourself an addict, alcoholic, fat, stupid, ugly. You stop saying that no one loves you. YOU STOP THE RECORD. You say "that's enough of that charade!"

You start telling a new story. You want to know a really good story about yourself? I'll tell you:

You are the light of the world. You are a child of God. You are beautiful. You are the Love of God. You are generous, kind, honest, gentle & joyful.

Finally, you stop killing yourself with all your limitations, self-hatred and doubt.

Let's repeat this lesson about death again, because it goes against everything you have learned in time & space. *Death is a thought that takes on many forms, often unrecognized. It may appear as:*

sadness
fear
anxiety
doubt
anger
faithlessness
lack of trust
jealousy

That's quite a list. Do you participate in any of the following: sadness, fear, anxiety, doubt, anger, faithlessness, or envy? If so, you are killing yourself. The resurrection is the SURMOUNTING of all of these things, which are really death. You stop harming yourself. You stop calling yourself names. You stop second-guessing yourself. You stop asking other people for their approval and opinions.

If you can see this lesson as it really is, it will begin to make perfect sense to you why the body appears to get old and sick and die, because you have been slowly killing it all along! Every day in a million little ways, you die a little. Finally, you make a decision to stop attacking yourself. You make a decision to renounce death in every form, and be happy.

This might sound like the craziest thing you have ever heard, but science has already proven that the way you think affects outer conditions. Have you seen Dr. Masaru Emoto's experiments with water crystals? It's amazing. He transmitted words of love and hate to water crystals and documented the results. A hate thought like "you fool" made a crystal chaotic and ugly, and a statement like "I love you" made a crystal harmonized and beautiful. Knowing this, wouldn't you want to experiment on your own body?

The vibration of love heals and restores.

The vibration of fear/hate deteriorates and destroys.

Now you can make an informed decision on which thoughts you want to keep and which ones you will get rid of. Even if you are skeptical, aren't you a little curious? Wouldn't you want to start practicing (even if only secretly) to see if this is true?

Spew out poison and it will poison you back. Extend love and it will transform you. You will get the results of your own thinking. The best part is that it's simple. You can begin today. You can start now.

The Holy Spirit teaches you to use your body only to reach your brothers, so He can teach His message through you. This will heal them and therefore heal you. Do not allow the body to be a mirror of a split mind. Do not let it be an image of your own perception of littleness. Do not let it reflect your decision to attack. Health is seen as the natural state of everything when interpretation is left to the Holy Spirit, Who perceives no attack on anything. Health is the result of relinquishing all attempts to use the body lovelessly.

We are finally allowing the blocks and obstacles to be removed so that God can shine into the world. What an amazing privilege and honor that is happening through us!

Last night I gave a talk on the internet, on this very subject, and I gave the gift of a clean slate. I said, "you are free of the past. You do not need to dwell on it any longer. You are free and innocent. You have been absolved of all your guilt. You can begin now by telling a new story."

Not more than one minute passed and some guy writes in and says about himself "I am an addict."

!!!!!

I couldn't believe it. I said, "THAT'S YOUR NEW STORY? I AM AN ADDICT. COME ON."

Never underestimate the insanity of the mind. If you are honest you will see you love your story of pain and suffering and addiction. And then one day you will become SO SICK AND TIRED OF BEING SICK AND TIRED that you will let the story go. Plain and simple.

A friend of mine wrote me a beautiful e-mail yesterday about how she lets everyone walk all over her and how she basically puts her life on hold waiting to see what everyone else's schedule is. Yesterday she made a decision she was done with waiting. She decided to stop waiting by the phone, inside, on a beautiful day. She decided to go shopping instead.

Now, this might not seem like the resurrection to you BUT I ASSURE YOU THIS IS AN EXTREME CASE OF THE RESURRECTION!!!

She made a decision to live. That's the resurrection. You decide to stop killing yourself. You decide to stop putting your life on hold. You decide to start living. You decide that no one has the power to hurt you. No one is doing anything to you. Whether you live or die is up to you.

Have you decided to stop telling your old story?

WHAT IS YOUR NEW STORY??

the day after resurrection.

Okay. Here we are. Resurrected. Risen from the dead. This is Jesus' gift to YOU. What does this mean in practical terms and what does this mean to you individually? It means that whatever came BEFORE this day has no more meaning for you. Your old story is back there in the ruins. You can stop telling it now. You've been reborn.

The choice is yours. Are you still clinging to old habits and limitations? Are you dragging old garbage with you? Why not let the old rugged cross go?

You are as God created you.

What do you love to do? What are you waiting for? You have been handed the keys to the Kingdom. From this day forward, you can begin telling a new story. You start behaving in ways that are in alignment with the new story.

Here are a few good stories:

I am the light of the world.

I am healed and whole and perfect.

I am here only to be helpful.

I am creative, gorgeous and generous.

I am happy.

I love to play.

A good place to start is in OBSERVATION. Listen to what you tell people about yourself. What are you saying? The power of decision is your own. You can step out of the black cloud, above the battleground and into the light. It's not mystical. It doesn't require hours of studying or long periods of contemplation.

It requires a decision to be as God created you. It requires a decision to be alive. It requires a new dedication to stop waiting for a future time in which things will change for you. Nothing external changes. YOU CHANGE. You change your mind and the world changes with it (not the other way around). Today is the day.

Undoing of fear

"You must do the thing you think you cannot do."
—Eleanor Roosevelt

look at your fears

I love Chapter 2 in *A Course in Miracles*. The most fundamental aspect of Chapter 2 is recognizing that the correction of fear is MY responsibility. It doesn't magically (or miraculously) disappear. It takes active participation to go right into my own thought system, recognize my own blocks and obstacles, and be willing to have them removed.

I love the analogy in Marianne Williamson's book *A Return to Love* about the rats in the basement. She said it's like these rats represent your fears and when you turn on the light, they go scurrying. You can't see them anymore, but they are still there lurking in every corner, in the walls, just waiting for you to turn out the light so they can return. She said you have to catch them individually and kill them one by one. Or in some cases, there are so many rats (fears) lurking, better to just knock the whole structure down, and start building from scratch.

This was my experience. I would surround myself with bright, happy people (which is the same as turning on the light in the basement) and all my fears would disappear. But the rats were still lurking, waiting for the light to be turned off so they could return. And they always did, but my response was always to find another form of light so I could forget about my fears for a while.

I would escape into books and movies and people and relationships and food. I simply wanted to forget about my troubles, pretend they didn't exist, until finally the day came when I was tired of running away from myself that I really prayed to find a solution.

The solution is simply this: LOOK AT YOUR FEARS. Step right into them. Whatever scares you, go do that. Are you scared of speaking in public? Go do that. Scared of being alone? Go do that. Scared of being with people? Go do that. Scared of writing and expressing yourself? Go do that.

Whatever you are afraid of, and it will be personal for you, go do that. You will see there is nothing to fear.

I then became really active in uncovering whatever fears were lurking . . . because . . . and here is my reason . . . I wanted to be a miracle worker.

Jesus says in Chapter 2: *"You can do anything I ask. I have asked you to perform miracles, and have made it clear that miracles are natural, corrective, healing, and universal. There is nothing they cannot do, but they cannot be performed in the spirit of doubt or fear."*

When I first began to practice *A Course in Miracles*, I did it for selfish reasons. I wanted to see miracles in my life. I wanted to be healed of deafness. I wanted to be free of alcoholism. I wanted every gift bestowed upon me. I wanted to be able to ask for whatever I wanted and receive it. I thought "Wow! How cool is this? All I have to do is get rid of doubt and fear and I'll be able to perform miracles!"

Let's just say, I got busy. I spent a lot of time alone, just simply reading the Course, looking at ways I could practice the instructions in my daily life.

There is a great one-liner in Chapter 2, in the section "The Function of the Miracle Worker" which I began to use on everyone I met: *Charity is a way of looking at another as if he had already gone far beyond his actual accomplishments in time.*

I transformed into a cheerleader right before my very eyes. If someone would express doubt to me about their own abilities, I would be right there cheering them on "You can do it! I know you can!"

And then that person would go and do the very thing they thought they could not do! Simply because ONE person had faith in them. Sometimes you have to loan your faith to others, until they begin to see their own strengths.

I have a friend who has total faith in everyone she meets. She is an inspiration to me and to everyone she meets. When I had the opportunity to move to New York to teach about God, I was filled with a tremendous amount of fear and anxiety. What did I know about God? Who was I to call myself a minister? But she stayed right there on the sidelines, always available by phone and e-mail, cheering me on—GO LISA GO!—until finally, I had faith in my own abilities.

So you see? She looked at me as if I had already gone far beyond my actual accomplishments in time. She cut out whole chunks of time for me and simply placed me at the finish line where all my goals were achieved and accomplished. This should be sufficient enough proof to show you that time is not sequential.

She showed me, by her demonstration, how to shorten time. Because I saw it work in me, I knew I would be able to do this for others. If you tell someone they are the best, they become the best. If you tell them they are perfect, they become perfect. If you tell them they are incredible, they become incredible.

It's a complete mystery, but it works. All the miracle does is shorten time.

So this is Chapter 2. I hope you get a chance to read it. Don't be concerned if you still experience fear.

Listen to this:

Everyone experiences fear. Yet it would take very little right thinking to realize why fear occurs. Few appreciate the real power of the mind, and no one remains fully aware of it all the time.

The mind is very powerful, and never loses its creative force. It never sleeps. Every instant it is creating. It is hard to recognize that thought and belief combine into a power surge that can literally move mountains. There are no idle thoughts. All thinking produces form at some level.

If this is not enough to make you want to begin to experience what *A Course in Miracles* has to offer, well, then, there is nothing more I can do or say. But this was a very exciting idea to me that everything "out there" was simply a reflection of thoughts contained in my own mind and that I could change the world by changing my thoughts.

So the final lesson of Chapter 2 is that each of us is making a decision in every moment to do one of two things: PROJECT or EXTEND. I am either making a world, or I'm extending myself to everything. That's it. There is no in between. Atonement is a total commitment. I either don't know who I am and I'm PROJECTING false images or I do know who I am and I'm EXTENDING the Love of God.

what frightens you?

We are allowing the blocks and obstacles to be removed. Remember, your active participation is necessary.

In Chapter 12: *Yet we have repeatedly emphasized the need to recognize fear and face it without disguise as a crucial step in the undoing of the ego.*

You must look directly at your fears. Write them down. Look at them. Face them. Turn towards them. Do not turn away, and do not ask for a miracle to remove them. YOU MUST LOOK AT THEM. Look at what frightens you.

Fear is a symptom of your own deep sense of loss.

How do you remove fear? What's the fastest way? By supplying the lack in others when you perceive it. Give yourself away. Do not attempt to do this alone. You can not remove fear in your living room, by yourself, meditating. I'm sorry. You cannot THINK your fear away. It doesn't work that way. Or if it does, it takes a very long time.

The fastest way is to give yourself away. Call a friend. Go find someone who needs help. Hit the streets. Go where it's scary. Speak up. Hold someone's hand. You will see the fear in YOU disappear as you begin to extend your love to THEM.

Your fear disappears along with theirs, and that's a miracle.

Remember, it's all just energy. The fear arises when you try to contain the energy within your own body, and control it. Don't do that. Extend it. If you don't feel joyful, well, GET OVER YOURSELF. Someone could use your help right now.

You're a miracle worker and there is work to be done.

My mother is a nurse, and she would never dream of bringing grief or misery onto the job. When she is there, she is there only to be truly helpful. It's all about the other person. She gives. And in her giving, everything is healed.

And now we are learning to extend that helpfulness to every moment in our lives. We don't compartmentalize. We don't take off our nurses cap just because the shift is over. We keep it on now, permanently, morning and night.

We are God's holy messengers. We are consistently vigilant and aware of who needs help and healing. In someone else's healing is our own healing, along with the world.

the correction of error

Chapter 9, "The Correction of Error" says we are asked to not correct anyone. Amazing, huh? To not correct anyone, ever.

NEVER EVER.

NEVER EVER NEVER CORRECT A BROTHER.

Let everything be exactly as it is.

Be wrong about everything.

Be willing to see things differently.

There is a girl around here who is sad all the time. I was getting really frustrated with her lately, to the extent that I wanted to grab her and shake her and yell "WAKE UP!" Or punch her lights out or something. She is doing *A Course in Miracles*. She knows better. Right?

But here, in these early chapters, especially Chapter 9, I am reminded of my own responsibility to not respond to anything except with love. Appreciation should be my ONE & ONLY response to everything.

Only appreciation is an appropriate response to a brother.

In the moment I see that I want to correct someone, or change something, it is a CLEAR INDICATION of the ego. MY EGO. That's why I'm saying today that I'm clearing him out. Enough is enough. I'm sending him far away. He's not welcome here anymore.

I want only to see with Christ vision. If my brother is sad, it is my responsibility to not respond to insanity but only to look beyond to the light that is there. That's my brother WHO IS ME. There is nothing outside of me.

Thank God.

conflict must be resolved.

I love Lesson 333. It says, *"conflict must be resolved."*

It cannot be evaded, set aside, denied, disguised, seen somewhere else, called by another name, or hidden by deceit of any kind, if it would be escaped. It must be seen exactly as it is, where it is thought to be, in the reality which has been given it, and with the purpose that the mind accorded it. For only then are its defenses lifted, and the truth can shine upon it as it disappears.

Did you read that paragraph? I want you to please read it again. Okay?

Conflict must be resolved. It cannot be evaded, set aside, denied, disguised, seen somewhere else, called by another name, or hidden by deceit of any kind, if it would be escaped. It must be seen exactly as it is, where it is thought to be, in the reality which has been given it, and with the purpose that the mind accorded it. For only then are its defenses lifted, and the truth can shine upon it as it disappears.

The reason I love *A Course in Miracles* is because it's always practical. It's not about pretending things are good, when you are miserable.

The miracle lies in the practical application, not in the examination of the problem or in hopeful wishing that the problem will go away, but in the PRACTICAL APPLICATION . . . ACTION . . . where you look directly at the problem/conflict/fear/doubt. You don't try to pray that the problem will disappear on its own. You look at the conflict. You name it. You own it. You make it personal. You say, "this is what is happening to me and I don't like it. I have a problem and I need help."

You look directly at the particulars and THEN you will be shown the answer. Then you will know what needs to be done. Then the "miracle" occurs.

Which is really not a miracle at all. It's just a change of mind.

You see the problem as it really is. You no longer are afraid to look at it. You admit you don't want the conflict, you don't need it, and you are willing to take action—every possible step—to be lifted into a place of freedom and joy.

But first, you must admit you have a problem. You must see there is conflict in your life that is causing you pain.

Step One in the AA program is to admit you are powerless. This is a great first step, and probably the scariest thing you'll ever do in your life. Admit you are powerless. Admit you have an unsolvable problem.

Step Two is "came to believe that a Power greater than ourselves could restore us to sanity."

Here is the entire basis of the miracle:

1. You admit there is a problem
2. You trust there is a solution.

Amazing, right? There is a Power greater than you who can restore you to sanity. In God, all things are possible.

Conflict must be resolved.

the undoing of fear

The phrase "fear not" is used 62 times in the King James version of the bible. It is a direct statement to not be afraid.

FEAR NOT!

Don't be afraid.

If Jesus says you have nothing to fear . . . well . . . then . . . won't you trust him??

Jesus simplifies it for us (in John 4:18) when he says, "There is no love in fear, but perfect love casts out fear."

There it is. Plain and simple. Perfect love casts out fear. That's the undoing of fear. If you don't want to be afraid anymore, then love everything with a perfect love that never changes, that never deviates, that gives all to all. If you do this, fear is impossible.

I used to be afraid of everything. I tried to conceal it with self-confidence but it was always lurking there right below the surface. I fooled most people, but I could not fool myself. I was afraid of losing the things I loved, and losing the things I'd worked hard to achieve. I was afraid of looking like a fool. I was afraid people were talking behind my back. I was afraid of being alone. I was afraid of being with people. I was afraid of being in a relationship. I was afraid of not being in a relationship. I was afraid of having no money. I was afraid of having too much money. I was afraid of responsibility. I was afraid of making a mistake. I was afraid I would be forgotten and left behind. I was always alert, always on-guard, always prepared in case the ride started to get a little bumpy.

I was living in constant fear.

I didn't want to upset anyone. I didn't want to do the wrong thing, but finally I realized the total burden on myself. The way out of fear is to love everything and everyone with a perfect love.

It is not complicated. It is the simplest thing in the world. If you are tired of being afraid, then start to love like God loves. Do not make distinctions. Just Love.

Fear disappears, automatically, in the presence of love.

Talking about fear does not get rid of fear. Understanding darkness does not dispel darkness. I know a lot of self-aware people who are still afraid. Only light dispels darkness.

I've used this analogy before: if you are sitting in a darkened room, it makes no difference how in depth you speak about the darkness or how eloquent you are in talking about the properties of darkness.

Most people can tell their stories of abandonment, fear & addiction better than most best-selling novelists. It doesn't matter. Talking does not equal action. The only thing that can dispel the darkness is getting out of your chair, walking across the room, and flicking on the light switch. Then you are in light. Do you see? No more darkness.

I used to think that looking at my negative behaviors could make me more enlightened and self-aware, but looking at the dark accomplished nothing for me. It was only when I made a decision to stop telling stories and to stop whining about my problems that I saw the entirety of the solution:

TO LOVE LIKE GOD LOVES.

The minute I started loving like God, darkness disappeared.

You can sit in darkness talking about darkness. Or you can turn on the light.

1. BE HAPPY.
2. THINK ABOUT GOD.
3. BE HELPFUL.
4. DO WHAT YOU LOVE.

Switch on the light.

Thinking about darkness and talking about darkness will never accomplish anything for you. There is no meeting place between light and dark. Either you are in the light or you are in the dark. There in no compromise. There is no in-between. You are either in hell or Heaven.

PERFECT LOVE CASTS OUT FEAR.

guaranteed way out of fear forever

There is a guaranteed way out of fear forever. Recognize you are doing it to yourself. If you are afraid, it is because you enjoy the feeling of being afraid. If you are in chaos, it is because you enjoy the feeling of chaos. If you are sad, it's because you enjoy the feeling of sadness.

Which means you are getting what you want, which means you should be happy!

Jesus says in *A Course in Miracles*: "*What if you knew you were dreaming? What if you knew this world was an hallucination?*"

He says, "*You would not react at all to figures in a dream you knew you were dreaming. Let them be as hateful and as vicious as they may, they could have no effect on you unless you failed to recognize it is your dream.*"

YOU ARE DREAMING. There is nothing happening to you at all. There are no other people out there doing things to you. YOU ARE DOING THIS TO YOURSELF.

Why do you continue to tell stories to other people about your own dramas?

Why?

Why?

1. First of all, you are talking to yourself.
2. Secondly, you are talking about yourself.

Begin to watch the words you use in conversation.

Do you talk about other people?

What are you saying about them?

Whatever you are saying about them is the way you feel about yourself.

This is a MIND-TRAINING. A systematic way to break out of your own limitation. Why tell a story about anything anymore? Why not just express and extend love and be happy?

Why not simply do the work you were sent here to do? You have been sent by God Himself . . . that His Will be done. That earth and Heaven may be One.

Why not simply be the LIGHT OF THE WORLD?

The only stories truly worth telling are the ones that make people happy. Everything else is a waste of time. We are here as the Teachers of God. We are not here to participate in the drama of this world. We are here ONLY to be truly helpful. Do you tell people about your night-time dreams in specific detail? Do you go on and on and on, telling everyone who will listen about the hurtful things that were done to you in your night-time dreams? Do you write lists about what they did, she did, you did, he said, she said, you said? Or do you wake up and realize it was a dream?

If you realize it is a dream, you would not give it one second of your time. You say "thank God that was only a dream" and then you would forget about it.

So then, why do we cling to our day-time dreams? Why? Why do we try to figure out our insane behavior? Why do we think about the people we hurt and that hurt us? Why do we replay the tape in our memory, constantly going over events that happened in the past (AND MORE ACCURATELY . . . EVENTS THAT DID NOT HAPPEN AT ALL!)

This is a dream of death.

You know how sometimes you have intense night-time dreams that seem very real . . . but by afternoon you can't even remember one detail? This is how it will become with your day-time dreams if you recognize they are not real.

You will stop meeting all your friends for therapy sessions, to go over the sordid details of your messy break-up. You will forget everything except the eternal Love of God which is within you.

Time to put your toys away.

If you complain about fear, it's actually because you enjoy the feeling of fear and terror. You may be able to fool yourself but you can't fool me.

Wanna know The Secret?

The secret of salvation is this: you are doing this unto yourself.

Whatever is happening to you, you are doing it to yourself.

You can choose to let the past go, in every detail, and be made brand new today.

emerging from conflict

"You must emerge from conflict to bring peace to other minds."

Period.

This sentence is from Chapter 2 in *A Course in Miracles*. *"You must emerge from the conflict if you are to bring peace to other minds."* There's no compromise involved in this. No trying to fix anything. No trying to solve your problem. No conversations with other people necessary. No trying to work things out. No therapy involved. You simply EMERGE from the conflict because you want to help God help you.

Do you see the necessity for releasing the past?

I've been going through a lot of physical stuff in this past week—starting with my head being paralyzed for five days. I was in the most pain I have ever endured in my life, but I emerged from it feeling totally renewed like the calm after a storm and I feel better than I've felt in a long time. MY HEAD IS CLEAR.

What was happening to me is a terrible pain in the entire back of my head, like in my brain. I couldn't move my head not even a half inch to the left or right. I felt very close to the brink of death. I felt like maybe I had a brain tumor. The pain was excruciating at times. But you know me with miracles . . . I let everything be exactly as it is. People were concerned, but not me. I kept saying "I'll be fine" even though I was not entirely convinced. I got advice to see a doctor, see a chiropractor, do something. But I decided to "do nothing." Be happy. If my time was up to leave this world, then I was ready to go. No regrets. I wasn't going to try to fix the pain. I let it be perfection. I let it be exactly as it is.

But it was so painful that I didn't sleep for 4 days because every time I moved (which was every 10 minutes) I woke up. My head weighed two tons. I couldn't move it off the pillow or couch without using both of my hands to lift it. Pretty scary. Like, what the hell is happening to me?

And then I had a thought that it was only energy. A LOT OF ENERGY, but energy nonetheless. Nothing to be afraid of. It was like a download of light had been given to me, and because it was unfamiliar, IT HURT.

I thought: okay, IF I've been given more light then it is not for me alone. It is for the world. And I have two choices:

1. extend it
2. be destroyed by it.

I chose extension. I spent all last week giving. I chose to be alive, not dead. I knew that every day might potentially be my last day. It felt marvelous. I took a couple of aspirin and used a heating pad when

Responsibility

the pain got to be too much. But I went out every day. I didn't lie in bed like a sick person. I took action. I laughed. I was my joyful self (but with a two-ton head). I wrote in a hand journal, bright entries of gratitude and love.

Everything is energy and if you do not give it a name (contain it, isolate it, try to fix it), it cannot crystallize. It will transform. It will integrate. It will convert. The minute you say it is cancer, it is cancer. Let everything be light and energy and you'll be fine.

And then, just as quickly as the whole thing came on, it was gone. Just like that. I could move my head again. There was no more pain, and I was free.

BUT WITH A WHOLE NEW DEDICATION.

I devote every day to extension, which is my natural state. I will extend the light and love within me, otherwise it will destroy me. The light is not for me alone. It was given to me to give to others, that they may receive it, and extend it to others. It becomes a huge interlocking chain of extension and forgiveness: of light and joy and happiness.

You see, when something like that happens to you it shows you clearly how PRECIOUS and SHORT time really is. You see how we take everything for granted. I did NOT realize that having the ability to move my head from left to right was a miraculous accomplishment. Now, I know better. Everything is a miracle.

Delay in time is tragic.

No more sitting around waiting for something to happen. No more waiting for external circumstances to be right, or for someone else to make a move before I can make a decision. The moment is NOW.

We have a function and a responsibility, a life mission. What it is for YOU is personal and the details will be revealed to you individually.

For me, I follow Jesus. He's my guide.

I went to Europe with Greta a few years ago, and she travels at lightening speed-up at the crack of dawn, following Jesus' guidance, going where he would have her go. I realized very quickly that if I didn't get out of bed in time, she would leave without me. She did not run things by me, SHE SIMPLY MOVED. It was evident that if I wanted to travel with her, I couldn't be a slouch. And that's how it is with Jesus.

You keep up with him. He speaks and you follow. You don't have a conference or a meeting to see what the group consensus is. YOU MOVE. You are constantly alert and ready. You stop being lazy. You don't get comfortable. You are constantly vigilant.

I love Paul's letter (in the bible) to the Thessalonians:

Now concerning the times and the seasons, brothers and sisters, you do not need to have anything written to you. For you yourselves know very well that the day of the Lord will come like a thief in the night. When they say, "There is peace and security", then sudden destruction will come upon them, as labour pains come upon a pregnant woman, and there will be no escape! But you, beloved, are not in darkness, for that day to surprise you like a thief; for you are all children of light and children of the day; we are not of the night or of darkness. So then, let us not fall asleep as others do, but let us keep awake and be sober; for those who sleep sleep at night, and those who are drunk get drunk at night. But since we belong to the day, let us be sober, and put on the breastplate of faith and love, and for a helmet the hope of salvation. For God has destined us not for wrath but for obtaining salvation through our Lord Jesus Christ, who died for us, so that whether we are awake or asleep we may live with him. Therefore encourage one another and build up each other, as indeed you are doing.

Undoing of ego

"Out, damned spot! Out, I say!"
—William Shakespeare, Macbeth

best advice ever.

How do you let go of the ego? Are you ready? Here is the best advice you will ever receive.

Are you ready? Here it is:

Never use the word "ego" again.

It's that simple.

Take the word right out of your vocabulary. Don't use it to describe you and don't use it to describe others. You are not an ego. Your brother is not an ego. Never refer to it again. You are Spirit. Mind. Light. Whole and perfect as God created you.

There.

That was easy.

Taking your place as savior of the world

"In the name of God, stop a moment, cease your work, look around you."
—Leo Tolstoy

"Everyone thinks of changing the world, but no one thinks of changing himself."
—Leo Tolstoy

you are getting what you ask for.

Do you realize that everything that is happening to you is happening because you want it? It might seem impossible to you that this be true if there is death and cancer all around you, but everything that is happening to you is happening because you asked for it and want it. Herein lies your total release, if you choose to accept to change your mind about what you want.

Look how uncompromising *A Course in Miracles* is, from Chapter 21, The Responsibility for Sight:

This is the only thing that you need do for vision, happiness, release from pain and the complete escape from sin, all to be given you. Say only this, but mean it with no reservations, for here the power of salvation lies:

I am responsible for what I see.

I choose the feelings I experience, and I decide upon the goal I would achieve.

And everything that seems to happen to me I ask for, and receive as I have asked.

Deceive yourself no longer that you are helpless in the face of what is done to you. Acknowledge but that you have been mistaken, and all effects of your mistakes will disappear.

Responsibility

How simple!

Total responsibility. You stop blaming other people for your problems and begin to see your own role and participation in the drama and chaos that is your life. You begin to look at your own judgments and fears, and you become HONEST with yourself.

You begin to see things in a whole new light.

There is nothing outside of me. It takes practice to see that I am the cause of everything that happens in the world. I am responsible for the destructions, for the wars, for the killings. It takes total vigilance. Every thing my body's eyes see are a temptation to believe otherwise. But the truth is still always going to be true. There is nothing outside of me.

Greta gave a great teaching years ago when we were in Italy. She said you must stop naming things. Names of people, places and things. She said when we name things it scatters the energy to the thing we have named. Boyfriend. Girlfriend. Job. Money. House. Children. We name all these things outside of ourselves, and the minute we NAME it, we have placed ourselves off the mark, and now we are standing "over there" in the very thing we have named. When you are repeating the name of God, you are standing in direct line of communication where God can raise you into a higher frequency. You begin to rise up to Him. But when you are naming people, places and things, you are still in linear time, but now, off the mark. God can't find you as you are contemplating how to fix worldly relationships. It's impossible to think of two things at once. If I am naming a situation or event, then I have forgotten the name of God. I can't think two names at once. I can't be in two places at the same time. So the only name that has any importance and meaning is God. Everything else must fall away.

It takes PRACTICE (mind-training) to stop rearranging my life to my own liking because the tendency, the old habit, is to organize, plan, fix, plot, write to-do lists, intend, visualize, and none of that has ever worked with absolute success.

I create whole dramatic scenarios in my mind about future events, invent whole conversations with people, imagining messages I will write, practicing conversations in my head, anticipating what they will say and do, and if that is not sheer insanity, I don't know what is.

And yet, it is the whole human condition.

Best to just draw a circle and see who comes in it. Stand in SINGULAR PURPOSE for God, and be vigilant to not let your mind wander, and allow the miracle to occur.

Best to simply be totally responsible for everything.

waking from disaster

We are living in chaotic times.

There have been crises of varying types at different periods throughout history: social, economic, national, global, political and personal. There are natural disasters of every conceivable kind—hurricanes, tornadoes, flooding, and global warming. There is mass devastation all over the world—airplanes crashing, ships sinking, people killing each other—but perhaps because it is not physically affecting you and your life, maybe you think you are exempt? Surely the earthquake in Pakistan that killed 20,000 people on Saturday doesn't really have anything to do with you or your life in Topeka, Kansas or wherever you live.

Lots of times we convince ourselves that what is happening "out there" has nothing to do with us, and doesn't affect us very much. We have been taught to lull ourselves to sleep and quickly adjust to whatever events are occurring, no matter how devastating. Wars. Murder. Terrorists. Suicide bombers. Hunger. Poverty. These are global problems and the headlines change so quickly that most people don't even register the violence and chaos that is occurring in the world. Instead, they have their own daily routine and bills and problems to think about.

Responsibility

You may think, "well yes, there are terrible things happening in the world but what can I possibly do to help? And besides, those world events, tragic as they may be, don't really affect me or my family."

This is the thinking of most people in the world.

But here is the fact of the matter:

You are continually and constantly losing the things you love. If you can be honest with yourself, you will agree that this is true. Everything is changing all the time—there is no constancy whatsoever. There is no safety or security anywhere you look. I don't know how anybody can stand it.

Perhaps...

You are in a great relationship, or have a "perfect" marriage, and the next minute your spouse tells you they don't love you anymore (not happy, in love with someone else, wants something more exciting and different) and they want a divorce.

OR

You have a thriving business, you're making lots of money and you think you are safe, until the day someone close to you deceives you, or the economy changes, and years of hard work are gone in a matter of days.

OR

One day you are perfectly healthy and the next day the doctor informs you your body is filled with cancer. One day you are perfectly safe and the next day you learn that the bank is taking your home away from you and you have nowhere to go.

Tragic events happen unexpectedly and without warning. They happen in your personal life as well as on a global level. The reason this is true is because there is no difference between a personal crisis and a global crisis. They are identical. Did you hear that? THEY ARE IDENTICAL. What is happening "out there" (bombing in New York city, flooding in New Orleans, a war in Iraq) is literally nothing more than a projection of the drama that is going on in your own mind.

Maybe you don't yet realize that the way you are handling your marriage or finances is EXACTLY the reason there are wars and earthquakes and hatred in the world.

The chaos of this world IS the conflict of your own mind.

Here is where a true revolution can occur.

There is a solution and there is work to be done.

My safety lies in God.

I believe the current crisis this world is facing is unprecedented. It is unprecedented because a vast majority of people justify their actions and blame someone else. They blame the government. They blame the economy. They blame their neighbor. They blame God. Once upon a time, in a magical faraway place, people took responsibility for what was occurring in their lives. When a person made a mistake, they admitted it. Perhaps not promptly (and maybe not publicly) but deep in their heart and mind they knew they'd done something wrong. Now? There is little responsibility for actions. In its place are justifications, excuses, and lengthy lawsuits designed to uncover the truth. Can you imagine a world where people owned up to their mistakes?

So we have an unprecedented crisis in the world that obviously calls for unprecedented action.

Unprecedented means "no previous example." Here are some "solutions" that have already been tried before in attempt to solve world and individual problems: raising money, giving money, asking for donations, volunteering, new taxes, new technology, new research, a bigger military, more machines, and creating more task forces and humanitarian organizations.

We've done all these things in the endless search for peace and yet . . . the problems of the world are only getting more chaotic and destructive. Doesn't this seem a little odd to anyone?

What would be an unprecedented action? Something that's never been done before?

INDIVIDUAL TOTAL RESPONSIBILITY.

You take responsibility for yourself as well as for all the problems and sickness in the world and other people. If you see it outside yourself, it IS your problem because it's NOT outside of you. Here's the beautiful part: You've been given a total solution. Love everything with a perfect love, and all problems and sickness disappears.

"I love you" heals all things.

This is how healing is accomplished.

If you accepted this kind of responsibility, you would never again blame anyone else for your problems. You would recognize that you are the cause of everything that is happening to you. Your days of attack and defense would be over.

All it takes is ONE teacher of God to heal the world. One wholly perfect teacher, whose learning is complete, suffices.

All it's going to take is ONE mind who has decided to take the leap into the unknown and not judge, not blame, not defend, not give in to *"the slightest sigh or the merest frown"* . . . and this world will be completely changed forever. One teacher who has made a decision to be happy and BE the demonstration and extension of the Love of God on earth, and this world of chaos and pain is over.

You'll be back home in Heaven, which is here and now.

You must recognize you made the world you see. Here is total responsibility. It is impossible to be driven by events outside of you, because there is nothing outside of you.

There are no accidents. Your mind determines what occurs during the day. Everything that seems to happen to you, you asked for and received.

how i woke from disaster

I can always only tell my own experience and how I woke from my own dream of disaster. I am a practical person. I needed clear-cut practical tools that I could begin to apply in my life. That's just how it worked for me. I honestly can't say how it will work for someone else. I can only express what worked for me. Thinking that the problem didn't exist or wasn't real did not create miracles in my life. Thinking about God did not make my problems disappear. Sure, I would be happy for a time, all light and airy, but that did not pay the bills and it did not fix my relationships. Love was not my only emotion. I would still find myself swinging from frustration to joy and back to frustration again. What finally caused me to SEE CLEARLY and TO RISE ABOVE THE CHAOS (to a place where miracles actually were occurring) was my dedication to come into a new level of maturity and to be responsible for EVERY action and thought.

I made a decision to be responsible for everything that occurred to me, with no exceptions.

Put simply, I finally stopped blaming other people for my problems.

I placed my faith in God and took total (not partial) responsibility for everything that was happening to me.

A Course in Miracles teaches quite simply that if you do what Jesus asks you to do, miracles will occur for you. If you are not seeing miracles, it is because you are not following his simple instructions. It means you are either compromising Jesus' message or interpreting his instructions.

Either God is mad or this world is a place of madness.

These are the choices that were presented to me in Chapter 25, "The Rock of Salvation." *Either God is mad or this world is a place of madness.* When I read this, I suddenly didn't care about being right in the world. I didn't care about justifying my actions. I didn't care about defending my position. Why would I waste even one second of my time worrying about anything once I had come to the sane conclusion that this world is a place of madness???

This world is a place of madness.

If you can accept this one sentence, then I assure you that you are on your way to waking from whatever problems and disasters you currently face. I promise you this is true.

Who cares about being right in a world that is crazy, insane and chaotic?

I used to spend hours and days and weeks trying to solve my problems as well as the problems of the world. I'd worry and think and scheme and plan and organize. I'd wrack my brains thinking of new ways to improve my life, my work, my marriage, my appearance and my finances.

But this world is a place of madness. Who cares about improving anything at all?? Why fix anything in a world that is flat-out crazy and will eventually fade away anyways? This world is a place of madness.

Having accepted this simple statement, I don't worry about anything anymore. I don't waste a second of my time wondering what someone meant by a passing statement. I don't analyze glances, or obsess over nonsense.

I've been sent here by God Himself and there is work to do. I don't have time for problems. I don't have time to waste worrying about disasters and chaos. It's all just madness anyway.

This world is a place of madness.

Now, I'm simply free to do the work of my Father. I am here ONLY to be truly helpful. I am here to represent Him Who sent me. I am here, in a body, as the total demonstration as the Light of Heaven on earth. I am here solely to extend the Love of God in the world.

And THAT makes me very happy.

there is no world or how i got sober

My friend Max said the most awesome thing tonight.

He said that it's impossible to bring truth to illusions but it *is* possible to bring illusions to truth. You CANNOT bring Heaven to this world (*A Course in Miracles* says you can bring a "touch" of Heaven here, but obviously that is NOT the same as being in Heaven where there are no levels or degrees or orders of difficulty) but you can bring this world to Heaven. Even though I've heard it before, read it before, practiced this thought many times, my mind sprung a chord when Max said it. I totally *GOT IT*—like, oh my God, THAT'S IT.

He said: if one person could "GET THIS" then that would be all that would be necessary for the whole world.

You gotta get out of this place. You gotta get out of the illusion. You gotta get out of the chaos. Above the battleground. Out of the conflict. It's impossible to make anything work here. It's a waste of time.

You gotta get with God.

You can't find a solution while you are standing in the problem. You can't get sober when you are standing in a bar drinking a beer.

YOU MUST LEAVE THE OLD SITUATION BEFORE THE NEW SITUATION PRESENTS ITSELF.

It's impossible to be in two locations at the same time. Impossible to be sober and drunk at the same time. Impossible to be asleep and awake at the same time. Impossible to be happy and miserable at the same time. You are either ONE or THE OTHER. Not both simultaneously. You choose.

There is still the temptation to think this world is real. Still the temptation that we can make our relationships work. Still a lingering thought that there is something here we can do, or something we want, or something we need to work out. We try to bring the Course (or spiritual ideas) into the illusion to make them work. But it will never work because the world is not real.

You simply must leave the old situation. You must rise above it. Don't try to figure out how to fix your current situation while you are standing it. You can't fix the war while you are standing among dead bodies and gunfire. You have to leave the battleground and go where there is peace.

This world isn't a real place. There are no holy/special relationships. There is no linear time. There is no past. There is no future. There is no conflict. There is only God.

THERE IS ONLY NOW.

A Course in Miracles always talks about two individuals coming together for a holy function, a purpose, an assignment, and it talks about forgiving your brother as if there are two people but there is only ONENESS. There is no "other." There are no separate bodies. There is no space between you and me. There is nothing except eternal reality, with no shifts, degrees, or intervals. There is no shady gray area. Either you are in love with your brother totally or you fear him still just a little (or a lot).

It's time to take the blinders off. There is no world. There is no need for healing. There are no bodies. You can love everyone without "knowing them" when you know yourself perfectly. You will have a perfect love for each and every individual in the entire world (past, present, and future) with no exceptions. Imagine that.

Imagine loving everyone. Imagine a world of peace and harmony.

Imagine that.

Then the question arises: What is this place? How did I get here? The only possible explanation is that it was a huge mistake. I mean, how else to explain it? Certainly this world of chaos is not God's Will for me. At a very early age, I began to question my existence. Death never made any sense to me. We are taught in the churches that God is all-loving and all-powerful and if that is true, what is death and divorce and separation? Certainly God did not create these things. At a certain point, you begin to see clearly that the whole screw-up is man made.

I've got all this innocence and joy and it's like I've totally landed at the wrong bus stop in the wrong part of town.

I keep getting dislodged. Carlos Castaneda talks about an "assemblage point" and he says that a good teacher (a warrior) will constantly dislodge the assemblage point, but because we are so rooted in habit it moves back automatically by itself to the old position. But he says that if you keep dislodging the assemblage point eventually it will be (and stay) in the new position. You must keep moving it. It keeps moving back. You keep shifting it. It moves back. You shift it. It moves back. But it's like every time it moves to the "new" spot it makes a deeper groove, until finally the day arrives when it doesn't shift back to the old spot.

It's how it was with me eating meat and drinking alcohol. I kept trying to shift my life (to a place where I was in a world where I was vegetarian and sober) but I always kept going back to eating meat, drinking martinis and smoking cigarettes. I seemed a hopeless case. Until one fine day, the miracle occurred and the cravings were gone.

There was no going back. All my efforts finally paid off.

Every time I made huge declarations "I'm finished" (with meat, with alcohol), I would feel like such a failure because I always went back to my old ways. I know now I was trying to shift myself in a new place. I would shift. I would "fail." I would shift again (break all my cigarettes in half, douse them in water, bury them in the trash, and pour whole bottles of vodka down the sink). I would stay in that "new world" for a couple days, but then I would crumble and find myself drinking and smoking again. I was completely powerless (for some odd reason, it never occurred to me to go to *Alcoholics Anonymous*). I thought I could get it on my own, without God's help. I was constantly declaring "This time it will be different." But it was never different, except for a few days. But something in me kept trying to shift, kept trying to change.

I wanted to be sober. I wanted to be happy. I wanted to be free from that prison house. I kept shifting the point. It was like I didn't have a choice. I was constantly making declarations "I'M NOT DRINKING ANYMORE" and for a few days I'd be a brand new person . . . but then the assemblage point would shift back and I would find myself in the liquor store again.

But that "world" was so painful to me, and I would TRY AGAIN to quit drinking. Constantly shifting the assemblage point. And then one day it just dislodged from its old position and I've never gone back to drinking (or smoking or eating meat) since.

I was one of the rare cases that quit drinking without the AA program, HOWEVER (big however) I later realized that I transferred my addictions and insanity over to my relationships and food. I hadn't actually solved the CORE problem . . . only the symptoms (alcohol, cigarettes, meat). But since I hadn't looked at the SOURCE of the problem (separation, a shutting off from others), more symptoms appeared: craziness in my marriage, along with food addiction.

I finally recognized and admitted: "I can't do this by myself. I have an unsolvable problem here." I finally joined the fellowship of AA, and lo and behold: my sanity was restored. My marriage improved. My food addiction disappeared.

The first step is admitting you are powerless.

It was difficult at first because I hate asking for help. I'm independent and stubborn. I prefer to do it "my way" even though my way fails 100% percent of the time. But the entire premise of *A Course in Miracles* is to ASK FOR HELP. It's the entire book. ASK FOR HELP. You can't do this by yourself. ASK FOR HELP. I'm always thinking, "Okay I'll pray about this and ask for a miracle" meanwhile closing myself off from human help. I kept all my skeletons hidden in the closet. I didn't want anyone knowing my marriage was in trouble or that I was eating a box of cookies a day. Definitely prayer works, whether you tell someone or not, but I'm finding there is a whole lot more healing available when you really truly finally ASK FOR HELP TO ANOTHER HUMAN BEING.

Here are the Twelve Steps of Alcoholics Anonymous (Reprinted from the AA Big Book, with permission of A.A. World Services, Inc.)

1. We admitted we were powerless over alcohol—that our lives had become unmanageable.
2. Came to believe that a Power greater than ourselves could restore us to sanity.
3. Made a decision to turn our will and our lives over to the care of God as we understood Him.
4. Made a searching and fearless moral inventory of ourselves.

Responsibility

5. Admitted to God, to ourselves and to another human being the exact nature of our wrongs.
6. Were entirely ready to have God remove all these defects of character.
7. Humbly asked Him to remove our short comings.
8. Made a list of all persons we had harmed, and became willing to make amends to them all.
9. Made direct amends to such people wherever possible, except when to do so would injure them or others.
10. Continued to take personal inventory and when we were wrong promptly admitted it.
11. Sought through prayer and meditation to improve our conscious contact with God, as we understood Him, praying only for knowledge of His will for us and the power to carry that out.
12. Having had a spiritual awakening as the result of these Steps, we tried to carry this message to alcoholics, and to practice these principles in all our affairs.

Copyright © A.A. World Services, Inc.

The Twelve Steps of Alcoholics Anonymous are great. It's about taking total responsibility by turning your will and life over to God. This action would be the END of therapy to anyone who cared to take this step. It asks that you admit that you are powerless, over whatever seems to be troubling you. Let go. Stop trying to solve your problem. It's not solvable. It can be alcohol, food, sex, relationships, money, pain, whatever is bothering you and ultimately ruling (ruining) your life. You just finally admit that you've tried everything to solve the problem, and you cannot. Then it's trusting that God can solve the problem, IF you let Him. You can't. God can. How simple!

That is the beginning of recovery. You turn your will and life over to the care of God. You stop running the show. You stop trying to figure out how healing is accomplished. You admit you are powerless, but that a Power greater than you can restore you to sanity.

I LOVE IT. It will make you totally vulnerable, but herein lies your strength. It's the journey into the deep caverns of your mind. You make an inventory, you admit you're powerless, and you begin excavating all the crap out of your mind, asking for help, telling another human being, turning to God, and letting the miracle occur.

be catapulted

There is no such thing as something outside of you. There is only love. That attack that appears to be coming from "someone else" is your own attack against yourself. I'm sorry, but you might as well hear it. This seems impossible to accept but it's true. There is nothing happening to you, except by your own decision. If you are being abused, you are doing it to yourself. If your children are being abused, you are allowing it to occur. If one million people are slaughtered in Rwanda (and in Iraq, Nazi Germany, and in individual homes around the world) it is because we, as individuals, hold hatred in our hearts and minds.

The explosion of an attack is the release of fear. It is energy (nothing more, nothing less) coming from the depths of our cells to our conscious awareness, and acted out in physical form. The forms range from subtle to brutal.

What is the solution? Let the explosion occur and let the healing begin. It's fear rising to the surface. Let it be converted to love. Let the explosion catapult you. Don't cycle back around again to your abuser. What has happened has happened. You can't change that, but you can make a decision to not be abused again. Don't stand in a fire when you see an open door to freedom over there. Walk away. Rise above the battleground—the slaughterhouse—and rest in God.

challenging the current thought system

It's curious for me to witness how much focus and importance is placed on PERSONAL ACHIEVEMENT in this world.

Responsibility

From the time we are all little babies, each and everyone of us was asked the question (by some well-intentioned adult): "What are you going to be when you grow up?"

This is the moment we begin to learn about the "importance" of money, fame, fortune, success, achievement and power.

Parents, teachers, and neighbors begin to define the PURPOSE for being in the world. The truth is, no one trapped in this little place knows for certain the meaning of life. Try to answer the question for yourself. Ask 20 people the question. You will get 20 different answers. Ask 5000 people and you will get 5000 answers. So we make it up as we go along, and hope for the best.

In my opinion the meaning of life is to be happy, but lately I've been thinking about how self-centered even this answer is. Do you see? Is this the meaning of life? My personal happiness?

The world teaches PERSONAL ACHIEVEMENT and SELF IMPROVEMENT. Look at the self-help sections in the bookstore. Turn on any talk show. Look at the magazines in the checkout aisle. It's all about how to improve yourself. It's all about YOU. How to be a better person, a better lover, a better friend, more attractive, how to succeed in business.

Can you see how self-centered we are? As individuals and as a society? We ask: What are my goals? What are my ambitions? What do I want? We spend all our energy focusing on something that is smaller than a speck of dust. Ourselves.

I'm having difficulty writing this piece because I know there is nothing outside of me, so all solutions and answers are found within me. But I want to go to a whole new level, and the only way I can do that is by challenging my current thought system.

Where is the new leadership going to come from? How do these changes come about? Throughout history, great change usually comes with great destruction. The old falls and the new rises up. That's typically how it works.

What is the solution?

SELF RESPONSIBILITY for every thought and action.

There came a point in my own awakening when I decided to give entirely of myself to others. I joined every cause to help humanity. I raised thousands of dollars to cure sickness, to help the environment and to raise awareness. I did volunteer work for several years cooking food for people with AIDS and reading to sick children in the hospital. But that wasn't the solution either. It was like putting a band-aid on an amputated arm.

Or as one great teacher once said to me: it's like rearranging the deck chairs on the Titanic.

The ship is sinking. Don't bother.

No matter how much time and energy I put in, the newspapers were still filled with horror stories. More people getting killed. More people getting cancer. More people unemployed. The divorce rate sky high. The national debt at astronomical figures. It was like we'd dug ourselves into a hole that we'd NEVER get out of.

I reached a point where I felt the absolute futility of trying to be helpful. This is the starting point, where you look at the CAUSE of the problem. For many years I'd been focusing on ME. I was in therapy. I read all the self-help books. I worked hard. I was a good person. But at the end of the day, I wasn't fulfilled. So I switched my focus to helping others. I became more social and active, a better listener, a better friend. But that didn't leave me feeling fulfilled either.

Something was always missing for me. It was like this nagging little question that plagued me constantly: How does one individual make a difference in this world??

And then, the miracle of all miracles: I started focusing on God. I forgot entirely about myself. I forgot entirely about my neighbor. I stopped trying to improve myself and I stopped trying to save the world.

I focused on God.

I put all my energy into thinking about God. God is Good. God loves me. God only gives. God is with me always. I started asking God what He wanted me to do. I began to practice talking to him, listening to him, being with him. New thoughts started to come into my mind. Life started to get more interesting. Curious and wondrous events would happen during the day. My relationships improved. I realized I never got sick anymore, and that whatever needs I had were "miraculously" taken care of with no effort at all.

Things weren't boring anymore. I felt entirely fulfilled. How do you teach this? I have no idea. I can only be a light in the darkness, an inspiration by my own demonstration.

Each of us is searching for something, waiting for something. All the self-help books say: Know what you want. Make lists. Set goals. Just do it. Believe in yourself. Aim high. Keep going. Never give up.

I've said these things. I've done these things. Be disciplined. Go the distance. Be focused. There's nothing wrong in these instructions, but my mind is beginning to expand beyond my own self-centered needs. I'm beginning to think of new leadership.

I presently have no clear-cut solution, but I do know the joy that I have found in total responsibility. It has shown me how to be honest, generous, patient, gentle, tolerant, and full of faith and grace.

My life has a PURPOSE now. A new direction. All because I made a simple decision to stop blaming the other guy for my problems. I stopped blaming circumstances. I stopped blaming the crappy weather. I said: I CAUSED THIS. You see? It's a shift in perception. Nothing more than a change of mind.

Every day and every hour and every minute, I return my mind to God.

I AND MY FATHER ARE ONE.

I AM GOD.

YOU ARE GOD.

We start teaching THIS to the children, to our neighbors, to our parents, and the world will change. The whole social structure will change. Each and every individual taking responsibility and their rightful place.

What is the meaning of life? I'm back to my original answer: to be happy.

And you'll be happy when you begin to have a relationship, a friendship, with God, not based on religion, theology, philosophy, or science. When you come without your past ideas about who God is, He will reveal himself to you.

The purpose of life is getting to know God, which is the same as getting to know yourself.

Then everything else will fall into place effortlessly.

accepting the atonement

The Atonement. Okay. Here we go. What is it? It is the final lesson that you need accept. I know what it is, but I've never had to explain it so please be patient with me.

Here we go. It is the recognition of the Oneness of all things. Atonement: At-One-Ment. At One with All Things. It is where you recognize that everything is YOU, connected to you, one with you, joined with you. It's where you lay down your sword and join another, without any qualms or description or hesitation.

You love another because you recognize that "other" is you and you love yourself. So you love them too. You don't wait to find out who they are (to see if you will like them) because you KNOW who they are because you know who you are! You see yourself as entirely worthy and lovable because you recognize your oneness with God, which means you see everybody else as entirely worthy and lovable. Because you love God. You see? It's completely circular. If you do not love yourself, then you have not accepted the Atonement. Once you realize that God created you and is one with you, and is you, loving yourself becomes automatic. You will be head over heels in love with yourself because you will realize that loving yourself is what loving God is. You will be thrilled to see everyone you meet because you realize it is the Christ standing in front of you, taking on the appearance of a human body.

If you keep even one little exception apart from this rule, you still must believe there is something outside of you. THERE IS NOTHING OUTSIDE OF YOU. This is what you must ultimately come to know. If there is one person who crosses your mind who you do not like, who angers you, who rattles your cage, who still doesn't "get it", YOU—not them—YOU—have not accepted the Atonement. You still believe in the separation and a world of separate bodies.

Once you know yourself, you will be rejoicing and celebrating every day of the year. Life will be one big party for you. There will be nothing to fear. No enemies. No sadness. No sickness. Only love.

Everyone will be a friend to you.

If you hate yourself, you do not know yourself, your brother, or God. In a very real sense, you know nothing. This does not need condemnation, but correction.

You'll hear often times references to a "circle" of Atonement, such as in King Arthur. A circle represents no beginning and no end. In King Arthur, it is a round table. There is not one seat that is better than any other. No head of the table. No leader. Just perfect equality. They all lay down their swords and come to this meeting place, without territory or nationality or stories. They come as brothers. It's a place of perfect peace and neutrality. No harm can touch you in the circle.

If you can accept the Atonement—which is recognizing your perfect Oneness with God and everything—you would have no need of the smaller lessons. If you could accept your own perfection today, you would not need 365 lessons because the lessons are leading you to the final realization of your own wholeness.

the power of decision is my own

Luckily, I get to choose the thoughts I think. Nothing is forced on me. In any moment I am free to change my mind and choose again. Here lies the beauty of training your mind in a systematic way. Nothing is happening to me that cannot be changed in an instant. There are no accidents. The power of decision is my own. If I am having a bad day, I can change it.

If I am feeling ugly, I can transform myself into stunning & beautiful in one instant, simply by changing my mind.

If I am feeling angry, I can choose forgiveness and be happy.

If I am feeling tired, I can change the thought and feel vibrant.

It's not difficult at all—usually I just take a deep breathe and stand up straight. The movement aligns me with God. Don't ask me how it's accomplished—I have no idea. All I know is that it works.

If I'm down, I remind myself to get up. Assemblage point UP. I force it to move and then I am in a whole new space. It's nothing more than a shift in thinking. It's really easy.

This world is an illusion. My mind holds only what I think with God. Your self-deceptions cannot take the place of truth.

Open your mind and clear it of all thoughts that would deceive and let one thought of truth occupy your mind:

My mind holds only what I think with God.

This is a great lesson. It says relax. *There is no hurry now, for you are using time for its intended purpose. Let each word shine with the meaning God has given it, as it was given to you through His Voice.*

We need only do the lesson to give us HAPPINESS and REST and ENDLESS QUIET, PERFECT CERTAINTY, and all our Father wills that we receive as the INHERITANCE that comes from Him.

Today is a special time of blessing and of happiness for us; and through our faithfulness restored the world from darkness to light, from grief to joy, from pain to peace, from sin to holiness. God offers thanks to you who practices thus the keeping of His Word.

no excuse, sir!

The army has a great slogan: "The difficult we do immediately—the impossible takes a little longer."

I love that. There is no order of difficulty in miracles. You can do the impossible if you take total responsibility for your behavior and actions.

Anyone who has served in the military knows that excuses for failure to perform are unacceptable. There is only one acceptable explanation and that is:

NO EXCUSE, SIR!

Even if you have a good excuse, it's still considered inappropriate to offer it. The only thing that might possibly get you off the hook is: NO EXCUSE, SIR!

I say this because as a teacher of God, there is no excuse for unhappiness, laziness or delay. I'm sorry. There is no excuse. I don't care if your mother just died. It doesn't matter if you are going through a divorce. Who cares if you are sick or have a headache or tumor?

There is no excuse.

Those are just stories you tell.

People talk a lot about conversion, about converting the darkness to light, and while this is a real event . . . it doesn't take time. It doesn't take you analyzing every behavior and action. All it takes is you remembering the simple truth. YOU ARE THE HOLY SON OF GOD HIMSELF. YOU ARE THE LIGHT OF THE WORLD. YOU HAVE BEEN ORDAINED TO USHER IN A NEW FORGIVEN WORLD. It takes one instant to snap out of it.

You think those army sergeants care if you're tired? You think they tolerate complaining? They would be shipping your sorry ass home. Either that or they'd have you up at 3:00 o'clock in the morning doing pushups in the pouring rain and mud.

The height of self-responsibility is: NO EXCUSE, SIR!

Stop making excuses.

I speak from deep personal experience. When the shit is hitting the fan, instead of getting upset . . . I get excited. First I am terrified, then an instant later I am happy again. It simply means a shift is occurring. Something new is happening. It is nothing to moan and complain about. BE HAPPY.

I mean, I'm not going to lie to you and say that I'm always laughing and having fun because there are times when I've literally lost the things I love—but in the next instant I REMEMBER THE TRUTH . . . that loss is impossible. I can't lose the things I love unless I value a body. Everything is joined with me perfectly, forever and forever.

This is the conversion. From darkness to light. How long, O teacher of God, are you going to analyze your situation? How long are you going to alternate between depression and happiness? Between confusion and certainty?

Either you "get it" today or you are resisting and denying the truth.

There is no acceptable excuse.

NO EXCUSE, SIR!

I wake up in the morning and no matter how crappy I feel, no matter what is going on in my life, I say, *"I am here only to be truly helpful."*

Everything good follows from that declaration. Today, I will make no excuses. I will follow God's Plan for salvation. I will be a happy learner.

the circle of atonement

We are all simply energy vibrating, in different frequencies. Some things are vibrating in low frequencies, some things vibrate in high frequencies. Each of us is literally in a different space and a different time. We think we live in sequential horizontal time, in the year 2007, but actually it's vertical. Some live in lower frequencies, and other live in higher frequencies. There's no judgment. That's just how it is.

The first time I really noticed this was once when I walked into a McDonalds. I was shocked. I actually could SEE energy for the very first time. I could see darkness around bodies. Everyone was all slumped over. Overweight. Sleepy. It was like walking into the Twilight Zone, or more accurately: slow time. I could feel the density, like being in sludge. The second I walked through the doors it hit me like a wave of hot humid air. It was like walking through a door into another world, like "What is this place????? Where am I????" I got out of there, FAST.

When you move out of a particular frequency, you are out of that frequency forever. Some might think this is a dramatic example, but you will find examples in your own life and find it to be true. You probably don't hang out with people who shoot heroin. That is a very low frequency. And if you ever find yourself in a room strewn with people who are shooting heroin, you will most likely have the same experience I had of "get me out of here."

The energy body cannot tolerate it.

The last time I was in NYC that very thing actually did happen to me. I got invited to meet someone and when I arrived it was a party in the very worst neighborhood, and no one was coherent. Everyone was spaced out on drugs at 2:00PM in the afternoon. The person who invited me was not there. I went in, said a prayer, stayed for a few minutes to see if there was any way I could be helpful, and then I left, knowing that all work is done and accomplished by the simple act of my asking the Holy Spirit that everything be healed.

In God, all things are possible. I never have to stick around to see the results because it's just my own healing anyway. There is nothing outside of me. I need only pray and offer myself that each and everyone find the peace and happiness we all are looking for. The only requirement is for me to be present in every situation, with the certainty that God is with me.

I noticed when I stopped drinking and hanging out in bars that all my drinking friends literally disappeared. The ones that stuck around stopped drinking. This is the miracle. It was because I was in a different frequency, and suddenly there were other friends in the new frequency who were compatible with my energy.

So I never get upset anymore when someone suddenly seems to drop out of the radar. I just know that everything is constantly changing. I am in a different frequency, and so I've always got my eyes and ears open as to how it's new.

My body used to be filled with sickness. I was in the doctor's office all the time, always looking for a pill to cure me. But then I got out of that frequency of thinking I could be sick, that sickness was possible, and suddenly, a miracle, I don't get sick anymore.

It's all just a big happy game.

In *A Course in Miracles* there is a great section in Chapter 14 called "The Circle of Atonement." It gave me a great practical exercise to draw my circle and stand with Jesus and call everyone in to join me.

Here is Jesus speaking, talking to you:

Blessed are you who teach with me. Our power comes not of us, but of our Father. In guiltlessness, we know Him, as He knows us guiltless. I stand within the circle, calling you to peace. Teach peace with me, and stand with me on holy ground. Remember for everyone your Father's power that He has given him. Believe not that you cannot teach His perfect peace. Stand not outside, but join with me within. Fail not the only purpose to which my teaching calls you. Restore to God His Son as he created him, by teaching him his innocence

And then it gets even better:

Each one you see you place within the holy circle of Atonement or leave outside, judging him fit for crucifixion or for redemption. If you bring him into the circle of purity, you will rest there with him. If you leave him without, you join him there. Holiness must be shared, for therein lies everything that makes it holy.

Come gladly to the holy circle, and look out in peace on all who think they are outside. Cast no one out, for here is what he seeks along with you. Come, let us join him in the holy place of peace which is for all of us, united as one within the Cause of peace.

Amen.

When I first read that, I knew that my responsibility was not to join anyone in their suffering or story. I was standing with Jesus inside a circle I had drawn. I knew that I simply needed to call others to join me to this place of peace, and not leave anyone outside. As for me, I have instructions to never step outside the circle. Never. I stand on holy ground, within the circle, calling you to join me.

I do not have to be concerned if anyone does not want to join me in perfect peace. I offer a solution that has worked for me, and they can accept or reject. We have free will. But the circle is always getting bigger and bigger. There are a LOT of us standing in it now. It's just great.

anger is never justified

Last weekend I cooked for a wedding and I made 40 individual salad dressings in plastic containers, because the bride specifically requested "salad dressing on the side." I had exactly enough salad dressing for 40 containers. There was none left over. It was a special raspberry vinaigrette that you can't buy in a store. I felt pleased and proud that I filled 40 containers exactly. Everything was going perfectly.

As I was serving the soup course, someone opened the refrigerator door and the shelf that the salad dressings were sitting on . . . broke. All 40 salad dressings came tumbling down with it, leaving a large greasy puddle of salad dressing all over the bottom of the fridge.

In the half second it took me to see what had happened, I realized that getting angry would accomplish nothing.

WHAT WAS DONE ... IS DONE.

What was getting angry going to accomplish? How was blaming someone going to put the salad dressings back in their containers? How was it going to turn back time?

It wasn't.

There was nothing to do. No one to blame.

The only question to ask was "Okay, now what do we do? Where do we go from here?"

For us the solution was to take the little salad dressing that was still in the bottom of each container (luckily, some containers did not turn entirely upside down) and drizzle it over each salad individually. It was supposed to be "on the side" but we had no other choice.

It turned out to be a good solution and everyone was happy.

More and more I can see there is no need to look to the past. We just keep going forward ahead. We learn from our mistakes. I learned to make sure the shelves are all sturdy before I put something on them. I make sure I have extra food from now on in the event of an accident.

Yelling at someone does not accomplish anything. Being angry accomplishes nothing. It's just a waste of time and energy. All it does is hurt you and the people around you.

Jesus says: Don't look back. Keep going forward.

A mistake requires correction. It does not require figuring out who is to blame.

you shall know them by their actions

I got home from work last night to an angry message on my answering machine: someone screaming their head off at me, totally pissed off. She went on and on. Screaming how I'd betrayed her. How she thought I was her friend. How I had stabbed her in the back. Etc.

I was completely and utterly SHOCKED.

First, I thought: *Anger is never justified.*

Second, I thought: This is someone who has *A Course in Miracles?*

Third, I thought: There must be some miscommunication.

Fourth, I thought: This is a teacher of God???

People show their true colors by their ACTIONS. You can always tell where someone is at in their own mind by WHAT THEY DO.

They can say they understand something, or practice something, but you can tell where they are by their actions. Like I can say I am on a diet (which I am NOT) but if I say I am on a diet and then I eat a hot fudge sundae then you can see where I really am—it's ACTIONS that tell the whole story.

It's the whole situation with our "leaders." It's the whole situation with the priests who abuse boys. They say they are our leaders or they say they are men of God, but it is by their actions that we KNOW them.

You say you practice *A Course in Miracles*, but do you really?

Jesus is uncompromising.

Do you give like God? Do you think like God? Do you love like God?

Responsibility

Are you unwavering in your thoughts and actions?

Are you entirely consistent?

They nailed Jesus to a cross and he did NOT say, "Screw you all to hell, you stupid bastards." No. He said, "Forgive them Father, for they know not what they do."

Judas betrayed him and yet Jesus did NOT run around having an angry tirade. He did not leave angry messages on his answering machine. Instead he went into the garden and prayed. He knew his own identity in God, which allowed him to remain in peace despite all the conflict around him.

I called my friend, who refused to take my phone call. I felt horrible. I didn't know what I'd done wrong. My hand was physically shaking, I was so upset. I was totally willing to accept whatever I'd done, apologize and ask for forgiveness. I was willing to be wrong. I can't stand conflict. I kept calling, trying to get her on the phone but she didn't want to talk to me. I was in a state of despair. I got into the bathtub and prayed. I needed help.

Within a few minutes, I felt entirely at peace. I closed my eyes and went home. I left the world entirely. In Heaven, there are no problems. I realized that nothing at all had happened. There was nothing to fix. I went to bed and slept like a baby.

This morning I was all ready to sit down with her for some long healing conversation and she came to me and apologized! She said there had been a miscommunication. She'd been all stressed out about other things, and she took it out on me.

I couldn't believe it. The power of prayer heals all things! She went from wanting to rip out my guts to asking me for forgiveness, all because God is good and prayer works!

Commitment

God

"In the faces of men and women, I see God."
—Walt Whitman

"O my brothers! God exists."
—Ralph Waldo Emerson

only God's opinion matters

At the end of the day, the only opinion we should really care about is God's opinion. Is He well pleased? Who cares about what other people think? Everyone has an idea about everything. People love to gossip. They love to talk about other people's mistakes. Why should this bother you?

IS GOD PLEASED?

Everything you see or hear is just a story and it's changing all the time. So why be concerned with gossip, news, or other people's opinions?

Only God's opinion matters.

I was trained in journalism. I was taught to question everything, including so-called facts. One event has 20 different perspectives depending on who you talk to. You learn to dig deeper than the surface to get the real story. You don't write an article based on hear-say and opinion. You go straight to the source, rather than speculating on what other people witnessed. There are deadlines to be met. You cut to the chase and get your story.

So every day I go to the Source. I check in with God. I find out what I need to know. I ask Him the important questions. He's the boss. Everything I need to know He will tell me.

Everything in the world is interpretation. Everything in Heaven is a fact.

What does God think of me?

Is He pleased?

Am I doing what He asks me to do?

Every day is different, and there are no set rules. Since I have no idea what miracles need to be accomplished, I make sure I check in with God every morning and often throughout the day. I don't try to figure out what I should do. I just ask. My day is not at random. God knows the larger plan and He tells me what needs to be done. This saves time.

I don't worry about other people.

God's opinion is the only opinion that matters.

the day is accomplished in God

I drove to the Madison airport last night to pick up my all-time favorite teacher, Greta. I know, I know, we're all equal, and I shouldn't play favorites, but whatever. She is the best. Her formal verbal teaching is fantastic, but it is her way of being, her demonstration, her total certainty and dependence on God that has taught me the most.

What a great gift when I finally recognized I can be myself, as God created me. She has taught me that I can stand anywhere, doing absolutely nothing, shopping, playing, reading, standing at the bus station, drinking a cappuccino, just feeling the peace of God, in harmony with everything, and that is how healing is accomplished. If something needs to be done, or if I need to speak a word, I will be told very specifically what to do.

Having already given myself and my life over to God for His purposes, I know that the day is set. Today is accomplished in God.

Time is already over, it lasted for a moment in my mind with no effect on eternity. Everything has already been accomplished in God and we're all back home in Heaven. I don't have to worry about a single thing!

I love the first paragraph in the original manuscript (called the Urtext) of *A Course in Miracles*. Here is Jesus speaking:

It is crucial to say first that this is a required course. Only the time you take it is voluntary. Free will does not mean that you can establish the curriculum. It means only that you can elect what to take when. It is just because you are not ready to do what you should elect to do that time exists at all. You will see miracles through your hands through me. You should begin each day with the prayer "Help me to perform whatever miracles you want of me today."

How great is that??

Jesus goes on to say that not only should you ask what miracles you SHOULD perform, but also to ask what miracles you SHOULD NOT perform. The key is to REMEMBER TO ASK!

Ask about everything, even the smallest tiniest details:

"Should I take a shower now or keep on working?"

"Should I make a phone call?"

"Should I say something or keep quiet?"

"What should I eat?"

"What should I do?"

"I need a new dress, what store should I go to?'

"Lord, What would YOU have me do?"

Help me to perform whatever miracles you want of me today

This saves time. Every day should be devoted to miracles. How fun.

my goal is God

I've done everything I've wanted to do in this world. Some people think if they were given a "death" sentence, you know, six months to live, they'd freak out thinking they hadn't done all they wanted to do. But that's not the case with me. I've done everything I've ever wanted to do. I've had the best friends. The best family. Eaten in the greatest restaurants. Traveled all over the world. Been around the block and back. I've done it all. I've lived in New York. Been to the ocean. The mountains. Lived. Loved. Laughed. Married my best friend. Worn Vera Wang and Oscar de la Renta. What more could a girl want?

I don't need anything else. I don't want anything else. Now, I give myself—my life, my body, all of it—over to the Holy Spirit for His Purpose.

My goal is God.

The coolest thing is that nothing is ever taken away. There is no sacrifice. I still get excited over birthday cakes, handbags, monogrammed towels and expensive stationary. I still love going to the movies. I still laugh hysterically at *Friends* episodes, no matter how many times I watch them. I am simply a brighter version of myself now. All the pain is gone. Now that I have found my center, I am no longer attached to things. It's like being a little kid—you can still want things and do fun things but you're not attached to anything because your attention is squarely in the present moment.

I love Chapter 17, about me & Jesus: *For he is risen, and you have accepted the Cause of his awakening as yours. You have assumed your part in his redemption, and you are now fully responsible to him. Fail him not now, for it has been given you to realize what your lack of faith in him must mean to you. His salvation is your only purpose.*

My goal is God.

Chapter 17, about faith: *Your faith must grow to meet the goal that has been set. The goal's reality will call forth and accomplish every miracle needed for its fulfillment. Nothing too small or too enormous, too weak or too compelling, but will be gently turned to its use and purpose. The universe will serve it gladly, as it serves the universe. But do not interfere.*

BUT DO NOT INTERFERE.

Once I had a total blowup where I screamed at the top of my lungs at a very good friend of mine and it sounded something like this: "YOU ARE SOUND ASLEEP IN A NIGHTMARE! WHAT THE FUCK IS THE MATTER WITH YOU? YOU DON'T HEAR A WORD OF THIS MESSAGE! YOU GO FROM LOVE TO HATE AT THE BLINK OF AN EYE! YOU'RE ENTIRELY INCONSISTENT! WAKE UP!"

So, that all happened. I don't know where that rage and intensity came from. It was like someone else yelling. It definitely got his attention. I didn't plan to explode like that, it just happened. He was speechless. He listened. He thanked me. He cried a little. We laughed.

And then I got home that night and I remembered that whatever I tell my brother is actually the message that I'm telling myself. I'm talking to myself. In this case, YELLING. I obviously must have needed to get my own attention. The words that I'm speaking to "someone else" are always my instructions to myself. You should have seen my reaction: FLOORED. SHOCKED. AND A LITTLE BIT EXCITED BY THIS NEW TURN OF EVENTS. It was all me, all the time. Nothing outside of me.

I was the one sleeping. I was the one sound asleep in a nightmare. I was the one who was entirely inconsistent. I was the one who couldn't hear a word of the message. I was the one that went from love to hate in a blink of an eye.

I was the one who needed to wake up!

I laughed out loud. If you don't interfere, Jesus will show you something new that you hadn't seen before. He'll show you a wider spectrum of colors and sights and you will be amazed.

And now I see how simple this course really is. I hear it entirely differently. I see the simplicity. I see the immediacy. I see that God doesn't hold anything back. It doesn't take any time.

I highly suggest reading the text chapters—one chapter a day—starting from the beginning. It will take you 31 days to finish. You will be amazed. Forget that you think you know what it says. Let go of that idea (and every idea) and come wholly empty-handed. Reports are coming in from all over, from other people who are reading the chapters now and having bright new experiences . . . just like me.

I want you to experience this gift for yourself: to feel the Love of God within you and to know happiness, peace and joy that never changes.

Lesson 189: *Simply do this: Be still, and lay aside all thoughts of what you are and what God is; all concepts you have learned about the world; all images you hold about yourself. Empty your mind of everything it thinks is either true or false, or good or bad, or every thought it judges worthy, and all the ideas of which it is ashamed. Hold onto nothing. Do not bring with you one thought the past has taught, nor one belief you ever learned before from anything. Forget this world, forget this course, and come with wholly empty hands unto your God.*

Is it not He Who Knows the way to you? You need not know the way to Him. Your part is simply to allow all obstacles that you have interposed between the Son and God the Father to be quietly removed forever. God will do His part in joyful and immediate response. Ask and receive. But do not make demands, nor point the road to God by which He should appear to you. The way to reach Him is merely to let Him be.

So today we do not choose the way in which we go to Him. But we do choose to let Him come. And with this choice we rest.

Father, we do not know the way to you. But we have called, and You have answered us. We will not interfere. Yours is the way we would find and follow. And we ask but that YOUR WILL, which is our own as well, be done in us and in the world, that it become a part of Heaven now. Amen.

(party time)

Finally, I see what this course is. It's not about worldly miracles. It's about being in true service. All practicing (forgiveness, no judgment, love, giving, patience, etc.) is only to remove the blocks and obstacles, getting me ready for God. So that He can take the last step. That's it! How marvelous.

My life is God's. What a privilege.

I'm done with conflict. I don't want it at all. Not in any shape nor form. I declare it finished. I want to be happy. I want the peace of God, and I mean it. I have no interest in protecting the body. I give it to God.

I have no use for it, so I'm donating it to Him.

"You have assumed your part in his redemption, and you are now fully responsible to him. Fail him not now. His salvation is your only purpose."

Amen.

i give my life to God to guide

I should NEVER say I will do something "later" (or that something will be a certain way), because having given my LIFE AND WILL OVER TO THE CARE OF GOD FOR HIS PURPOSES everything is constantly getting rearranged in my schedule. I can make tentative plans for a future date, and I can hold a job and show up on time, and when I say I will be somewhere then 9 times out of 10, I arrive early and do the thing I say I will do. But then there are days when I'm led down a completely unexpected path going where God would have me go.

I have a good story. A couple years ago I was in New York at the airport, heading to Wisconsin. I got to the ticket counter and the woman there said: "We're sorry Miss Natoli, but you are probably going to miss your connecting flight in Detroit."

I became like a child in that moment. I literally could not comprehend what she was saying to me. I just stood there. Then I said, "what should I do?"

She said, "Well, go sit over there and I'll see what I can do."

About ten minutes later, she comes over and says, "There is another flight leaving around the same time and if we put you in first class, you will be closer to the front of the plane and there's a better chance you will make your connecting flight. Now, it's not guaranteed, and we can't promise anything, and if you miss your flight there is nothing we can do. We can't put you up in a hotel, and there are no other flights leaving till tomorrow morning."

Um. Okay.

I had bought one of those cheap Expedia tickets that the airlines hate, and so they were not going to accommodate me with a free hotel. I said yes to first class, but I couldn't even enjoy it because I was so worried that I would miss my connecting flight.

Low and behold, I missed my connecting flight. I got to the ticket counter and they said "We're sorry Miss Natoli, there is nothing we can do."

I just stood there. I was scared. I didn't have any money. I don't own a credit card. I didn't want to spend a night in the airport. I didn't even know if it was allowed. I literally did not know what to do. I just stood there like a little child, because that's how I felt in that moment. Scared and lost and alone with no one to help me.

Then I remembered that Jesus is standing with me. I remembered that I am here only to be truly helpful. I remembered there is nothing to fear. I remembered that I'm a messenger of God, letting myself be led where God needs me to go. I don't know what anything is for. I don't know where I'm going. But there is One Who does know and he is standing with me and takes the journey with me.

This change of mind took less than one minute. In that one minute, one of the ticket guys had a change of heart (while I had a change of mind, funny how that works) and he said, "Well, let me see what I can do."

He went into the back and I saw him talking to another woman and then he came back and said, "We can put you up in a hotel."

I began squealing in excitement and then all the ticket counter people started squealing along with me. It was suddenly a big party.

He gave me a taxi voucher, made a phone call and sent me on my way. I got to the hotel and my room turned out to be a wedding suite. I had a huge California king size bed, a gigantic hot tub, chocolates on the pillows and breakfast included.

The next morning in the taxi was a guy who was completely STUNNED to see me. He said "I can't believe it's you. I have been watching you since yesterday!"

We followed exactly the same route. We both started our day in New York. The airline bumped him up to first class (along with me) and then they put him in the same hotel, and he had seen me during breakfast.

He asked what I did and I told him I'm a minister. I talked about God and Jesus and *A Course in Miracles*, and this guy, a grown man, a movie executive from L.A., started crying his eyes out. He said "you're not going to believe this, but I've been praying for a miracle for a very long time."

He was convinced I was an angel sent by God.

I'm convinced that there is a switchboard operator in Heaven who receives prayers from people and then connects them with the appropriate messenger of God. A prayer goes up and operators start a "search" on who is the closest and best teacher for that individual, where both teacher and pupil can come together in a learning situation.

That one event taught me to stop praying to reorganize events to go "my way." How do I know where God needs me to be? I've stopped praying for traffic to move faster, or for people to act a certain way. I stopped praying for things to go my way. I don't know the plan of God. BUT HE KNOWS, and I am willing to go wherever He would have me be.

I've said "YES!" to a life of service. I've said "YES!" to being truly helpful. I've said "YES!" to accepting my role as Savior.

God's gifts are yours, entrusted to your care, to give to all who chose the lonely road you have escaped. It is you who teach them now. For you have learned from Christ there is another way for them to walk. Teach them by showing them the happiness that comes to those who feel the touch of Christ, and recognize God's gifts.

And so having made this commitment, I can't really say where God is going to have me go. Life just becomes one big adventure. When it seems like things are not going MY WAY, I remember that things are going GOD'S WAY.

In order to get me to a different location, to wherever I can be helpful, it usually takes the form of a disruption. It usually looks like something is going wrong. But now I know that in those moments, everything is going right.

I know that God goes with me. I know that I'm completely taken care of even when it looks like no one cares and I can't see the solution. When all seems chaotic and hopeless, I know there is a larger plan occurring and I trust in God.

There is nothing to fear, even when it looks like I am in danger. Trust is the first characteristic of a teacher of God. Trust.

Have a little faith that you are exactly where you are supposed to be, even when your plans are being sidetracked. Trust will solve every problem now.

in God, all things are possible

This is not an appeal to magic. It is not dependent on any of the rituals you have devised. It is inherent in the truth of what you are. Ask for anything and you will receive it. Ask for healing. Ask for love. Ask for understanding. Ask for guidance. Ask for miracles. Ask for anything. You have been promised full release from the world you made. You are worthy. You are entitled. You do not have to "do anything" to earn God's favor. Ask and your request is granted. Your wish is the Holy Spirit's command. God loves you as you are, because He created you perfect. If you feel less than perfect, it is your own misunderstanding and mistake. If you feel your behavior and actions need correction, that is up to you. God created you perfect. Whatever bad behavior is in you (anger, grievances, intolerance) these are things you taught yourself. God created only a perfect Son who knows only how to love. Everything that has been added on top of that is your own false learning. A mistake is a mistake. It's not something to cry about. It can be corrected. Go ahead and ask for something. Don't be shy. Just ask. What have you got to lose?

to know your brother is to know God

I know a lot of people who say they love God, but they say they hate someone in their life. To which I say, YOU DO NOT KNOW GOD. When you know God, you will recognize that God is the physical person and He's everyone and everything and everywhere. He's not some guy in the sky.

Here is Jesus speaking:

My trust in you is greater than yours in me at the moment, but it will not always be that way. Your mission is very simple. You are asked to live so as to demonstrate that you are not an ego, and I do not choose God's channels wrongly.

You are a mirror of truth, in which God Himself shines in perfect light.

It also talks about the Atonement: about loving yourself and loving God and loving your neighbor because it's all just ONE thing.

The Kingdom of Heaven is you. What else but you did the Creator create, and what else but you is His Kingdom? This is the whole message of the Atonement; a message which in its totality transcends the sum of its parts.

There it is—the Atonement: You are the Kingdom of Heaven. You are what everything is.

Your gratitude to your brother is the only gift I want. I will bring it to God for you, knowing that to know your brother is to know God.

I repeat: TO KNOW YOUR BROTHER IS TO KNOW God.

If you are grateful to your brother, you are grateful to God for what He created. Through your gratitude you come to know your brother, and one moment of real recognition makes everyone your brother because each of them is of your Father.

Are you ready? Listen to this:

As you come closer to a brother you approach me, and as you withdraw from him I become distant to you. Salvation is a collaborative venture. It can not be undertaken successfully by those who disengage themselves from the Sonship, because they are disengaging themselves from me. God will come to you ONLY as you will give Him to your brothers.

Here's more from Jesus:

God is praised whenever any mind learns to be wholly helpful. This is impossible without being wholly harmless, because the two beliefs must coexist. The truly helpful are invulnerable, because they are not protecting their egos and so nothing can hurt them. Their helpfulness is their praise of God, and He will return their praise of Him because they are like Him, and they can rejoice together.

The truly helpful are God's miracle workers, whom I direct until we are all united in the joy of the Kingdom. I will direct you to wherever you can be truly helpful and to whoever can follow my guidance through you.

Isn't that amazing? Jesus will direct you to wherever you can be truly helpful, until everyone is united in joy. He'll take care of everything.

Total Dedication = Total Power

"Until one is committed, there is hesitancy, the chance to draw back, always ineffectiveness concerning all acts of initiative and creation. There is one elementary truth, the ignorance of which kills countless ideas and splendid plans; that the moment one definitely commits oneself, then providence moves too.

All sorts of things occur to help one that would never otherwise have occurred. A whole stream of events issues from the decision raising in one's favor all manner of unforeseen events, meetings and material assistance which no one could have dreamed would have come their way.

I have learned a deep respect for one of Goethe's couplets: "Whatever you can do or dream you can, begin it. Boldness has genius, power and magic in it. Begin it now!"
—W.H. Murray

the missing piece of the puzzle

Living a devoted life—a commitment to God, to serve and to be truly helpful—leaves me in a state with a tremendous amount of energy, enthusiasm and joy.

I spent a lifetime wanting to get "on track" and "aligned" but I was always just slightly off-center, constantly thinking that some time "in the future" circumstances would adjust themselves so that I would know WHO I AM and WHERE I'M GOING and WHAT I'M DOING.

But I was always searching . . . never arriving. It was like a big puzzle. If only I could find the missing piece, then everything would become clear and make sense. As it was, I couldn't see the whole picture. I kept trying to add more pieces into the puzzle, thinking that would solve my problem. It seemed like the relationship piece was missing, the money piece was missing, the perfect body piece was missing, the ideal job piece was missing, the more time for travel-and-relaxation piece was missing.

I would think I didn't live in the right location, or didn't have the right credentials. I was either too young or too old. Either I had too much experience or not enough. My problem, looking back now, is that I had no idea who I was, where I was going or what I wanted. I was wandering aimlessly through life waiting for something to happen even though I had no idea WHAT that "something" was. I didn't know what I wanted to happen. All I knew is that I felt a sense of incompleteness. I felt some piece was missing.

Often I would think, "this can't be life." Nothing held any meaning for me. What's missing? What's missing? What's missing? I searched and I searched and searched.

What was missing?

1. COMMITMENT.
2. GOD.
3. LOYALTY AND TRUST.

I wanted to be attached to something BIG. I wanted my life to have meaning. I wanted to make a contribution and to feel successful and important. I wanted to be noticed and seen and heard.

But I had a lot of false ideas about success wrapped up in social conditioning: money, big houses, private jets, fame, celebrity culture. I lost sight of the IMMEDIACY of the importance of my life in the small details.

I falsely believed I needed external recognition to be considered a success. My heart was in the right place—to want to inspire people to remember God—but I started to fall under the spell of society. I believed the lie that I needed validation and compensation. What began as a simple desire to make a difference in the world became a struggle to make people notice me. I constantly felt other people were holding me back from being my best self. I thought "if only I could get my foot in the door (of a magazine, a television station, a radio station), then I could begin to shine."

And finally there was that AH-HA moment when I realized that I DO MAKE A DIFFERENCE. It has nothing to do with fame, money, or recognition.

My life is a success already.

So here we are again, back at the starting point: it was just a shift in perception. I changed my mind and I began to see things differently. Nothing external changed. I changed.

I realized that I make a difference to my family, to my friends, to co-workers, and to strangers on the street. I began to notice just how very much my presence in the world was affecting everyone around me. I saw how much my happiness is contagious to other people. I saw that a smile has the power to immediately lift someone out of depression. I found that taking the time to write someone a love letter changed the quality of my day. Reaching out to someone restored me to my sanity.

This was the MISSING PIECE.

A LIFE DEVOTED TO BEING TRULY HELPFUL.

I see that my life does have meaning & purpose, and where I found this meaning is in God. I'm here as HIS representative, a shining light in the world. There is no future moment when things will click. It's all here right now . . . in the small details.

the wish for constancy

The constancy of joy is a condition quite alien to your understanding. Yet if you could even imagine what it must be, you would desire it although you understand it not. The constancy of happiness has no exceptions; no change of any kind.

How can you know joy while you still think outside events are happening to you, that were somehow not caused by you? You would be forever at the mercy of things you had no control over. How could you be consistently happy? It would be impossible.

While you still think the world is real, with separate bodies, you will sometimes be happy and sometimes be sad. You will think other people are causing you happiness or depression, without recognizing: YOU ARE THE CAUSE.

While you do not recognize the TRUE SOURCE of everything that is—God—you will merely be shifting your emotions based on what you think you see.

This is why it is so essential you realize it's a dream because otherwise you will think someone is doing something to you when in truth NOTHING IS HAPPENING TO YOU AT ALL. It's an illusion. What you think happened, never occurred.

Until you see this, you are trapped in time & space. Escape is impossible. You will be forever at the mercy of events that seem outside of you, happenings that come to you that seem to be not your choice.

But here is a fact: It's all you. Everything that is happening to you is by your own decision. Period. No exceptions. No compromise. You are responsible for all of it. You are the cause of everything that appears to happen to you.

All of it. The good times. The bad times. The pain. The peace. All the pleasure. All the loneliness. All the sickness. All the chaos. Your co-worker who is driving you crazy. Your wife who is being a bitch. Your husband who is having an affair. Your love life, or lack of one. The car accident you were in. The store clerk who is rude to you. All of it. You want it. You asked for it. You got it.

So the question is: WHAT ARE YOU ASKING FOR? WHAT DO YOU WANT?

I'll tell you what I want:

I want the peace of God. I want to be happy. I want to be truly helpful.

Beyond this, I don't have a clue what I'm supposed to do (in the specifics) but I know it's gonna be good.

be yourself

Everything is shifting so fast lately, I can't keep track anymore. The only thing that is constant is God. The only thing that is constant is that I want to MAKE PEOPLE HAPPY and be GORGEOUS FOR God.

Recognizing this personal mission, which I have chosen for myself, everything else in form shifts to meet this goal. Everything that is happening to me simply re-aligns itself as I keep my MISSION clear in my sight. I let everything change to meet the goal. I am willing to let every worldly thing go that interferes with my only goal: God.

The only thing that matters to me is salvation.

I have a friend who used to tell me I talk too much so I made a decision to change myself to keep the friendship. I turned down the brightness button on me so that we could stay friends because he's a really good guy. I took the request seriously because if someone is telling me to be quiet, that must be the Voice for God speaking to me. But I recognized almost immediately it was simply a state of limitation because being quiet interferes with my ULTIMATE GOAL of making people happy and teaching *A Course in Miracles*. I love to talk. I love to love. I love to give. I am happiest when I am with other people, giving of myself.

Why would I change myself?

I am as God created me.

I set up dream figures to keep me in a state of limitation and littleness, when God is asking for me to decide for my own magnitude, which is His Magnitude.

I'm a talker. It's my fundamental nature.

Anyone who knows me knows how I am—I walk into a room and I shine. I don't wait for inspiration to strike. I don't hover around the edges of a room, quiet, waiting for people to approach me. It's not my nature. I am the kind of girl who makes the first move. I have no problem walking up to strangers and introducing myself. I have no problem holding someone's hand or striking up a conversation.

I like to talk. If someone is sad, I say something to cheer them up. If someone is crying, I make them laugh. I'm built that way.

So I had to make a choice: keep the friendship OR keep my promise to God. I've been changing myself my whole life to make people like me. Finally, I'm not going to do that anymore. I am going to be myself perfectly. I am going to be the brightest star in the universe, because that is what I am. Jesus says our names are written in the stars.

This is where it sometimes gets difficult because YOU DO HAVE TO MAKE CHOICES.

I used to have an atheist boyfriend and I loved him dearly, and I thought we were going to get married and be together forever, but obviously when I decided to dedicate my life to God . . . that relationship shifted. He had every quality of the perfect guy. We lived together for four years. The first few years were incredible, and when things started to go bad I kept thinking he was simply going through a rough patch but that eventually we'd go back to the way we were. We were great together. He was sweet and funny and smart and generous. HE ADORED ME. I ADORED HIM . . . but . . . he didn't believe in God and I really wanted to be with someone who shared my love of Jesus.

I actually hid my *Course in Miracles* book in a closet, and I only read it when I knew he wasn't coming home for several hours, like it was pornography or something.

I changed my fundamental nature to keep the relationship intact. I kept quiet about my passions. I gave up having friends because I was afraid to lose him. I cooked, read fiction, took baths every night and was in bed by 10:00PM. I prayed that my boyfriend would change so that I could be myself again.

What insanity! Almost immediately, the relationship started to disintegrate. Where once we were friends, now we started to despise each other. I lived in hell for six months, trying to hold it together. The more distant he grew, the sweeter I became. We never had a fight because I was afraid to turn into a bitch, for fear he'd use that as an excuse to leave me. I kept thinking, with patience, I could make it work. I cried almost every single day. Finally I got the courage to leave him and then I spent another year in hell, devastated that we broke up. At the time, I couldn't see the larger picture. It didn't occur to me that God had something better in store for me.

Now my life is totally different in every imaginable way. I am myself again, and my Course book sits right out on the coffee table.

So the lesson here is simple: be yourself.

Stop clinging to relationships and situations that are keeping you in hell. God is waiting to give you something much better. He is waiting for you to loosen your tight grasp on reality.

Be yourself.

Relationships

"It's always worthwhile to make others aware of their worth."
—Malcolm Forbes

married by accident by the moonies

Last night someone asked me to describe my marriage. She was excited by the possibility of living a life devoted to God and be married at the same time. She wanted advice from me about making a marriage . . . holy.

I had to laugh. As if I'm the expert.

I told her I have one relationship and it's with God. My holy relationship is with everyone I meet or see or think about. There is nothing outside of me. There are no other people. There is only me in one singular relationship with God, and everyone is included in that love.

There is always a tendency to try and transform a special romantic relationship into a holy relationship. So that you feel joined in purpose with another, joined in God.

But that's not it. For me, it doesn't work like that. There is only ONENESS. You can't do this together with another individual, except in the totality that you are doing this together with everyone. We go to God alone, and yet, here is the paradox: you can't get to Heaven without your brother by your side, holding your hand.

My commitment to the people who seem to be external to me IS my commitment to God.

I love being married and I am the luckiest girl alive, but God comes first.

Putting God first makes me the best I can be. It makes me a better person. It makes everything easy and effortless. It puts things into perspective. I believe the saying that "the family that prays together, stays together."

Jesus lives smack in the middle of our marriage between us. He eats dinner with us. He watches movies with us. He drives in the car with us. It's a threesome, and it works.

For me, I needed to learn about commitment and it was given to me to get married. My whole life I was like the wind, fluttering from one event to the next. I was wildly independent, and terrified to sign anything on the dotted line. I always wanted to know where the emergency exits were for my speedy escape. I'd had one relationship in the 90's that ended badly, and I didn't want to get hurt again. So I closed off my heart saying I would never put myself in a situation in which I could be hurt ever again.

But when you have a lesson you need to learn (in my case, commitment, trust, and opening my heart) there is no stopping Jesus.

No question about it, the way I came to be married is an astonishing story. Married by "accident" in a mass wedding ceremony by the Moonies one unsuspecting day in September 2002.

It's a good story:

We were in NYC for two weeks. We stayed at a Hare Krishna place in the East Village, which was cheap and included breakfast. We gave them all our money on the first day we arrived so that at a minimum we knew we'd have a roof over our head and one good meal a day. We had $50 left over in our pocket, on our first day in NYC. We decided to take all that money and rent a room to teach *A Course in Miracles*.

Fifteen people showed up and one woman said, "You two definitely need to stay here and continue teaching *A Course in Miracles*. This city needs you."

We were like, "Um, we have no money, no jobs, and we just gave our last dollar to rent this room."

She was adamant. She said, "New York needs you. You have to stay." She said, "my ex-husband and his new wife are moving to Canada and they have an apartment in Grammercy Park. Here. Let me give you his phone number."

So Bastiaan called this guy—who turned out to be from Holland, just like him—and they had a 10-minute phone conversation in Dutch and when he got off the phone, he turned to me and said "if we want, the apartment is ours."

I couldn't believe my ears. We had no jobs, no money, no security deposit, no references and someone in the nicest part of Manhattan is offering us their apartment?

It made no sense to me whatsoever, except in the remembrance that there is a God and this is *A Course in Miracles*. So we went the next day and picked up the keys. Within a few days, we both found jobs working in celebrity catering companies.

Around this time, I had seen some beautiful origami paper flowers in the Hare Krishna place. I asked where they came from because I wanted to learn how to make them. I was put in touch with some Korean women who invited us to an office in midtown for an afternoon of tea and flower instruction.

Bastiaan was totally into it. It was the funniest thing. I thought for certain he'd be bored but he loved it.

They spoke practically no English and we spoke no Korean, yet we got along splendidly. At one point, someone asked if we were engaged.

Bastiaan said "Yes."

I said, "No."

The woman left the room and came back with an American minister and a whole lot of other ladies.

The minister said, "So there seems to be some disagreement between you. You (Bastiaan) say you are engaged and you (Lisa) say you are not. Which is it?"

Um.

I don't even remember how we responded. I just remember that time seemed to stand still and freeze. They gave us a talk about how people needed to join in commitment and union, one with each other and one in God, and only then could the real work begin. They talked about how there is no energy in individuals staying separate, but that by joining together in God something new can occur.

They showed us a video.

They invited us to a mass wedding ceremony that Saturday. They told us to dress up. Somewhere in the back of my mind I had an idea that maybe it would be our wedding day. I didn't know what to expect. It seemed too far out there to get married without having a conversation about it, and that probably we would just distribute Course materials.

But I still wanted to look nice . . . just in case.

I still had no money. I felt desperate. I had nothing to wear in my suitcase. I went to the Goodwill shop and found the most perfect dress in the history of perfect dresses. It wasn't a wedding dress, but it was beautiful and I wanted it.

It was $10, which would normally be a bargain for the world's most perfect dress except that I didn't have a dime to my name.

I stood there wondering what to do. How could I make this dress mine? It fit me perfectly. I loved it. Cream colored, to the knee, low back and it had my name written all over it. You know how when you just KNOW something is yours? Well this dress was mine.

I reached into my pocket and felt the Hare Krishna key! I remembered that when I returned the key I would get a $10 key deposit back!

$10!!!!!!!!!

I was out of my head with excitement. I was supposed to check out of the place that very day. I couldn't believe it.

I asked the clerk at Goodwill if she would hold the dress for me. I also asked if there was tax on the dress. She said no. It was $10.

I ran back to the Sanctuary, returned the key, got $10, and ran back to Goodwill and bought the dress. Mine, all mine!

So that Saturday Bastiaan and I packed a suitcase full of Course material and made our way to the New Yorker hotel on 34th Street. We walked in and there was like 5,000 people and not an empty seat in the house. The Korean women came rushing over to us, all happy and excited that we showed up. They were snapping their cameras at us, giving us flowers, kisses and hugs like we were family.

They took our suitcase away and ushered us right to the front with all the other brides and grooms!

Everything happened so fast. Almost immediately the ceremony began and there was no time for contemplation or discussion. Like the universe was conspiring to get us married: like QUICK! GET THIS THING GOING BEFORE THEY HAVE A CHANCE TO REALIZE WHAT IS HAPPENING!

haha. That's what it felt like. Like an orchestrated event, set up by God Himself.

We exchanged vows. We laughed a lot. They pronounced us husband and wife. Afterwards we distributed booklets, and they gave us slices of cheese pizza. That was our wedding day. We decided to go to city hall and make it legal, since it already felt accomplished. I promised to love him, and he promised to love me. It's not make-pretend. A promise is a promise. When you join in God . . . you join in God.

Only a radical shift in purpose could induce a complete change of mind about what the whole relationship is for. It would not be kinder to shift the goal more slowly, for the contrast would be obscured, and the ego given time to reinterpret each slow step according to its liking.

So, we were given a RADICAL SHIFT in the most dramatic way possible. Single, then married . . . with no discussion about it.

It says in *A Course in Miracles* what God has joined together cannot be undone. It's a lesson I remember in those times when it feels like we are falling apart and are separate from each other. Nothing in time works. The Course says there will be a sense of failure and aimlessness BUT THIS IS THE TIME FOR FAITH.

Abandon not your brother. Have faith in your brother in what seems to be a trying time. The goal is set. Your relationship has sanity as its purpose.

For now you find yourself in an insane relationship. Now the ego counsels thus: substitute for this another relationship to which your former goal was quite appropriate. You can escape from your distress only by getting rid of your brother.

NOW, He asks for faith a little longer, even in bewilderment. Abandon Him not now, nor your brother. This relationship has been reborn as holy.

It's the best thing that has ever happened to me. It's not always easy. There are still times when I want to run away. There are still times when I want to scream. I have been known to smash glass and throw sugar bowls. I don't try to be June Cleaver.

In those moments, I let things fall apart. I let myself fall apart. I don't try to smooth things over or make things nice. Because everything is changing all the time. When a shift is occurring, it often looks disruptive and messy.

I let it change. I trust in God that I'm not going to be abandoned.

I don't know what marriage is. I don't know how to make it work. I know Bastiaan is a gift from God. He makes me laugh. He inspires me. I love him. But that's as far as I get. I can't formulate an idea about domesticity.

I am certainly not the kind of girl to settle down and get comfortable. I'm the light of the world. Light doesn't settle. It shines. I'm just too wildly independent. I value freedom above all else. Free to be myself. Free to be like God.

God is my one & only

Married life. It's good. But—let's be honest here—I LOVE it when my husband goes away, and vice versa.

It's like a tropical vacation without ever leaving the house.

There is some really nice stuff in the Course about FUNCTION and how each of us has a specific function that we alone can fulfill . . . *"a part for only him."* Sometimes there is a tendency in couples to become attached at the hip or to feel like it's "you and me against the world", and I know that there is a whole lot more energy when you stand alone.

Don't get me wrong—I love Bastiaan and I love being married to him—but some things cannot be shared and one of those things is your relationship with God. There is no substitute for it. *A Course in Miracles* is very specific. It says: *"You have one relationship and it's with God."*

What does this mean? It means—in truth—you have one relationship and it's with God. Everything else is an extension of THAT relationship. The love I feel for Bastiaan is my love for God. They are the same. It is the same love I feel for my friends and the cashier at Wal-Mart and the homeless person on the street and the guy yelling profanities on television.

It's all the same. Equal love. When you have a relationship with God—when it's your ONE relationship—everything blends into One Love. I don't know if this is explainable. It is an experience. When you experience the Love of God, you want to share it with everyone equally. It's not containable. You want to hug strangers on the street.

There's a song I love called "Pass it On":

That's how it is with God's Love

Once you experience it

You want to sing

It's fresh like spring

You want to pass it on.

I wish for you my friend

This happiness that I've found

You can depend on God

It matters not where you're bound

I'll shout it from the mountain top—PRAISE God!

I want the world to know

The Lord of love has come to me

I want to pass it on

So you see? It's an experience. The Love of God is an experience. You want the world to know. You want to pass it on. How anyone could do this as a couple is beyond me. Which is NOT to say that two individuals cannot come together for a higher purpose. It's my marriage. But it has nothing to do with us as a unit. Again, I don't know if this is entirely explainable.

In Chapter 25 in *A Course in Miracles*, here is what it says about your brother: "*He has no need but this; that you allow him freedom to complete the task God gave to him.*"

Isn't that lovely? This is why I love my marriage. It's unlike anything I've ever seen in a marriage. It defies all logic. We are joined as one . . . yet . . . totally free.

Bastiaan has no need except that I allow him freedom to complete the task God gave to him. And vice versa. I have no need except freedom to complete the task God has given to me.

I'm really grateful.

More from Chapter 25: *Such is the Holy Spirit's kind perception of specialness; His use of what you made, to heal instead of harm. To each He gives a special function in salvation he alone can fill; a part for only him. Nor is the plan complete until he finds his special function, and fulfills the part assigned to him, to make himself complete within a world where incompletion rules.*

Forgiveness is the only function meaningful in time. Forgiveness is for all. But when it rests on all it is complete, and every function of this world completed with it. Then is time no more. Yet while in time, there is still much to do.

DID YOU HEAR THAT?

Yet while in time, there is still much to do.

WHAT IS THERE TO DO?

FORGIVE.

And each must do what is allotted him, for on his part does all the plan depend. He has a special part in time for so he chose, and choosing it, he made it for himself.

What is your special function?

That you let him (your brother—which is every person in the entire world, everyone you meet, see or think about) . . . That you let him understand that he is safe, as he has always been, and will remain in time and in eternity alike. This is the function given you for your brother. Take it gently, then, from your brother's hand, and let salvation be perfectly fulfilled in you. Do this ONE thing that everything be given you.

Amen.

commentary on the state of marriage/divorce

You can't control energy. In a world in which everything is energy vibrating, it is impossible to keep things static. It's impossible. I used to hear about people getting divorced and I'd think "Oh well, if only they knew how to communicate with each other they could have worked it out."

But that's impossible in a world of energy, with everything vibrating on different frequencies. The only way energy could be harmonized is if one energy was either speeded up or slowed down. It would have to be the case.

Most people agree with this on a basic level—they say you have to keep pace with the changes in your spouse. I think this is a nice idea in theory, but I think it's impossible in a world of energy. I don't think energy can move faster or slower by making a conscious decision in a human brain. I think you can TRY to do this for a while, but then suddenly the energy simply wants to move at the pace it is moving.

In terms of bodies (and spouses), it takes on the appearance of having different interests. One person wants to do one thing and the other person wants to do another. Suddenly you don't feel like spending so much time together. You are not attracted to each other anymore. Energy attracts and repels. It's positive and negative. It has nothing to do with love which remains unchangeable.

But in form, in time, in space, in bodies, in a world of matter . . . things that appear solid DO CHANGE because energy is constantly moving.

There is no getting around this.

Here is a little science class for you: Energy is defined as the ability to do work. Due to a variety of forces (heat, light, electrical, mechanical, gravitational, magnetic, nuclear), energy has many different forms. Energy is in everything. It can be broken down into two categories: potential (stored) and kinetic (moving) and is stored in two ways: renewable and non-renewable.

Energy can be transformed into another sort of energy, but it cannot be created and it cannot be destroyed.

What does this have to do with relationships? We'll get to that.

So everyone is constantly wondering why marriages fail. They go into therapy to talk about it. But does this make any sense? Really.

Look at it. Either energy is harmonized or it is not. Either you are moving at the same speed or you are not. Energy is constantly being transformed from one thing to another.

When you talk on the phone, your voice is transformed into electrical energy, which passes over wires or through the air. The phone on the other end changes the electrical energy into sound energy through the speaker. A car uses stored chemical energy in gasoline to move. The engine changes the chemical energy into heat and kinetic energy to power the car. See? Energy doesn't stay the same. It changes. Food is stored energy. It is stored as a chemical with potential energy. When your body uses that stored energy as it becomes active, it becomes kinetic energy.

You see? Energy starts out as one thing and by the time it reaches its destination, it's entirely different.

Energy moves and transforms from one thing to another. It doesn't wait on time or events. It doesn't have a brain to think about cause and consequence. It moves. It doesn't hang around to compare itself with other forces of energy. It is what it is.

I don't think there is anything to discuss or fix. I think this is the point where being the SAVIOR OF THE WORLD becomes difficult for a moment. You make a decision to stand in total singularity with God. You let everything change to meet the goal. You don't slow down. You keep rushing toward the light with Jesus as your guide.

In every instant I have to see who is standing beside me. It's not something I can control. Having given my life and will over to God for Him to use for His Purposes, I find that most things in my life are eventually disrupted.

It's momentarily devastating and sad—you think you lose the things you love—but then there is the reminder from *A Course in Miracles*, Lesson 249: *"Forgiveness ends all suffering and loss."*

Forgiveness paints a picture of a world where suffering is over, loss becomes impossible and anger makes no sense. Attack is gone, and madness has an end. What suffering is now conceivable? What loss can be sustained? The world becomes a place of joy, abundance, charity and endless giving. It is now so like to Heaven that it quickly is transformed into the light it reflects.

So you see? Change your mind. Forgive. Choose to see things differently. No matter what happens to you, no matter how devastating—you lose a job, you lose a marriage, you lose a limb, you lose someone you love—remember that loss is impossible.

You cannot lose anything or anyone, ever, because nothing is outside of your mind. Those you love are with you forever. No one goes anywhere because there is only you, and death is impossible.

The world of time is the world of illusion.

wanted: a holy relationship

I get quite a lot of relationship questions, sincere questions. The main running theme is people trying to make their "special relationships" into "holy relationships."

I'm sorry to say it doesn't work like that. Your holy relationship is the one you have with God, which includes everyone you meet. Every relationship is a holy relationship if you make this decision. A holy relationship is the one where you realize the person you are talking to and interacting with is, in fact, YOU, a perfect whole part of you, not separate from you, joined with you, one with God.

When you realize the person you are talking with is Christ Himself, God Himself, the relationship instantly becomes holy.

If you are looking for ways to improve a ROMANTIC SEXUAL relationship, you should try the self-help section of the bookstore. I cannot help you in that department. Your relationship with the guy or girl you are trying to date/marry/get into bed is already holy by the very nature of what God is. Physical closeness is a sorry substitute for the Love you'll experience when you know God.

I say this, but people still write to me with questions about how to make their boyfriend into a more loving spiritual person. Here is what I say to them: Stop focusing on your boyfriend and start focusing on yourself. Focus on God.

During my first year of marriage, Bas and I almost got divorced twice. It was a doozy of a year. Since I thought I lost him, I let him go. We stopped talking. I didn't wait by the phone. I was very upset to be losing the love of my life, but I knew that my unhappiness was only affecting me. I knew that crying would not help the situation. So I started focusing on myself. I deepened my relationship with God. I made new friends. I did things that made me happy.

And an interesting thing happened: our marriage was saved and made brand new. When we came back together again, we were both totally different people: happier, more appreciative, and grateful. The Holy Spirit took our marriage and washed it clean.

That was a good lesson: Just focus on yourself and have a relationship with God.

During this time, I read the international best-selling book *He's Just Not That Into You* and it's GREAT. It is one great book. It was like it was dropped in from Heaven for me. It's written by two Sex in the City writers, Greg Behrendt & Liz Tuccillo. It's insightful, on-the-mark and true. I read the entire book one afternoon from start to finish, and it changed my entire perspective. It made me stop feeling sorry for myself.

If he's not calling you, he's just not that into you. If he's not asking you out, he's just not that into you. If he's not sleeping with you, he's just not that into you. True, true and true. This book is written for women and its basic message is: You're fabulous! Stop wasting your time on dead-end relationships.

I love that. You're fabulous! You're gorgeous! Start living! Stop waiting around for other people.

Please don't try to make someone love you or like you or appreciate you. This is a waste of time. Don't try to turn hatred/dislike/disinterest into holiness. Just recognize that your brother is your savior. That guy that's not calling you is literally you, so don't chase after him. Just look at your own thought patterns and ask yourself where you need healing, where you need forgiveness, and where you need to start giving a little more of yourself.

If someone is being stand-off-ish with you, ask yourself if you are treating other people in this way. Often times you cannot see that the very behavior you despise in others, is exactly how you treat people.

I think a great relationship book would be: THERE'S NOTHING OUTSIDE OF YOU.

You realize all these shadow figures you see are YOU. You would stop chasing outside of yourself for love and peace and happiness. But in the meantime, I think there are some good rules to follow.

I think men and women screw up relationships just by their general neediness and craziness. It's the search outside themselves which always fails. Believe me when I say I've tried every variation of cute, funny and charming. I've done the domestic goddess thing believing the best way to a man's heart is through his stomach. I've tried being motherly. I've tried worldly and independent. I've tried sex kitten. I've done The Rules. I've played hard-to-get.

None of these things work, except for temporarily, because we each have built in RADARS that can spot when someone is being needy and inauthentic. What I've finally learned is that these are all just stupid rules for manipulation because I felt incomplete and thought I needed a man and a relationship to make me feel whole.

One day I made a decision that I was done with romantic relationships. They are far too restrictive and limiting. Truly. I was simply going to be happy and free and do things that I liked to do.

I'm happiest when I'm alone with God. It's really true. It's a relationship that gives me everything and that works. My mother freaked out when she heard the news. "What do you mean you're never going to be in another relationship? Don't say that."

The result?

I've become a magnet for love.

It's true. Without even trying, I've stumbled on the solution I'd been looking for all these years.

JUST BE YOURSELF!

Just give of yourself. Be yourself. Love. Give and then give some more. Stop trying so hard. Relax.

I was reading through my Hotel Employee Handbook and it could be the next international best-selling relationship book.

HOTEL RULES & GENERAL GUEST SERVICE HINTS AND TIPS:

1. APPEARANCE IS IMPORTANT.

First impressions do make a difference. Lasting impressions are made instantly when meeting someone new. The belief that is held by most people is that you can't provide care and exceptional service to others until you have given that same care and concern to yourself. Personal appearance is crucial to our guests overall impression of our hotel.

2. VERBAL COMMUNICATION:

Think before you speak, speak clearly, confidently, and use a warm friendly tone. Acknowledge the guest by name when speaking to them.

3. NON-VERBAL COMMUNICATION:

Actions speak louder than words.

-Lean forward

-Smile

-Nod

-Make eye contact

-be focused and attentive

-open posture (don't cross your arms or turn away)

4. Attitude:

-Always be helpful, positive and courteous.

-You should have a smile and a warm greeting for every guest that approaches you.

So there you have it.

Everything I really need to know I learned from my Hotel Employee Handbook book!

Be Yourself. Give. Love. Stop waiting by the phone. Be active. Get involved. Relax. Trust in God.

There's nothing outside of you. You will attract everything you need to you by the simple fact that you are a magnet for love.

walk away

I have said that one of the most spiritual books I have ever read is the relationship book *He's Just Not That Into You*. It may not appear at first glance that "forget the jerk" would be very spiritual advice, but let me explain.

This journey is about coming to know yourself. As God created you. It is not about taking abuse. It is not about being ignored. I know many good Course teachers that stay in hell trying to "convert" their brother from an image of hatred to an image of love. Don't do that.

You may say, "but my brother is myself!"

I say: there is nothing outside of you. Stop looking to shadow figures to see where you are in your own mind.

I played that game for a long time. I thought that what I saw "out there" was a reflection of my own inner state of mind. This is exactly what *A Course in Miracles* says, and I was trapped for a long time trying to "change my mind so the world would change with me."

I was very confused for a very long time because the Course also says the world I see is of my own making and does not exist. I was like "alright, let me get this straight. I made the world but it's not real??"

I was so confused. I wanted proof of the world's unreality, until I realized that's a complete waste of time. Why would I test God? I decided to ask myself simpler questions: Am I an illusion or unchanging Spirit? Am I the light of the world or not?

Jesus, who was completely awake, continued to look on a world of hatred. You think he tried to convert the dark images? No. You think he used his brothers as a mirror image of where he was in his own awakening? No. He knew himself. He knew God. In this recognition, he simply went about his way: practicing forgiveness, extending love, healing the sick, remembering God, and speaking the truth. They nailed him to the cross. Do you think he thought to himself, "there must still be areas where I need forgiveness because I'm not looking out onto a happy world?"

No.

He was wide awake. He said, "Forgive them Father, for they know not what they do."

Once you know yourself, you are free. You don't play a game of looking out at your projections to see where you are in your own mind. You stop using your physical sight. You see with Christ vision. You stand in singularity with God, realizing your own holiness, innocence & perfection.

If someone is treating you like crap, WALK AWAY. If someone is ignoring you, WALK AWAY. If they are not giving you the love you deserve, DON'T WASTE YOUR TIME.

Would you react at all to figures in a dream you knew you were dreaming??

A Course in Miracles says, *"Don't abandon your brother"* and while this is certainly true, you shouldn't abandon yourself or God in the process.

A Course in Miracles says, *"Side only with that which will never leave you."*

This is God.

God will never leave you. Do not be deceived by physical bodies. Everything in form will eventually fall away. Greta once said to me, "What has a beginning MUST have an end." All form has a beginning. All relationships have a beginning. All marriages have a beginning. And they all have an end. That simplified it for me.

But there is CONTENT beneath the form that endures forever.

Jesus says to his disciples in the bible that if you go into a house and you are not received, then to leave that house and shake the dust off your feet. (Matthew 10:14).

WALK AWAY.

He also says: "give not that which is holy unto the dogs, neither cast pearls before swine, lest they trample them under their feet and turn again and rend you." (Matthew 7:6)

What does all this mean? It means STAND WITH GOD. It means if you are being abused, ignored or cheated, then don't be stupid, walk away. That hated thing you see is in another world, in another frequency of time, in the past, over and gone.

People say, "But he's my brother! I have to stand with him until he sees the truth! Until we are joined together as one!"

I say: you are going to be here a very long time.

There is nothing outside of you.

I remember the moment I stopped lingering in time. I actually even remember the year. It was 2001. I was in my room at Endeavor Academy and Jesus appeared. He said (in his most exasperated voice): "LISA, DO YOU HAVE ANY IDEA HOW LONG IT TOOK ME TO GET YOUR ATTENTION?????"

He said "STOP LOOKING BACK! STOP LOOKING TO SEE IF YOUR BROTHER IS COMING WITH YOU! JUST KEEP YOUR EYE ON ME AND FOLLOW ME!"

He said that when I step out of the world into Heaven, everything comes with me . . . because everything is me.

This was the turning point when I started keeping my eye on Jesus as my only guide. I stopped looking to my brothers to see where I was in my own mind. I stopped waiting for them to catch up to me, to be standing by my side.

You see, I've always been helpful. I've always checked to see if everyone around me is okay. My mother calls me The Peace Maker. She used to beg me to come home for holidays because she knew if I was there, everything would be okay. I have this ability to calm people down and make people feel safe.

But finally, how long will this take?? To calm every single person down in the entire world? This is an impossible situation. *A Course in Miracles* says that when healing occurs in my mind, it occurs for all the world. I heal my brother by healing myself because my brother is myself. ONE IN THE SAME.

If you think you see a physical body out there, separate from you, you are screwed.

Stop trying to heal your brother. Stop trying to make him love you. Stop trying to see the effects of the miracle in physical form. You are wasting your time and there is work to do.

Just stand with God. Follow Jesus. Don't get distracted by shadow figures. Keep your eye on the goal. Do not look back. Straight ahead, with only Jesus before you. He will light the way.

do not tolerate nonsense

I was forever trying to figure out how it was possible that all the seemingly solid bodies and objects I saw outside of me were actually only projections of my own mind, and were actually not there at all. It sounded like something straight out of a Star Trek episode. But I have an open mind and was willing to entertain the idea as possible and true.

Obviously it's common knowledge now that everything is energy vibrating.

Everything is energy moving in different frequencies: slow, fast, medium speeds. For example, take water. It's two parts hydrogen and one part oxygen. In a slow density, it is solid, like ice. in a fast frequency it is invisible, like vapor, sometimes it's liquid, but it is always the same properties of two parts hydrogen and one part oxygen. It never changes, though its appearance changes depending on how fast it is moving.

So with "people", everyone I see is me, only in slower or faster frequencies. Sometimes I am looking at myself from the past, sometimes I am looking at myself in the future. And this is the reason why attacking someone or defending myself makes no sense whatsoever.

I can only love.

The only benefit I have ever found in a case where I do find myself justifying some behavior or explaining myself to someone is that I LISTEN to whatever words I am saying to the "other" because these words are my own instructions to myself.

Even as I am typing these words, I am aware they are for me. I am reminding myself of what I already know. It's called mind training.

There was a letter from someone yesterday who is in a long-term abusive relationship, and she was really asking for help to see the situation differently, realizing there is nothing outside of her, and if there is abuse in her life it is her own self-hatred.

She thinks that when she loves herself more, her boyfriend will miraculously change. Now, perhaps that is true, but it's a LOT FASTER to walk away from the situation and never look back. If you don't want to see abuse in your life, and you've changed your mind, walk away from it. Do not tolerate nonsense. Refuse to be part of someone else's dream. This is the fast track. You walk away from one world and into another world. Literally.

This is not denial. If a house is burning down, ablaze in flames, you don't stand in the middle of the fire, praying to God to be saved or for the situation to change. You walk away from it. The path to God is forever practical.

When you make a decision you want to see a change in your life, very often the circumstances and scenery change.

I used to get caught in thinking that as long as I saw violence and chaos and sickness and death that I wasn't doing something properly. I was constantly trying to change my thinking to change the images outside of myself.

It doesn't work that way.

Again, think of Jesus. He offered only love and they crucified him. You think that slowed him down? He went all the way. He didn't pause to wonder if he should pick up a sword and beat the hell out of those guys. He knew the instructions that were coming from God and he followed them. The journey to the cross was "the last useless journey" and my total gratitude to Jesus for doing it for me.

I have a friend who asked me, "What will you do when they come up with undeniable proof that God doesn't exist?" I had to laugh. I said, "That would be like someone coming up with undeniable proof that YOU don't exist! I know you exist, so you can't prove to me you don't. I know you perfectly!"

No one can prove to me that God doesn't exist, because He does exist. I know him perfectly. It's not a matter of belief or faith anymore. It's knowing.

That's it. I know God. I am not concerned at all with the chaos that is this world. It's not real.

Believe me, the reason I do the work I do, to stay in constant awareness of my purpose and function for God, is because I feel the pain and suffering of those still trapped in time. My heart goes out to those on the streets, in the battlefield, in abusive loveless relationships: to the sick, the lonely and the afraid.

Nothing makes any sense to me here. I used to look for meaning in the world, but there is none. But there is meaning in God.

And herein lies the reason I got VERY HAPPY when I found *A Course in Miracles*, because finally, I located the true Source of the problem: it was in my mind and in my thinking. As I change my mind, the world changes.

It's a solution that works.

Certainly I still help where there is a need. I go wherever God would have me go. The whole teaching of Jesus is to be in service to your brother. Give him your coat and your cloak, and walk with him two miles. Give and then give some more. But I'm no longer concerned with trying to fix the world. I don't go looking for things to heal.

It's a relief to know I am the PROBLEM as well as the SOLUTION.

Finally, I can relax and feel the peace of God shining within me now.

Amen.

adamantine particles

If I had 5 minutes to tell the world the most important thing I have learned, I would tell them about adamantine particles.

It's a term that comes from Glenda Green's book *Love Without End*.

Adamantine particles are real (yet invisible to the human eye) love particles that you send out through your heart. This is the idea of sending Christ out before you to make your path straight. He goes before you re-organizes everything before you physically get there, removing all obstacles and all stones you might have tripped on.

This is how I personally live my own life, and it works!!

Before I go anywhere, I take a few minutes to be quiet and acknowledge Christ and His Love (you can call it God or Jesus or your higher power or love, whatever works for you) and then send this Love, this force out through your heart into the spaces before you get there.

Send out love and light from your heart and send it out into your day. Send it to all the people you will meet. Before you do anything, see love going out before you as INVISIBLE LIGHT PARTICLES into the room you are about to enter, into the shower, into the car before you get into it, into the plane before you board, into your workspace before you walk through the door. Send Christ before you, allowing the love to enter the space and make straight your path.

This is seriously the most powerful practice I know of. It will completely & utterly transform your life. ACKNOWLEDGE HIM, SEND HIM OUT BEFORE YOU AND HE WILL MAKE STRAIGHT YOUR PATH.

Love is what you are. Light is what you are. Open your mind for the Light of God to pour into you. Open your heart for the Love of God to pour out of you into the world. When you actively send love and light and blessings from your heart to all the places and people you will meet and encounter, everything around you will transform. Have fun with this one!

Miracles

"There are only two ways to live your life. One is as though nothing is a miracle. The other is as though everything is a miracle."
—Albert Einstein

every day should be devoted to miracles

Jesus says:

Every day should be devoted to miracles. The purpose of time is to enable you to learn how to use time constructively.

Ask me what miracles you should perform. This spares you needless effort, because you will be acting under direct communication. That the miracle may have effects on your brothers that you may not recognize is not your concern. The miracle will always bless you.

A miracle is a service. It is the maximal service you can render to another. It is a way of loving your neighbor as yourself. You recognize your own and your neighbor's worth simultaneously.

A miracle is a correction. It does not create, nor really change at all. It merely looks on devastation, and reminds the mind that what it sees is false. It undoes error, but does not attempt to go beyond perception, nor exceed the function of forgiveness. Thus it stays within time's limits. Yet it paves the way for the return of timelessness and love's awakening, for fear must slip away under the gentle remedy it brings.

Miracles are expressions of your own state of grace, but the action aspect of the miracle should be controlled by me because of my complete awareness of the whole plan.

Jesus knows the whole plan. Shouldn't we be asking him what to do? He knows and he'll tell us. We simply have to ask.

ask & receive : what do you really want?

I just made Bastiaan laugh big-time. He did an assignment for his *Time To Teach* class called "What do you really want?" and so he asked me the question and I said, "I want to be gorgeous."

He laughed.

Apparently the correct answer (according to *A Course in Miracles*) is "I want the peace I God" and "I want to be happy."

But I'm ALREADY happy all the time. I'm ALREADY at peace. I have certainty and joy and laughter. Miracles are all around me. These things are accomplished and set. My mind has transformed. So why would I request something I already have??

It would be like owning a particular item and then asking for the same identical item. That would be insane. You wouldn't ask for something you already possess. He laughed. He said, "Well, you're certainly HONEST."

And I'm thinking: well, honesty IS the second characteristic of a teacher of God.

Like finally, we stop playing the spirituality game and become real. You know? I'm not here to be Mother Teresa. I do not pretend to be a saint. I don't attempt to be pure and holy and innocent. These traits are inherent in WHO I AM. I am pure. I am holy. I am innocent. I am as God created me. I'm also passionate and joyful and sometimes my life looks like a train wreck. It is not a tidy package where everything is wrapped in pretty paper in a satin bow. I say what's on my mind. Sometimes I forge ahead full-speed without thinking of consequences. I make mistakes. I step on toes. I don't always say the right thing.

BUT THAT'S THE PURE BEAUTY. This is where it's lovely. It's pure creation. I'm not a soundtrack of a bubbling brook that soothes and calms. I don't wait to have a perfectly clean house until I invite people in. I don't wait until I look a certain way to start living. I say: THIS IS THE MOMENT.

I know a lot of people who either don't say anything or they only say the words of *A Course in Miracles*. I can't imagine a worse prison. I think they are afraid if they open their mouths the truth will be revealed: that they are just like the rest of us with hopes and dreams and wishes and desires.

I mean, come on. It's total freedom to be yourself. I'm a teacher of *A Course in Miracles* and you know what I just did? I went out and bought the latest issue of *Vanity Fair* because it's the Style Issue and I live for the Style Issue of *Vanity Fair*. Like, why would I stop doing the things I love just because I serve God now?

I love *Vanity Fair*. It makes me happy. So I buy it. Is it spiritual? Totally. Whatever makes me happy is how healing occurs. I'm perfectly myself. So anyway. I want to gorgeous. It's what I really want.

It's accomplished.

what would you do if you knew you couldn't fail?

What would make you happy? What would make you feel alive? What have you always wanted to do? What if you knew all power was given to you in Heaven and on earth? What if you knew the universe supported you in all your desires and was just waiting for a signal from you?

What would you do?

Think about your childhood. The clues to unlocking your present happiness are contained in that child.

I always loved pens, paper and notebooks. I loved books. I lived in the library. I won every reading contest every summer, without fail. I wrote a letter to Santa Claus when I was 7 that says: "Dear Santa,

I've been a very good girl this year. Please bring me 12 pencils and some paper and I will give you 5¢. Love, Lisa"

There are the clues. I wanted to be a writer.

But what's interesting is that it never occurred to me to be a writer. I knew I loved writing letters and in a journal, but it never occurred to me to pursue writing as a career or profession. I didn't think I was good enough. I thought I'd open a bed & breakfast or a restaurant. But writing is what I love to do. It's the place where time disappears.

If you could spend all the rest of your days doing what you love, what would it be?

The clues are in your childhood.

step back and let Jesus lead the way

I've always been a forge-ahead kind of girl. If I have an idea, I don't stop to think about consequences. I'm all action, full-speed ahead. But then *A Course in Miracles* goes and says, "*I will step back and let Him lead the way.*" So I started to practice stepping back and letting everything be revealed to me.

I have a tendency to swing to the extremes. I rarely do anything in the gray area of half-way in-between. Either I do something totally or I don't do it at all.

A Course in Miracles says, "*Do nothing.*" I liked this idea and for a long time I decided to put it to the test. Except that it's impossible to do nothing. My idea of doing nothing was reading fashion magazines and lounging around, waiting for something to happen. I would take a bubble bath or watch a movie or go shopping or read a novel. But that's not doing nothing. That is the mind preoccupied. Other times I would get quiet and pray or I would read the bible and think about God. But that's still not doing nothing. Sometimes I would sit in a chair or lie on my bed and say "okay, I'm gonna be still and do nothing." But that's not doing nothing either, because the mind is still waiting for something to happen. I even stopped working for several months thinking hahaha, look at me, I'm doing nothing. You want me God, come and get me. The end result of that brilliant stunt was that I had no money.

Doing nothing is a total paradox because it's total action.

Prayer

"I have been driven many times upon my knees by the overwhelming conviction that I had nowhere else to go."
—Abraham Lincoln

how i learned to pray in Venezuela

We had a little situation last night that required Jesus and a lot of prayer. One of the guys from the advent turned out to be our very own private Judas. I am not even going to go into the details because it's too complicated, but to make a long story short . . . he was lying to us from Day One. He ended up stealing a computer from the center, as well as $500 from the donations. It was one lie after another. I had a funny feeling about the guy from the first moment I saw him in a shirt & tie, sitting in the back of the room. He claimed he was a lawyer but he is really overweight with zero confidence and when I saw him sitting there in a tie, it was like seeing a little boy playing dress up in daddy's clothes. It was all wrong.

But you know, when someone tells me their profession I have a tendency to believe they are telling the truth.

So we got a phone call last night that he had sold the computer, took off with the money, bailed on his hotel bill, and was nowhere to be found.

He was not answering his cell phone.

Though he was leaving text messages on everyone's cell-phones saying YOU WILL HATE ME AFTER TONIGHT and then PLEASE DON'T HATE ME and LESSON 34 I COULD SEE PEACE INSTEAD OF THIS.

We all got together and prayed about it, and it was the most amazing experience because I asked everyone to remember that we do not pray that circumstances change, but rather we pray to remember the truth. We pray so we remember we are Teachers of God and we pray that we remember we have a function on earth to be truly helpful.

We prayed to see this guy in the brightest light possible. We prayed to see past his errors, past his mistakes, past all appearances, past every perceived sin. We prayed that we release him from his past (which was that he was NOT a lawyer, but actually had spent several months in jail and was wanted for several crimes) and we sat there praying, and while we were praying someone walked through the door with a computer and it turned out to be the stolen computer, in perfect condition. Returned to us. I could not believe it.

That is Jesus for you.

So, the money is gone but the computer has been returned and most importantly: our minds have been restored to peace.

I know that *"All things are lessons God would have me learn."* I know that there are no accidents and that a happy outcome to all things is certain.

And now, I know how to pray. That was a lesson that God needed me to learn. I no longer pray for circumstances to change. I let all things be exactly as they are. NOW I pray that my mind be changed. I pray to see differently. I pray to remember the Truth. I pray to remember I am a Teacher of God, here only to be truly helpful. I pray that God work though me that His Will be accomplished, on earth as it is in Heaven.

prayer as a daily reminder that God is with me

> God is my life. I have no life but His.
>
> How incredible is this lesson?
>
> I love it.

My life is God's.

I have no life but His.

I am here only to represent Him who sent me.

I am the holy Son of God Himself.

I am here only to be truly helpful.

I was mistaken when I thought I lived apart from God—me here and God out there—I was mistaken. We are not apart. He is not out there in the clouds. He is not off conducting other business waiting to get a prayer from me to bring me back into his awareness.

He's literally not apart from me. He is me. I am Him.

We are one, together.

The only reason for prayer is for me to remind MYSELF of God's presence in my life. God does not need reminding, but I do. I pray so that I remember God's presence.

Prayer is nothing more than a reminder to myself. It's like a little rubber band around my wrist, making sure that I never forget that God is with me constantly, since He is me.

Prayer does not call in outside forces to help. It simply gets me back on track, aligned with the truth and this action calls in FORCES UNSEEN.

Prayer shines away confusion, allowing light to come into my mind. Prayer reminds that:

God is with me.

God is in me.

God is me.

I and my Father are One.

I literally am what God is.

That's an amazing thing. He is my Source. He is everything that is around me. He is the food I eat. He is the air I breathe. He is the water and the trees and the ground and this house and He's every person I meet.

I see God's shining face in every person I look upon.

He literally is everything that IS.

God is.

He is my home, my love, my inspiration, my kindness, my joy, my happiness.

God.

He is here and everywhere.

I will not forget or be distracted.

Heaven On Earth

What is Heaven?

"Heaven is not a place nor a condition. It is merely an awareness of perfect Oneness, and the knowledge that there is nothing else; nothing outside this Oneness, and nothing else within."
—A Course in Miracles

the great adventure

Today is the day. No looking back. Today is the day. This is a day of special celebration. It is the time Heaven has set for you to receive your treasure. This day is holy, for it ushers in a new experience for you.

Today is the day.

A Course in Miracles is merely the travel brochure.

The book is not the adventure itself, just merely the instructions about how to get to the destination. Now you make a decision to journey out past the stars, and straight into Heaven. You put down the travel guide, and YOU GO. You stop studying, you put aside the books, the groups, and you decide TODAY IS THE DAY. You lay aside learning, you cease all your planning, you stop waiting around for circumstances to be right, and you prepare yourself for an adventure of a lifetime.

You make a move finally.

You stop wondering what Heaven is like, and you simply go there because that is your ultimate destiny and destination.

With *A Course in Miracles*, it doesn't matter how much you understand the language of the words contained within the pages. It doesn't matter how great you are as a teacher. How much people love you. None of that matters. *A Course in Miracles* is merely the travel brochure. Finally, you must put it down and GO. Leave the concepts. Leave the fantasy of wondering what miracles are in store for you. Leave the future-type-thinking that love will come to you someday.

The time has come for you to go directly to the EXPERIENCE of what is being offered to you.

It's one thing to look at a sunny bright PHOTO of a beach with clear blue water. IT'S A WHOLE OTHER STORY TO BE SITTING ON THAT BEACH, feeling the sand, feeling the sun, feeling the water.

Time to have an experience. Time to leave the photo behind and step into the real experience of knowing what it feels like to have no sickness, to feel loved by all, to have no problems, and to be perfectly free and joyous.

It's like wondering what a peach tastes like and listening to someone else describe it. This will never give you the full benefit of knowing what a peach tastes like. You must bite into one yourself. There is no other way. You could find the best peach experts in the field or the most-cutting edge weekend workshop and this would never come close to your own experience of the simplicity of biting into a peach directly.

No one else can do it for you. YOU must take the journey. You must take the first step. You must take the bite. You must take the action.

YOU.

It's time to stop wondering what Heaven is like, time to stop listening to what other people have to say about it . . . and go there yourself.

There's a ticket with your name on it. You can go there now. No more saying you haven't finished looking at the entire travel brochure yet. No more saying you're not ready. No more saying you are a "student."

It's never a matter of being ready when a plane is scheduled to leave in 8 hours. You prepare yourself to the extent that you are willing to make the trip. From that point of willingness, the only thing left to do is get your butt to the airport. You don't plan some more to make more money or find a more appropriate time to travel when the plane is leaving today and you are holding a ticket.

YOU SIMPLY GO.

Put down the book and GO.

How long will you keep reading? How long will you keep searching for some little nugget of truth? How long will you keep getting together with others to discuss the ideas?

Some people spend their lives scouring the internet for more information about a specific destination. Meanwhile, the destination is sitting right there, one plane trip away!!! RIGHT THERE. You could have gone at any moment and experienced it first-hand.

And so it is with Heaven. What are you waiting for? IT'S RIGHT THERE. You can go there now. You can leave this little place of pain and loneliness and spring into Heaven. Today. You can leave the world and GO.

Today is the day your plane ticket says you are scheduled to travel into Christ's Presence. Right into the Heart of God.

Happy forever. No more conflict. No more pain. No more sickness. No more misery. No more doubt. Nothing but peace, joy, happiness and laughter. Why would you wait to go to a place like this when it is being offered you to go there today?

Your body becomes sanctified today. It's only purpose being now to bring the vision of what you experience this day to light the world.

Here is the journey you make and start today, with the EXPERIENCE this day holds out to you to be your own. Time to put down the book. Time to finally experience the destination directly.

TIME TO GO THERE.

Today's the day. Have fun. Bon Voyage.

Time & Space

"A human being is part of a whole, called by us the Universe, a part limited in time and space. He experiences himself, his thoughts and feelings, as something separated from the rest—a kind of optical delusion of his consciousness. This delusion is a kind of prison for us, restricting us to our personal desires and to affection for a few persons nearest us. Our task must be to free ourselves from this prison by widening our circles of compassion to embrace all living creatures and the whole of nature in its beauty."
—Albert Einstein

life is a temporary assignment.

When you start thinking of life as an assignment, it gets a whole lot easier.

You think:

I'm from Heaven.

I've been sent by God on a mission.

I am here only for today.

Sir Thomas Browne says your time on earth is "but a small parenthesis in eternity."

What an amazing idea. The YOU that is YOU lives forever. You think you are 20 or 30 or 50 or 100. But actually you are 4000 years old. Or 40,000 years old. Or 100,000 years old. Or older. You can't die. You can't get old. You live forever.

Who YOU are is eternal. You are energy. You are light.

Are you increasing your energy by remembering the truth OR are you dissipating the energy and killing yourself slowly?

Are you preserving the altar of God within you OR are you destroying it with unloving actions and behaviors?

This world is so small. Look at it. The most you could live is 120 years. That is a blip. It's a blink of the eye. That is nothing in the grand scheme of things. And yet we take it so seriously. We think this is all there is. We think we are born into a world, we have some good times and some bad times and then we die. If you are religious you think you either go to Heaven or to hell. But that is a childhood story, a myth that we've been told, like the story of Santa Claus or the Easter Bunny.

These are stories that are made up to make us feel good about ourselves. It's exciting to think there is a Santa Claus who flies in a sleigh with reindeer on Christmas Eve and comes down chimneys and leaves toys and gifts. But it's not true. You know it and I know it. It's as fake as the story that you are born into a world with a separate body. It's a fairy tale. Sometimes the story has a happy ending and sometimes our hero faces tragedy. But in all cases, no matter how happy or tragic the adventures, the story always ends in death.

Who would want this story to be true?

Could this really be life?

Somewhere in you is a memory THIS ISN'T LIFE. You know it.

I know it. Everyone knows it.

I knew it when I was five years old. All children question their existence on earth, but no one seems to be able to give an answer that makes any sense. We all just accept the fairy tale.

Who is reading these words? Is it your body? Think about it. Get logical for a second. Your body without the life force that is within you would be a heap on the floor. So, what is that life force?

Are you your body? Or are you something much greater that is allowing you to think and laugh and live? Which are you?

This alone will show you the body is nothing.

What makes you move? Can a body think? Can a body love? A body without the energy within is just a pile of skin and bones, soon turned to ashes and dust. It cannot rejuvenate itself. It cannot do anything. It's nothing.

If you have ever witnessed a person "die" and seen their body lying on a bed or in a morgue, you KNOW that's not them. You know they have gone somewhere else. You know they didn't die. You know that they are ever-present.

Think about it.

All our loved ones are with us now. They didn't go anywhere. Where would they go?

And yet there is something in me that makes this body of mine animated. I am walking and talking and sleeping and moving and doing all the things a body does. The body is a vehicle we move in. It's like a car—it gets you from Point A to Point B.

But the car itself it not capable of laughing and living and loving. It's just a vehicle for the driver. It's a pile of metal and parts. You can love it, but you would not mistake it for the driver.

Without the driver, it doesn't go anywhere. It doesn't do anything.

So, we start honoring the Spirit within. We start realizing we are not our bodies. We have them to use, and just like a car, we take care of them, but our cars our not who we are.

And yet we find ourselves in the world. Why are we here? What is the purpose? Are we here for our own needs OR is there something else going on?

When you start to realize how small this world really is, you will be a whole lot more open to giving of yourself. You will worry less. You will laugh more. The body is a means of communication. Nothing more. And nothing less. Death is impossible.

What you do here on earth determines your role in the universe. There is a whole lot more going on than meets the eye. Believe me. It's true.

You've got angels all around you, and God standing with you. You have helpers on stand-by that are just waiting for you to ask for help. They are waiting for you to acknowledge them. They are waiting to assist you. Won't you speak to them?

a hologram of light reflection

There is a reason why I am happy all the time. Would you be interested to know where my constant joy comes from?

I will tell you:

Nothing I see means anything.

It's the reason I'm happy. I am not even here. I'm a memory. A hologram. A light reflection. This world is over. It's not solid. It's not real and everything that seems to occur was over a long time ago. I don't have to worry about anything.

Herein lies your total freedom.

You're dreaming.

Everything that has happened to you in the past or that you are anticipating happening to you in the future has already occurred. The world was over long ago and you are simply looking at a memory thought pattern that appears real. It is an illusion, a hologram and there is nothing solid at all here.

You might as well hear it. You know it already. Everything that is happening to you is already over. Time is over. Space is over. Nothing at all is happening here. This is the reason why there is no order of difficulty in miracles. The world is not a real place.

I totally love Lesson 8 which says, *"My mind is preoccupied with past thoughts."* It says when you are thinking about the past or anticipating the future your mind is actually BLANK.

This is so funny to me, especially when I think about how many people try to achieve a "blank mind" by meditating. What they do not realize is that THEIR MIND IS ALREADY BLANK as they think about all the things they are doing in the world.

I think this is the difficulty a lot of people have: they try to not think at all. They try to empty their mind of all ideas and thoughts. But there is nothing happening in that space. The mind is ALREADY blank.

The practice is to get you to start thinking

1. with God
2. like God
3. as God

Because you are God.

The only time you are really thinking at all is when you are thinking with God. It's marvelous. They only time you are really alive is when you are remembering your True Identity, One with all things.

Human beings ACT and REACT.

God ONLY LOVES and CREATES.

Which is it going to be for you?

the world is redeemed through you

"Your ministry begins as all your thoughts are purified."

As each thought is transformed, it takes on the healing power of God's Mind which saw the truth in it, and failed to be deceived by what was falsely added. All threads of fantasy are gone. What remains is unified into a perfect Thought that offers its perfection everywhere.

I've been losing track of time. The day starts then ends and one minute it is February and the next minute it is June. One minute it is 1975 and I am dancing in tap shoes, my hair in a ponytail, and the next minute it is 2007 and I am . . . well . . . haha . . . dancing in tap shoes, with my hair in a ponytail.

Nothing ever changes. I am exactly as I was created. Just a happy little kid, doing what I love.

Whatever falsity and nonsense I picked up along the way in my human condition about guilt, sin, jealousy, competition, sadness, sickness, loneliness, grief, worry, anger have been erased from my mind. They are false lessons. I thought I needed them to protect myself but once I realized these emotions never served me, I was free to let them go as defense mechanisms. They never worked or protected me in the past so why should I call on these false lessons today or in the future? They never worked. All they did was make me miserable (guilty, jealous, lonely, sad, sick, angry). These negative emotions did not protect me. They did not change my circumstances. Being depressed accomplished nothing. Nobody cared. While I was moping around in a frown, everyone else went on with their lives.

The moment arrived when I could see with clarity that I was only hurting myself.

Might as well just SNAP OUT OF IT, GET OVER MYSELF and be happy.

Happiness is knowing you are never alone. It is knowing you are safe, protected and loved. From that moment I was right back to where I started as a little girl—no cares in the world.

I've had an "adult life"—the education, the success, the failures—only to see the only real true happiness comes in moments of realizing I have everything and I don't need to do anything. I don't have to worry about what other people say or think or do. The only joy comes from not having a single care or worry in the world. Waking up happy, playing the whole day through, and falling asleep exhausted at night.

Living the day like there is no tomorrow because here is the FACT OF THE MATTER: there is no tomorrow! There is only today, only this moment, now. This is life. Being totally present to let the day reveal itself, in all its splendor, glory and wonder.

A Call to Service

"Determine that the thing can and shall be done, and then we shall find the way."
—Abraham Lincoln

i am here only to be truly helpful.

My favorite prayer, as you all know by now, is from Chapter 2 in *A Course in Miracles*. It is the first thing I think when I wake up in the morning. I have trained my mind to say this prayer before I allow any other thought to enter, because otherwise I'd be lying in bed for a half hour thinking about past and future events. This prayer erases all that. It places me right squarely in the present moment. It works for me and it will work for you:

I am here only to be truly helpful.

I am here to represent Him Who sent me.

I do not have to worry about what to say or what to do, because He Who sent me will direct me.

I am content to be wherever He wishes, knowing He goes there with me.

I will be healed as I let Him teach me to heal.

My next thought is "Coffee" and this gets me out of bed.

you can be like God, starting now.

This year, starting now, you can see with Christ vision. You can make a decision to see everyone as God sees them. Starting now. You can live every day as if it is your last day on earth. You can live every day as if it's your first day on earth. You can be like God, because that's what you are.

God = You.

You can boldly declare you are here, in body form, only to be truly helpful. No more trying to figure out your problems. No more procrastination. Today, we take our place among the saviors of the world.

Say to yourself:

In me is love perfected, fear impossible and joy established without opposite. I am complete and healed and whole, shining in the reflection of God's Love.

We are the bringers of salvation. We are the holy messengers of God who speak for Him, and carrying His Word to everyone whom He has sent to us, we learn that it is written on our hearts. We bring glad tidings to everyone.

I love that. We bring glad tidings to everyone.

Last week someone criticized herself, calling herself fat and ugly. I was appalled. This woman is extraordinary. I quickly offered a different way for her to look at herself. I reminded her of all her good qualities—funny, smart, generous, and beautiful—and this remarkable woman got instantly happy. She said she needed a "good dose of Lisa." You can be like this for everyone you meet. Give someone a dose of yourself. Give them a shot of love. Give them a blast of light. Give them a slice of Heaven.

I told her to wipe the word "fat" and "ugly" right out of her vocabulary. I told her "never say those words, ever again." When I was little, my parents taught me and my sisters to never say the word "hate." Never ever never ever NEVER. "DO NOT SAY HATE." That word was NOT allowed, ever. And so it is with other words and phrases. You can wipe them right out of your vocabulary. You can change the way you look at yourself (and others) because there is ALWAYS another way of looking at everything and everyone. You can stop attacking yourself, starting now.

You can be like God, starting now.

i choose the second place to gain the first place

Step back and let Him lead the way. Why struggle to find your way when you have been given a Guide who will show you exactly which way to go? I take the second place and Jesus leads me, and I gain the first place.

I don't practice this just in my mind. I practice it in my daily life. If someone is trying to cut in front of me in the supermarket, I let them cut in front of me. What do I care? I'm here only to be truly helpful. If someone needs a break, I offer it.

If someone is fighting with me, I let them be right. What do I care? I am willing to be wrong in every situation. I take the second place to gain the first. Jesus says you can't possibly know the whole larger big picture. You can't possibly know what kind of day someone is having.

So why not just offer someone the "benefit of the doubt" and be kind to them? What have you got to lose?

If someone wants to cut in front of you, let them.

If someone wants to be right, let them be right.

You see people all the time RUSHING TO THEIR DESTINATION. Once you wake up, you will see there is nowhere to rush to. There is only the location you are in, here & now. Everyone is constantly trying to get somewhere. It's the whole human condition. They RUSH RUSH RUSH. They GO GO GO.

Well, let them.

One day they will know the universal law that once you allow yourself to SLOW DOWN you are SPEEDED UP.

This is a true statement. Try it for yourself and see. Allow yourself to stop rushing and take the time to be quiet and pray instead.

Count your blessings or make a gratitude list instead of making a to-do list. Try it. What you will notice is that all the things you used to rush to accomplish are now being accomplished by God. Everything becomes effortless. You don't have to do anything. When you slow down, everything falls into place.

Time gets readjusted to help you do all the things you need to do.

Jesus says: *"Here again is the paradox often referred to in this course. To say, "Of my own self, I can do nothing" is to gain all power. And yet it is but a seeming paradox. As God created you, you have all power. The image you made of yourself has none."*

Try this and see. Stop trying to make things work. Give up. God will lend you His Strength. Give some time to God and watch the rest of the day be lit by miracles. Take the second place. Step back. Let Him lead the way. God's Will for you is happiness and eternal peace. You need not struggle. Ask God to lend you His Strength and His Grace and it is given to you.

Heaven is a decision

I love this lesson. You have to CHOOSE Heaven. It's not given to you, rather, you have to choose it. You have free will. You must make a decision that peace is what you want.

Creation knows no opposite.

In Heaven, which is all around you, there are no opposites. There is nothing to choose from. There is only Oneness. Yet here, in time and space, you believe there are alternatives to choose between.

All day long you are confronted with choices: should I have tea or coffee? Should I take the subway or a taxi? Should I sleep in or get out of bed? Should I watch TV or go for a jog? Should I live in the city or the country? Should I keep my hair long or cut it short? Should I wear a skirt or pants? Should I say I'm sorry or should I wait till they say it first? Should I send this letter? Should I make a phone call? Should I be still and do nothing? All day long, a thousand choices seem to confront you.

Yet there is only ONE choice to make: Heaven.

All the other choices are completely and utterly meaningless, and will fall into place effortlessly when I make the decision to be happy. Nothing else matters. Tea or coffee. Skirt or pants. Job or no job. Relationship or no relationship.

Heaven is chosen consciously.

It's true. And yet, how can you choose the only alternative there is until you have seen all the other alternatives and recognized how very similar all roads and choices are?

I choose to be happy.

For a long time, I kept thinking I needed to make a decision about my marriage. I would make a mental list of pros and cons, pluses and minuses, weighing all the information to try and make an "informed decision."

In truth, I just want to be happy. That's the only decision I ever need to make.

In this way, I rise above my marriage, above all the questions and doubts I have, remembering only that Bastiaan is my MIGHTY COMPANION in this journey back to God. He's not mine to possess. He's in my dream to help me, along with everyone I meet.

Would you react at all to figures in a dream you knew you were dreaming?

I wonder if I can explain this in a way that makes sense. I rise above time and space, outside of daily events, I go as high as I can go into the Thought of God, and there I rest.

I literally loose myself from my marriage, from all my friendships, from my identity, from my job, from every learned concept. I literally leave a location by rising above it.

Let me illustrate this. Imagine a horizontal line. This is your life. Birth to death. Sequential time. Where the line begins is where you are born and where the line ends is where you stop being in your body. Obviously, death is impossible, but there is a point in time when you leave your body, and in the world we call it death. We can all agree on this.

Birth _____ Death

Okay. So you have a line. You are standing somewhere in the middle of it. This is your life.

At various points on this line, events occur. You had your first birthday, you rode a bike, you graduated from high school, you graduated from college, you traveled to Europe, you won an award, you got sick, you got better, you got married, you had a baby, etc.

All these events led you up to the point you are now.

Birth _____ present _____ Death

You are standing at the present point, somewhere between your birth and death. You have certain ideas of probable events that will happen to you. You will get a new car, a new job, a new relationship. One thing is inevitable: you will die. This is how everyone in the world thinks.

But you see, the miracle snips out certain intervals and makes death impossible. You have the God-given ability, along with God's Power, to altar your life and make it whatever you want it to be.

Everything that happens to you is by your own decision. There is no exception to this fact.

Maybe in your time line you are destined to get cancer. Or be in a car crash. These are just ideas. They have no meaning except the meaning you give them. It's a dream. But let's say there is cancer in your future.

The miracle is a sudden shift into invisibility, that transcends the body. Okay? Does this make sense? The miracle entails a SUDDEN SHIFT from horizontal to vertical perception.

From the point you are standing right now, you can rise above the horizontal plane and land, say, in the year 2012 and snip the whole event right out of your life. Just rise above time and space and drop back in AFTER the event was supposed to have occurred. It's easier than brushing your teeth.

To your body's eyes it may appear like nothing has changed. You may think only five minutes passed, when in fact, five years passed. You are in a totally new location, no matter what the body's eyes report. If you can trust in this, your physical world will shift. The body is denser than the mind and sometimes it takes a while to catch up with itself. Just trust and be patient.

Miracles are your natural birthright.

Maybe there is an abusive relationship in your future. You can skip right over, as you start listening to instructions, and you will never even know that you missed it. You might hear a voice that says, "I don't really want to go to that party tonight. I'd rather stay in and read." Just from listening, you may save yourself the misery of a failed marriage just by staying in that night. Or the voice might tell you to go buy some bread, and while you are out, you meet the love of your life in the supermarket. You could miss an accident because you realized you forget something at home and had to turn around. You don't even know what events you missed and bypassed because you altered your direction. These are not accidents.

You simply start listening to the voice inside your head and following its simple instructions. If something tells you "turn around", then turn around. Don't worry about making a mistake. Often, it might seem like nothing at all is different. It might make you late for your meeting and maybe you get fired. Don't worry about it. Just listen and follow. A lot of people report that sickness or a life-altering event is the best thing that ever happened to them. It made them have a new appreciation for the little things or it taught them to be calmer and more peaceful. Knowing this, it's impossible to judge what is occurring.

Remember, all time is going on all the time. There is no such thing as sequential time. No one is in the same space as you, nor the same time as you. Some people are light years ahead of you. Some people are thousands of years behind you. LOOK AROUND. There are people still stuck in the Dark Ages. They say they hate blacks and gays and women. They still use their bodies to get what they want, by use of violence, attack and threat. They have NO IDEA the power of the mind to manifest. They have not evolved. They are from hundreds of years ago. They are old ideas.

On the other end of the spectrum are people who can transport themselves from one location to another simply by using their mind. There are "individuals" in such a high frequency of energy that you cannot see them. In fact, some people cannot see you! Next time you are at the supermarket, look around. You will see that you are invisible and people can't see you. Some people will bump right into you, and then say "I didn't even see you!" It's because you are in a different frequency and, in fact, they didn't see you!

Have you ever had a conversation with someone and realized they didn't hear one word that you said? It's not because they weren't paying attention. It's because you are both operating on different frequencies. They literally did not hear what you said because they literally COULD NOT hear what you said. Often times you will have to harmonize your energies in order to communicate. You might have to speak their language. You might have to drop down a notch. Then they can hear you. It's why Jesus used parables. People could not hear direct truth. But they could understand simple stories.

Start to observe. You will be amazed when you realize that everyone is in a different time and a different space than you.

When this becomes quite logical in your mind, you will begin to operate with love. You will want to be in a high space, because it feels good. Things are easy and effortless. You might even begin to feel "better" as you read this paragraph. I am holding a high vibration for you to enter. It is my gift to you. The door is open. There is a whole other dimension of reality. You can walk right into the other world. You can leave time and space altogether. You can go to the past. You can go to the future. Just look around you. You can breathe easy now. You can relax.

Just the mere introduction of these ideas into your current thought system is enough to speed you on your way. This is called the COLLAPSE OF TIME.

The miracle has the unique property of abolishing time to the extent that it renders the interval of time it spans unnecessary. The miracle shortens time by collapsing it, thus eliminating certain intervals with it.

This is a very basic instruction.

How is this accomplished? It's quite simple. Choose to be in a higher consciousness. Choose love. Choose to be as God created you.

Happy Birthday.

my happiness—my salvation—comes from me.

My salvation—my happiness—comes from me. It doesn't come from anywhere else. It doesn't come from another person. It doesn't come from money. It doesn't come from friends or family. It doesn't come from external situations.

It comes from me. Happiness is a decision I have made. It's a choice.

I want to be happy . . . nd so . . . I am.

It's that simple.

I could think up a dozen reasons that could send me into a pit of blackness: I have bills, I don't make enough money, I could get sick, I could get into an accident, my marriage could crumble, I could lose my job. But instead of thinking these ideas, I choose instead to be happy.

I choose instead to live in the ADVENTURE OF LIFE rather than worrying about things that are seemingly happening around me, or that happened in the past, or that could happen in the future.

Stuff happens all the time. The popular term is "shit happens" so I might as well be happy.

If shit happens, for no apparent reason, why worry about it?

Another popular thing people say is "it's always something."

Just when you think you get your life sorted out, the car brakes down, a fire erupts, an unexpected bill comes in the mail, or someone gets sick, dies or leaves. It's always something.

If this is true—AND IT IS—then why spend even one second of my time trying to sort it out? If things are breaking down and falling apart all the time—as a fact of life—I might as well be happy. RIGHT?

I turn my eyes to Heaven and ask God what He needs for me to do. He's asked me to be the light of the world. I turn my attention away from the chaos and ask God how I can be helpful.

I keep my eyes fixed on Heaven. I rise above the battlefield. It takes practice to do this, but once I got the hang of it, it's the easiest thing in the world to do.

I have the power in me to be a bright spot in someone else's dark world. It's impossible to do this if I'm standing knee-deep in my own crap. I can't be bright if I'm dark. I can't be happy if I'm sad. I will not hide my light behind doubt or insecurities or endless worrying.

I made a promise to God to shine light and extend love in this world. It's that simple. I'm here for Him, our Father. My relationship is with God. I'm not here to participate in the chaos that is this world.

I'm all light, along with you.

Peace

"We shall find peace. We shall hear angels. We shall see the sky sparkling with diamonds."
—Anton Chekov

is world peace possible?

In this world of chaos, destruction and war, peace seems impossible. Yet God promises that peace is possible even here. HE PROMISES. However, you must see differently for this change to occur. Here is what Jesus says in *A Course in Miracles*: "But it is true that the world must be looked at differently, if His promises are to be accepted."

A Course in Miracles says "there is no world" but it also says "God loves the world." It's a total paradox. It says, "*What the world is, is but a fact.*" IT IS A FACT. It is not nothing. It is real to anyone who believes in it. The world's problems are not real, but that is meaningless to anyone who believes in them.

Jesus says: *"Peace is impossible to those who look on war. Peace is inevitable to those who offer peace. It is not the world that makes peace seem impossible. It is the world you SEE that is impossible."*

So we do not seek to change the world, we seek to change our MIND about the world. We choose to see only peace, in each situation, in all circumstances—despite every appearance. Anyone who has ever tried to bring about peace by external means knows the futility of the task. It is impossible. There is no end to the problems here. But a Savior, someone with the ability to bring about the salvation of the world, sees only peace. He sees only the solution. He sees only love. He looks beyond the appearance of the problem (hatred, fear, war) and sees peace. He sees the Love of God shining in every living thing.

World peace is possible. Are you ready to take your place among the peacemakers of the world? Are you ready to join in the solution?

Are you ready to usher in a new forgiven world? God needs teachers to speak the truth and extend the light of Heaven on earth that peace becomes possible even here.

Christmas : peace on earth, goodwill toward men

I'm grateful that I've been given a total solution that works.

This Christmas I ask that God use me, actively, to give this message of hope and miracles to those who need it. I pray to be given the means to offer a solution (of perfect peace) in such a way that is practical and useful. I got it good at the Academy where I am surrounded daily by 250 people dedicated to being happy and helpful.

So it's shocking every time I travel, to see how much pain and suffering still exists in people's daily lives. It seems like life is getting worse in the world, not better. The main theme is fear about money and security. Another big theme is a feeling of being trapped with no way out.

I'm not even looking for horror stories but I keep meeting people who are telling me about their loneliness, their children's dead-end future, their money problems, their addictions, their fears, their worries, and the constant pain of living in the world.

Christmas is supposed to be a time of joy but I get the sense that for 90% of the population, it is a time of sadness and stress.

People spend money they don't have. They fight over who gets the kids. There's the loneliness that comes from not being with family. Of feeling loss over those who have left us. It's a time of regret for divorce and death, and mistakes made that cannot be undone.

The whole meaning of Christmas is lost entirely. It's like people try to get back to that feeling of warmth and magic, they try to recreate it with a tree and presents and lights and family dinners, but it's like there is always something fundamental missing from the picture.

That something is the memory of God. It is the memory that you are never alone. It is the memory of a star, a light in the darkness. It is the memory that nothing is lost. It is the memory of baby Jesus: an innocent little child that is you.

It's the feeling of something magical. A feeling of hope and anticipation where before there was only dread and despair. It's a feeling of a life of possibilities, of newness . . . and well . . . that feeling of Christmas morning when you come down the stairs as a kid and realized Santa was there during the night. You see the presents, the filled stockings, the lights and you know that life is bigger than yourself.

You know that Santa came down the chimney and that there were flying reindeer on top of the house. And most importantly, you know that you weren't forgotten. You know that despite all your naughtiness, Santa still brought you presents. He still put you on the NICE list.

It's a feeling of being loved and safe and warm.

How do you recreate this magic when there is no family, no gifts, no stockings over the fireplace? How do you find this place of peace and anticipation when you are alone and afraid? How?

The only way I know how is to have a purpose in life. It is to be part of something larger than yourself and to feel connected to the Source of creation.

For me, it is to believe in miracles.

In my worst down-and-out moments, in a place of devastation and loneliness when I cannot see a way out, I remember God. I bring myself back to the present moment, here and now. I count my blessings. I write a gratitude list, either on paper or mentally.

I change my mind. I don't change my circumstances—I sit right where I am and I change my mind. I remember that I have a function in life and somehow, for me, this is enough to change my mood from dark to light in one instant.

From Chapter 15:

This Christmas give the Holy Spirit everything that would hurt you. Let yourself be healed completely that you may join with Him in healing, and let us celebrate our release together by releasing everything with us. Leave nothing behind for release is total, and when you have accepted it with me (Jesus) you will give it with me. All pain and sacrifice and littleness will disappear in our relationship, which is as innocent as our relationship with our Father, and as powerful.

So will the year begin in freedom and joy. There is much to do and we have been long delayed. Accept the holy instant as this year is born, and take your place, so long left unfulfilled, in the Great Awakening. Make this year different by making it all the same. And let all your relationships be made holy for you. This is our will. Amen.

on listening, hearing and being a bombshell

I hear these questions all the time: How do you experience peace? How do you hear the Voice for God?

It's simple: You must listen and be quiet. You must turn off the cell phone once in a while, get away from the computer. You must go out into nature or into a quiet room, or wake up early in the morning when no one can disturb you. Shut off the internal dialogue. Still your mind and God will reveal Himself to you. He is waiting to be known.

To hear God speaking, you have to listen. It's like this with people. You can't hear them while you are talking or when your own mind is filled with ideas. You can't hear what someone says to you when you've got the TV blaring, someone on the cell phone, the kids screaming in the background and your mind preoccupied with a million other things.

When you are still an instant, when the world recedes from you, when valueless ideas cease to have value in your restless mind, then you will hear His Voice.

When you want to hear a friend speak, typically you will go to a quiet place, just the two of you, and you will listen and hear. You stop all the endless mind chatter. When you are focused and attentive you can see and hear truly. Everything becomes crystal clear. You start relating to God exactly the same way you relate to your best friend. You give your full attention.

It's marvelous when there are no distractions. When you can give yourself the gift of HERE & NOW. The most marvelous thing of all? What your brother says to you is God speaking to you directly! Your brother is God! The Holy Spirit is in him, and His Voice speaks to me through him. I hear God as I am willing to listen to what everyone has to say to me! God is trying to speak to me. I love it.

Knowing this, I listen. I really want to hear what other people have to say because I really want to hear what God has to say. I'm curious. He's not distant. He's right here, in my brother.

In Chapter 9 of *A Course in Miracles*, it says a beautiful thing. It says, *"Your brother may not know who he is, but there is a light in his mind that does know."*

Isn't this amazing?

My brother, the atheist, or the murderer, or the wife-beater carries the Christ unknowingly within him! And although he knows it not, there is a light in his mind that does know!!!

Isn't this incredible? The miracle proceeds without anyone's awareness. It goes forth and heals all things. You could be the slowest, dumbest or most wicked person in the world and you still carry God with you.

Jesus asks, *"Is your faith in him (your brother) strong enough to let you hear?"*

I love *A Course in Miracles*. It's so practical. It's so contemporary. It's so current. It applies to every situation without exception. It's all-inclusive. It's for me.

Yes! Yes! Yes! I want to hear my brother because I want to hear God. I want to start listening. I want to hear.

And what if your brother is not speaking loving things to you?

Listen to this:

Everything you perceive is a witness to the thought system you want to be true. Every brother has the power to release you, if you choose to be free. You cannot accept false witness of him unless you have evoked false witness against him. If he speaks not of Christ to you, you spoke not of Christ to him. You hear but your own voice, and if Christ speaks through you, you will hear Him.

Did you get that? "IF HE SPEAKS NOT OF CHRIST TO YOU, YOU SPOKE NOT OF CHRIST TO HIM."

How amazing. Everything you SEE is a reflection of what you THINK.

I, Lisa, think about God all day long. It's what I do. And as a result I am constantly surrounded by people who want to talk about God. This is no accident. This is my mind. This is my dream. This is my show. I am the director and the lead actress. I am the star in my own life. I never go out of character. My part is the happy bright reflection of the Love of God on earth. I tried out for the part and I got it. My part is Gorgeous for God.

What character are you playing? What part do you want to play? Do you want the lead role in your own life? Or do you want to be a supporting character? Or an extra? Are you a victim or a star?

Are you one of the good guys or the bad guys? Are you helpful or harmful? Look at your life. Is it a sitcom? Is it a drama? A tragedy? An uplifting romantic comedy? A Lifetime movie that inspires? Look at the way you carry yourself. YOU ARE PLAYING A PART.

Like any good actor/actress you get into a new characterization simply by changing your mind, your thoughts, and actions. It's simple. It's not complicated. Yes, it takes work. Yes, you may have to study other people's behavior who you wish to be like. But with practice, you can win an Academy Award (or at a minimum a nomination in that category) in this thing called your dream.

I play the Bombshell. My favorite book in the world is *The Bombshell Manual* of Style written by Laren Stover. It's the most beautiful book on the planet—full of light and love and joy and laughter. Everyone should own a copy of this book. It's a dose of happy medicine. I keep this book on my nightstand and read it when I want to feel good. Even my husband laughs. One night he was lounging on the bed, flipping through the book (out of curiosity, he said) and he read something, looked up at me and said, "This description is so totally YOU".

Here it is:

The Bombshell is never bored, therefore, never boring. She never pretends to be anyone other than herself. She is not censored, careful or contrived. She doesn't read the rules, or follow the rules, or color her hair to the latest trend. The Bombshell has her own sense of ethics to which she is always true.

My husband said, "It's like the author studied you and then wrote the book."

Except that it happened exactly the opposite: I studied the book and became the character. This thing called "life" is a happy game we play. You get to have fun. It's not complicated. You get to be yourself. It's not serious business.

Was I born a Bombshell? DEFINITELY NOT. I was awkward and frumpy and average. I wore black. I was moody and isolated. Somewhere along the way I decided I didn't like that character, so I chose a different one. It's that simple. I decided that being a Bombshell was probably a fun way to go through life, and so far it's been great. I get to be compassionate, authentic, and glamorous. Va-Va-Voom.

I get to be a Bombshell because I choose to be one.

I am grateful to Laren Stover for inspiring me to be my brightest self. This is the gift of perfect strangers. She doesn't even know me. I'm just someone who read her book, and it changed me forever.

I love you Laren!

express only truth

There was a time in my life when I was swayed by everything people told me. I used to let people tell me who I was. Good or Bad. Ugly or Beautiful. Charming or Despicable. I actually listened to these voices. They were never consistent, but I listened as if it was truth.

I listened to advice despite that ten different people told me ten different things. I tried to figure out which advice was best for me, based on whether I thought someone was speaking from the Holy Spirit or whether they were speaking from the ego.

Someone recently wrote me an e-mail saying "the Holy Spirit told me to tell you" . . . and then he wrote that I'm an ego, and he began to list all the ways he could help me.

I laughed.

He's telling me that I am a thing that I am not and that he can help me. I'm not an ego. I'm not a body. I'm not any of these things. Why is he instructing me how to get rid of the ego? I'm not an ego. Does he see me as an ego? Who's he seeing?

A good teacher expresses only the truth. He expresses only the light that he sees. He literally does not see an ego. He does not see error. He sees only love.

A good teacher does not see falsity and then try to correct it. He does not see error and then attempt to forgive it. A good teacher sees only the Love of God in everything.

Hopefully we are at the point in the journey when you recognize there is no need to correct anyone. There is no need to "help" anyone, unless they are asking you directly for help. Jesus did not go around asking people: do you need to be healed?

He did not go seeking for egos or sick people trying to help them. He knew the world was not his home, just as I know the world is not my home. He let everything be exactly as it was because he knew who he was!

He could not even see sickness. He saw that many people believed in the illusion of sickness but he himself could not see it. He only saw love. He saw only God. He saw the complete unreality of the world.

He let people come to him. He did not seek out people for healing. He let all things be revealed to him. He reached out his hand and offered love. He let himself be totally available and those who needed help & healing found him.

This is the journey. We are coming to know Who we are. We are recognizing ourselves.

I'm grateful to be surrounded by such great lights. I'm thrilled and excited to be a part of this new space in time.

Perfection

"The moment one gives close attention to anything, even a blade of grass, it becomes a mysterious, awesome, indescribably magnificent world in itself."
—Henry Miller

be perfect

"Be ye therefore perfect, even as your Father which is in Heaven is perfect."
—Jesus Christ of Nazareth

I've been looking at the idea of PERFECTION lately.

I know that the me that is me, the part that is eternal and changeless is perfect, but then I look down at myself and see something quite less than perfect. But is this thing I am looking at . . . this body . . . is it me? Obviously my body is not what I am, but I do equate it with myself and judge myself according to its appearance. And then I try to fix it, and well . . . that has never worked. I've actually gotten down to my ideal weight before, and still felt miserable, so that's obviously not the solution.

Most people think "I'll change first and then I'll be happy" or "as soon as I lose 50 pounds, then I'll love myself" or "If I quit drinking, then I'll have more time to do the things I really love" or "as soon as I make more money, then I'll be generous."

But this is actually backwards. First you be happy. First you love yourself. First you make more time to do the things you love. First you be generous. THEN YOU CHANGE AUTOMATICALLY. Then the excess weight starts falling off you. Then you lose the desire for alcohol. Then money starts flowing to you, effortlessly. You change your mind first, and then the outside picture changes.

Finally, I see that perfection is accomplished as I begin loving myself—TODAY. Loving every inch, all the good and the bad, all the flaws, all the imperfections. NOW. Today. Right this minute. I see how easy it is to go to the finish line today, to go directly to the goal I am hoping to achieve: that I am perfect as God created me, and that I feel safe, secure and at peace. I go to that point today, no matter what my body looks like.

Today.

Most people agree that nature is perfect, in all its chaos, in its so-called imperfection. Leaves on the ground, flowers blooming and dying, snow, rain, sleet, wind, sunshine, clouds, storms, lightening, and thunder. In its diversity, lies its perfection. Nature has an ability to harmonize and balance and we call it perfect.

Trees come in all shapes and sizes and each one is perfect without being judged against another tree. Each stands on its own without comparison. Seasons come and go and most people are grateful for a rainy day every now and again. A lot of people get terrifically excited by a massive storm.

So, why not embrace your own seasons? Why not let yourself be all that you are—sunny, rainy, stormy, dark—and not judge yourself anymore, and let yourself be perfect in all your moods? You are as God created you.

Just be yourself.

Most people call their pets perfect even if the pet is blind, with a broken leg and a ripped off ear. Think about it. A pet is pure love. Nothing bothers them. They exist to love and be loved.

So we call nature perfect and we call our pets perfect, but when we talk about ourselves we say, "No one is perfect."

Most people have an idea about perfection which includes a description of the body. Ask someone, anyone, if they think they are perfect. The mass majority of people say, "I'm working on it" or "I'm not there yet" or "I'm too fat" or "I'm too old" or "I've got stretch marks" or "I've got wrinkles" or "I have to wear glasses."

Almost everyone's ideas are wrapped up in a body, which is just plain stupid.

So, this is what I am looking at lately. Really being honest, and not denying the truth about myself. I am perfect. I love myself. I love God. I love you. I love this day. I love my body. I start from this premise and let the details of what I have to do next be revealed to me.

your determination to be holy

How willing are you to be holy?

Holy and innocent is what you are—as God created you. It is your natural state. It's already accomplished. The question is: How willing are you to SEE it in yourself?

All it takes is a "little willingness" to see your own holiness, your own innocence, and your own perfection. The Holy Spirit asks only a little and gives a lot.

TRUST NOT YOUR GOOD INTENTIONS.

Do not try to be holy. Whatever you think is "holy" are your old ideas based on things you have learned in the world. Perhaps you think to be holy is to be a saint, or to never make mistakes, or to always be nice and sweet and gentle. This is NOT holy. This is the world's idea of holy.

Let the Holy Spirit SHOW YOU what holy is.

Here is Chapter 18, Section IV:

Humility will never ask you to be content with littleness. But it does require that you be not content with less than greatness that comes not of you. Your difficulty with the holy instant arises from your fixed conviction that you are not worthy of it.

What an amazing idea. All that is really asked of each of us is the willingness to be as God created us. Don't worry about what anyone else is doing. Just focus on yourself.

Here's how it works for me: I think of myself as a dwelling place for God. An empty shell. A body for God to occupy that His Will may be done "on earth as it is in Heaven."

My body, thus, has become a means of communication for God.

Herein lies my holiness, innocence and greatness—pure & untouched—because it comes from God. You see? My holiness is what God is. It's not something that I made up. It contains all the love and light in the universe. It is passionate. It is gentle. It is active. It is quiet. It is lovely to behold.

Half the time, I sit in amazement at what is occurring in me and through me even though it's happening in my own body. I think "I'm so lucky to be me." I get to hang out in my own company 24-hours a day. This is not arrogant. This is how you will think of yourself also when you come to know that God dwells in you. Jesus walks with you. You are never alone. You are in the finest company on the planet. No one is luckier than you. You will never be bored again. Life becomes a grand adventure, a happy game you play. You will look in the mirror and be amazed by your grandeur.

I don't really know how it happened, except that I had the WILLINGNESS to know my own holiness. I wanted it above all else. I didn't want to be a limited human being anymore. I didn't want to be trapped in meaningless petty grievances anymore. I wanted to be bright and happy. This was my one wish on every birthday candle and every shooting star. I didn't want money or fame. I wanted transformation. I wanted to look in the mirror every day and be thrilled with the person looking back at me.

This was my one desire. My one wish. Total transformation.

And it was granted because God always answers all prayers.

look only to what is the same

If you look around you, it will become clear that every individual is constructed in a different way. We each have a different energy configuration, and we appear different. We are different colors, different races, different backgrounds, different religions, different levels of success or poverty, sickness or health, skinny or fat, beautiful or ugly. Most people spend their whole life relating to these differences, as if this is the person. This is the state of the world. We go by what our body's eyes tell us. We relate to the form.

WE RELATE TO THE DIFFERENCES.

As you come into a new awareness, you begin relating only with what is the SAME. You begin to look for qualities that are inherent in everyone. You stop seeing Paris Hilton as different than you, and realize she wants exactly the same things you want. She is no different.

As impossible as this sounds, she wants her life to have meaning and to make a difference in the world. It's what we all want.

You begin TO SEE that we all desire exactly the same things. We want security, peace, lasting love, and happiness.

Each and every individual wakes up in the morning confronted with their own mind. Maybe one wakes up on luxurious 1500-thread count Egyptian cotton sheets and another wakes up on the street covered by a dirty blanket or a shack in Africa, but the CONTENT IS THE SAME.

One wakes up in an 80-year old body and another wakes up in a 20-year old body.

BUT THE CONTENT IS THE SAME.

THEY ARE CONFRONTED WITH THEIR OWN MIND.

This is true across the board.

It doesn't matter what your body looks like or what the external situation look like. Every single individual, without exception, wants exactly the same things.

To feel loved and to feel safe.

Practically everyone I know is faced with the "inevitable" situation that the body ages, gets sick and eventually dies. You will be depressed until you know that the YOU that is YOU is eternally creative and that sickness and death are impossible. Then you will be ridiculously happy every day, and life will become a grand adventure.

Everyone who walks upon this earth has a memory (no matter how dim) that there is "something else." We spend our lives searching for this missing piece of the puzzle, the thing that will make us complete and whole.

Most people mistakenly look for their completion in a new relationship, a new location, a different job, more money.

BUT THE CONTENT IS THE SAME: We are all seeking for our own completion: to be healed and whole and happy.

Knowing this, you will begin relating differently to everyone you see. You will begin to look past differences and look to what is the same. Here, all barriers are left behind. You stop thinking you are better or worse than anyone else. You see we are all exactly the same.

This kind of thinking will improve your life dramatically.

a contemporary Jesus

Gisele Bundchen is my new hero and inspiration.

I love it when I stumble upon Teachers of God in disguise. It's the greatest thing when I see someone who has never heard about *A Course in Miracles* and yet who practices all the lessons in their own life.

I read an interview between the supermodel Gisele and Oprah Winfrey. It's incredible. She talks about loving yourself, being honest, and realizing that beauty is something inside of us. She says, "If you love yourself and accept yourself, that shows on the outside."

She talks about appreciating everyone. Respecting everything. Not taking anything for granted. Happy with no money. Happy with money.

Sounds like the lessons of *A Course in Miracles* to me. Be happy. Be honest. Only appreciation is an appropriate response to your brother. Don't judge. Know thyself.

Here are more inspiring words by the lovely Gisele: "When you're good to yourself and you accept yourself and you're honest and you understand yourself, and you're not judgmental—that is confidence."

I LOVE HER.

I actually stumbled upon her by accident. Certainly I've seen photos of her in Vogue and every other magazine on the planet, but it wasn't until a few days ago when I heard she was wearing a $12.5 million dollar bra in the Victoria's Secret Fashion Show that I started to get curious. I did an internet search and read interviews by her, and in every single one she is just plain NICE.

A total angel with wings, matching lingerie, and a $12.5 million dollar diamond bra.

A contemporary Jesus.

I love it when I find individuals who lead by example. People who are simply out there, living their lives, as bright shining stars. People who have never heard about *A Course in Miracles*.

My other inspiration is Elle Woods (Reese Witherspoon) in *Legally Blonde*. It's my all-time favorite movie. I show it to Course groups as a perfect demonstration on how "to be."

"Just be like her," I say.

Elle Woods is a perfect Teacher of God. She exists only to be truly helpful. She's perfected all the lessons. She's Gorgeous for God. She still gets upset, but she quickly gets over it. She doesn't bad mouth anyone, but she also doesn't let anyone trample over her. It's not like she's dancing around on the Good Ship Lollipop. She's simply being herself, and it's lovely.

If you have not seen the movie *Legally Blonde* (I & II), you should definitely rent them today.

Obviously, if you know me, you know I use Jesus as my original source of inspiration but it's still exciting to find contemporary role models. You know, happy individuals who don't have a mean bone in their body. These characters definitely exists. I personally know lots of them. I'm surrounded by angels.

Jesus is definitely alive, walking around today. I see him everywhere I look.

why i am vegetarian

Someone confronted me at work tonight about being a vegetarian. I was sitting there minding my own business, eating a salad, when suddenly the question rang out, "Why don't you eat meat?

Oh boy, here we go. I looked up and there were 20 meat-eating servers waiting to hear my response. It's impossible to answer this question honestly without causing controversy. Usually I say, "It grosses me out."

But the conversation NEVER ends there.

They always want to know, WHY? Where do you get your protein? Do you eat fish? (no) What about chicken? (??) If you don't like to eat things that have been killed, why are you eating salad? Plants are living and were killed for consumption. Etc.

What's the real reason I don't eat meat? The honest answer? It grosses me out. I love animals. I was taught not to kill. When I was a girl I used to kick over ant hills and squash ants till they were dead, until one day my mother told me not to do that. She said the ants worked hard to build their homes and didn't deserve to die. I was taught to be compassionate and kind to all living things.

So I was told not to kill the ants, and yet we ate hamburger and chicken for dinner. One day I looked down at my plate and realized there was a dead animal on it. It was no longer a "protein source." It was no longer a gourmet meal, with sauce. It was a dead animal. From there, my meat-eating days were numbered. I cut out red meat and stuck to chicken and fish.

But then someone said to me that everything is energy vibrating. Animals have consciousness. When they are killed, they feel the pain of their own death and that pain is then trapped in their flesh.

So, when I eat animal flesh, I am mixing the energy of death consciousness in with my own energy. I am literally eating death, pain and suffering. Now the dark energy is in my body, and I have to deal with it.

When I heard this, I almost threw up. I never touched meat again. My meat-eating days were over. I felt I had enough problems in my own life to deal with, without adding additional chaotic energy into my system. This is the real reason I am vegetarian. This is the real reason I don't eat meat. I don't want to consume death consciousness. I want a clean, pure system.

And it's been my experience that you don't tell this to a table of meat eaters.

The next question everyone wants to know is "What do you eat?"

I EAT WHAT I WANT.

I am a foodie. Food is my passion. I have a degree in hotel/restaurant management. I love to cook. I love fresh fruit. I love a 4-course meal. I love cupcakes from *Magnolia Bakery* in Manhattan. I love *The Cheese Factory Restaurant* in Wisconsin. Breakfast is my favorite meal. I love vegetables out of a garden. I think no kitchen is complete without a blender, a juicer and a food processor.

I went through a whole healing with food. It came when I stopped eating processed crap. I can't explain scientifically what happened to me but food was like a drug to me for many years. I was definitely addicted to food and dieting. I was addicted to creating a perfect body. Some days I felt like a crazy person. I began to suspect that the chemicals and preservatives in processed food had the same numbing effect as drugs and alcohol. I couldn't prove it but I decided to experiment. I gave up eating crap. I started eating whole fresh food, lots of fruit and salads. I started treating myself with love. I began viewing myself as a temple to God.

Almost immediately, my food addiction was healed. I wasn't hungry anymore. I stopped binging. Fruit smoothies healed me! I heard that a lot of people overeat because their bodies are not getting the nutrients they need from fruits and vegetables.

This is the point where it can get a little tricky for those practicing *A Course in Miracles* because if the body is not real, then food has no meaning, right? TRUE. But again, you know when something is fundamentally OFF and you need to make a change.

I knew I had an addiction that needed healing. I needed to go deep into my thought system and be honest. I wasn't going to deceive myself with statements like "There is no world" and "I need do nothing."

I knew I needed help. I prayed. I listened. I prayed some more. It was given to me to stop eating meat. To stop eating crap. When I first got to the Academy, the first thing the Master Teacher said to me was, "THIS ONE SEDATES."

He nailed it. That was exactly my problem. I sedated. I used food and alcohol to fill an empty hole where God should have been. So my solution was to stop sedating. To stop abusing myself and to allow the Love of God to sustain me.

I let go of attack thoughts, begin treating myself with love, and I was healed.

Grace & Gratitude

"Everybody can be great because anybody can serve. You don't have to have a college degree to serve. You don't have to make your subject and verb agree to serve. You only need a heart full of grace. A soul generated by love."
—Martin Luther King, Jr.

"The hardest arithmetic to master is that which enables us to count our blessings."
—Eric Hoffer

what is grace?

"Grace is acceptance of the Love of God in a world of seeming hate and fear."
—A Course in Miracles, Lesson 169

my way vs. God's way

I am back in Wisconsin now. We had a great trip, but it's always good to be home. I was not able to get on the same flight as Bastiaan, so we flew separately giving me yet another opportunity to remember I don't know anything. At first I was upset and kept trying to persuade the flight attendant to PLEASE look again to see if there was another seat. PLEASE PLEASE PLEASE there must be something, one seat available, I've never seen a flight entirely booked, etc. my husband is on that flight, my bags are on that flight, etc. but to no avail. There were no seats left. I was not getting on that flight and I was not getting my way.

MY WAY.

When you start to realize how many times you try to manipulate events to get your way, you will be startled.

The program of *A Course in Miracles* asks that you let everything be exactly as it is. You let yourself be shown and guided and led so that HIS WILL can be accomplished.

My plan vs. God's Plan.

This flight attendant was giving me DIRECT INSTRUCTIONS about where I was meant to be—Terminal F at 4:45—but I kept trying to make things different, being a big adult baby. I was practically whining. "I want to go home! Whaaaaaaaaaaaaaaaaaaaaaaaaaa."

It was shocking to me when I actually HEARD myself, as I must have sounded to the flight attendant.

A total baby, and a total bitch.

As I was walking to the next terminal (on the other side of the airport in Chicago, a 10-minute walk) I had a chance to remember my only purpose is happiness. Without my joy, God's joy is incomplete. Without my smile, the world cannot be saved. While I am sad, the light that God Himself appointed is lusterless and dim and no one laughs because all laughter but echoes mine.

Lesson 100: *Your joy must be complete to let His Plan be understood by those to Whom He sends you. They will see their function in your shining face, and hear God calling to them in your happy laugh.*

Remembering this lesson, I quickly got over myself. I came to my senses. I remembered the truth. I remembered that I have a function to fulfill. I am here only to be truly helpful. Suddenly I was happy and the scenery changed before my eyes. I noticed how friendly all my fellow passengers were. I noticed how peaceful I was waiting in the terminal. I realized I hadn't had a free moment to myself until now, a whole block of complete and absolute solitude, where no one could reach me by phone or e-mail. I recognized my gratitude and I had a great trip home. Two seconds earlier, I was having a terrible time but with a simple change in perception, the whole scene changed before my eyes. That's the miracle.

I don't know the Plan of God. I don't know where I will be sent but I do know I am His Happy Messenger. I do know that without the Teachers of God . . . there is no hope in this world.

Now we have work to do, for those in time can speak of things beyond, and listen to words which explain what is to come is past already. Suffice it, then, that you have work to do to play your part.

So the New Year is upon us. Resolution Time. Last year my resolution was to be truly helpful (and also to go to the movies at least once a week) and I think I did a good job with keeping my promises. This year my resolution is grace and gratitude and *"to play my part to bring salvation a little nearer to each uncertain heart that does not beat as yet in tune with God."*

thank God

I am feeling terrifically grateful. I am happy every single time I come into the PRESENT MOMENT and remember THIS MOMENT IS ALL THERE IS. So simple, yet so easy to forget. Today I am reminding myself of the TOTAL PERFECTION of me, my life, my brothers, my marriage, my living situation, my work situation, my money situation, and God.

1. I have everything I need.
2. There is nothing lacking.
3. I am grateful.

I believe that a new moment can only arrive when you have accepted the total perfection of the moment you are currently in, RIGHT NOW. You come into a total acceptance of your circumstances, without wishing they were something else. Why? Because the thought of MORE or DIFFERENT is a limited idea. It is an idea based on deprivation that you will somehow be better off (happier, more peaceful) in a different situation, different circumstances, different location. IT'S NOT TRUE. Everything you are searching for is right here for you to find, in this very day.

You can be happy now because happiness is what you are.

I used to read motivational books by famous rich self-help authors and I'd think, "Yea, well, it's easy for YOU to say everything is perfect! You have everything!"

Well, I'm not rich or famous. At this very moment, I have no money (no wait, that's a lie. I have change in my purse. Let me go count. Okay, I have $1.27 in dimes, nickels and pennies), no gas in my car, no job, and I don't know where my next meal is coming from . . . and yet I love my life.

How is this possible?

Because God is with me. I am perfectly safe. I am loved. I know I won't starve. I know things are fine. Everything I need is inside of me, not outside of me.

I could be anywhere and be happy. This is a sure indication of total freedom. You no longer depend on external things for your own comfort. I will tell the truth: I woke up this morning worrying that my phone is about to be shut off because I can't pay the bill. I caught the thought, realized that worrying is what death is, and I started counting my blessings. It's impossible to worry and count your blessings at the same time.

I thought about Immaculee Ilibagiza. Google her. She's extraordinary. She hid in a cramped bathroom for three months in Rwanda with seven other women, during the massacre in 1994. Her entire family was brutally slaughtered and she discovered God during that time. If she can emerge from a situation like that as a shining bright star, full of grace and peace, then I THINK I will survive on 1-meal a day and no phone.

You must begin by loving all that is, now. It doesn't matter if you live in jail or a penthouse on Park Avenue. It doesn't matter if you are sick or well. Your life—right this minute as you read these words—is perfect. It's so simple. In total acceptance of perfection, IN THIS MOMENT, is everything given and received

THEN . . . the landscape changes.

You don't pretend you live in a mansion when you live in a motel room. You give thanks for the motel room. You don't pretend you are healed when you are sick. You give thanks for your cancer. Count all the ways it has been a blessing to you. Don't tell me there is nothing good about cancer. It is giving you something. Just be honest—maybe you get to stay home and not work, maybe it gives you extra attention and love—just be honest. And when you realize you no longer need sickness to get the love you deserve—healing will occur.

So be grateful for everything. It's all good.

Purpose

"A ship is safe in the harbor, but that is not what a ship is for."
—Ralph N. Helverson

"How far would Moses have gone if he had taken a poll in Egypt? What would Jesus Christ have preached if he had taken a poll in the land of Israel? What would have happened to the Reformation if Martin Luther had taken a poll? It isn't polls or public opinion of the moment that counts. It's right and wrong and leadership."
—Harry Truman

you are the light of the world

What does it mean to be "the light of the world" in practical terms?

It is to be like the sun that shines in the sky: to rise in the morning and shine and shine forever. The sun doesn't do anything else. It doesn't judge. It doesn't plan. It doesn't attack. It doesn't defend its position. AND IT CERTAINLY DOESN'T GO DARK. It simply shines bright all day long. It doesn't have varying degrees of brightness. It is not sometimes super-bright and sometimes kind of bright and sometimes just a little bright. No, the sun is always the same. It never varies. Even when the clouds are covering it, it is still exactly the same—A BRIGHT STAR.

This is my function as the light of the world: to be a bright star.

I rise in the morning and I shine and I shine forever.

How simple is this??

TO HEAL IS TO MAKE HAPPY.

Finally, at long last, I "got it." I saw there is nothing to convert and nothing to do as far as this world goes.

I could spend a million years writing down my list of grievances and making amends. But that will take a very long time. It suddenly occurred to me one day "why not just let the past go?"

I mean, REALLY LET IT GO.

Then there is nothing to forgive. One day I simply realized that I could be born again and brand new. In that instant, which is every instant, the world around me was also brand new with no reference to the past.

This is the only way to live—to see with the eyes of a child, in perfect wonder where everything is constantly revealing itself as brand new.

I kept thinking this would happen "magically"—like an angel or Jesus himself would appear in my bedroom and do "something." I didn't know what this something was, but I can tell you: I wasted a LOT OF TIME waiting for something miraculous to happen to me which would give me the indication to be bright and happy.

It doesn't work like this. YOU MUST CHOOSE. You choose the time when you make a decision to be happy because finally you just get tired of a meaningless existence that seems to go nowhere.

For me, more than anything, I wanted a purpose and a function in life. I wanted to be part of THE GREAT CRUSADE that ushers in a new world. I wanted to be one of God's helpers, to stand among the saviors of the world.

It's what I definitely wanted. I asked and I received.

I wanted a job working for God.

It's a decision I made.

If you don't want the job, that's fine too. Not everyone wants to be a doctor. Not everyone wants to be an accountant. And not everyone wants to be the light of the world.

You get to choose.

It's that simple. You can do this today, right here, right now. No more waiting for circumstances to change. No more waiting till you get the right job, the right relationship, more time, more money, etc. You suddenly say: ENOUGH IS ENOUGH. I will begin today.

I will be bright and happy because I'm tired of being sad and miserable.

The new beginning is that simple: you get sick and tired of being sick and tired. You find that your old story bores you and that your self-loathing has become quite ridiculous. You say: ENOUGH IS ENOUGH. I'm done with attacking myself. Done with hating myself. Done with abusing myself. I'm going to start being a little nicer to myself, starting now. It's that simple.

Perhaps you don't know how to be happy? I didn't know either at first. But it's like a job. When you first get hired to a new job, often you have no idea how to accomplish many of the tasks given to you. BUT YOU LEARNED. Someone trusted you enough to hire you and so you must have in you the ability to do the job you were hired for. Right? You didn't just say "oh well, I don't know how to do that." You asked someone to show you. Otherwise, you would lose your job. If your boss gave you a list of work-related things to do and you didn't know how to do them, you would learn.

You would find a mentor. You would ask for help. You would watch other people around you. This is what happens in the workplace, and suddenly before you know it, you're are accomplishing all those impossible tasks effortlessly. Suddenly you are an expert. You see new people coming into the job who have no clue (just like you once did) and you think: oh, if only they knew how easy it is going to get!

It's exactly the same with being happy. You will learn how to do it, and you will be changed in the twinkling of an eye.

you are the savior of the world

You have been called by God Himself. You have been by ordained by God Himself. Your name is written in the stars.

What would you say if Christ appeared to you in all His glory, saying, "Choose once again if you would take your place among the Saviors of the world."

What would you say? *For He HAS come, and He IS asking this.*

Are you ready to take your place among the saviors of the world?

How willing are you to forgive your brother?

How much do you desire peace instead of endless strife and misery and pain?

The power to heal the Son of God is given you, because he must be one with you. You ARE responsible for how he sees himself. But reason tells you it is given you to change his whole mind, which is one with you, in just an instant. And any instant serves to bring complete correction of his errors, and make him whole. The instant that you choose to let YOURSELF be healed, in that same instant is his whole salvation seen as complete with yours. Reason is given you to understand that this is so. For reason, kind as is the purpose for which it is the means, leads steadily away from madness, toward the goal of truth.

You ARE as God created you, and so is every living thing you look upon, regardless of the images you see. What you behold as sickness and as pain, as weakness and as suffering and loss, is but temptation to perceive yourself defenseless and in hell. Yield not to this, and you will see all pain in every form wherever it occurs but disappear as mists before the sun. A miracle has come to heal God's Son, and close the door upon his dreams of weakness, opening the way to his salvation and release. Choose once again what you would have him be, remembering that every choice you make establishes your own identity as you will see it, and believe it IS.

Here is time collapsed. You are the decision maker. You decide how long you will be a human being having a human experience. You decide when you will take your place as the Savior of the world. No one can stop you. YOU DECIDE. No one else. Things are still going to happen to you. People are still going to act the way they act.

The question is:

HOW WILL YOU REACT?

WHAT IS YOUR RESPONSE?

How does the Savior react? How does God react?

Love and Appreciation and Helpfulness are the only appropriate responses.

The other day someone wrote me a letter about Jesus. I was thrilled. I was reading it with excitement. Everything she wrote was 100% true. I loved every word of it. Then the next day I got a letter from this very same person apologizing for attacking me. I was stunned! No one was attacking me. Apparently the letter was written as instruction for me.

But having accepted the Atonement for myself, I saw only love. It was the most dramatic evidence to date of how much my mind has changed. Someone "attacks" me and I take it as a compliment. I couldn't believe it! I laughed out loud at the miracle of my own transformation. All I remember was a beautiful letter about Jesus that someone took the time to write for me!

As the savior, you see every moment as another opportunity to be GRATEFUL.

YOU SEE EVERYTHING AS A GIFT.

You don't waste EVEN ONE SECOND bad-mouthing your brother. NOT ONE SECOND. You never say an unkind word. This Course is uncompromising. There is no room for error.

Either you are:

1. entirely demonstrating the message of Jesus and you are home in Heaven, consistently happy and at peace.

OR

2. you are being a human being, with all the limitation, sickness and fear, with occasional bouts of joy, followed by doubt and depression.

There is no compromise between these two states. Either you are on a rollercoaster (sometimes happy, sometimes sad) or you are in Heaven where there are no degrees or intervals.

There is no in-between. Which is it for you? Are you extending love? Are you showing appreciation? Are you expressing gratitude? Are you happy? Are you at peace?

Or are you waiting for external things to change so you can change? Are you affected by other people's emotions? Other people's behavior?

This is a very simple course. It's not complicated. You might be wondering how this is all accomplished. You might be wondering how you can let your OLD STORY go. You might be wondering how you can forgive. You might be wondering how you can stop judging yourself and others. You might be wondering how you can accept your own perfection.

It's very simple.

It's the function you have accepted as a Teacher of God. It's like any job. You are given a job description and you just do it. It's not complicated. You are the savior of the world.

THIS WORLD NEEDS LIGHT. IT NEEDS YOU. IT NEEDS INDIVIDUALS WHO ARE DEMONSTRATING THE ENTIRETY OF HEAVEN ON EARTH.

Won't you do this? For the Love of God? For the healing of your brother?

Will you take your place among the saviors of the world?

what is charity?

I had a great Christmas. Bastiaan is here and we're having a really good time—simple and relaxing. We spent Christmas Day at my mom's house with my sisters, and now we are at my dad's house until Thursday, then back to Wisconsin.

So, Christmas. The time of year when everyone thinks of charity. Salvation Army. People who have less than we do. Families who need help. Giving.

But what is charity really? What does it mean?

Here is the DICTIONARY definition along with *A COURSE IN MIRACLES* definition. These two contrasting descriptions will demonstrate, hopefully, how everything in the world has many meanings. We often learn things in time that are not altogether true, and in many situations: entirely false. Jesus says we have been badly taught. *A Course in Miracles* teaches to let go of every idea about everything *("make no exceptions")* so that you can be shown its true meaning.

CHARITY:

DICTIONARY DEFINITION: *"generous actions or donations to aid the poor, ill or helpless. Something given to a person or persons in need, alms. Leniency in judging others, forbearance. Christian love; agape."*

A COURSE IN MIRACLES DEFINITION: *"Charity is a way of looking at another as if he had already gone far beyond his actual accomplishment in time."*

Isn't this amazing? You place your brother further along in time than he thinks he is. You see in him what he cannot see for himself. This is true charity. You see the potential in others. You see the spark. You see the light. You see the love. You see the creativity. You see what your brother is capable of accomplishing. You look beyond appearances. You look beyond form. And you see what is truly there.

This is charity.

What a great way to start the new year. By seeing in everyone the light that is truly there. To see in your co-workers more than they see for themselves. To see in your children, husband, wife, girlfriend, boyfriend, mother, father, brother, sister WHAT IS TRULY THERE.

Most people, because of childhood (or adult) disappointments learn to suppress their creativity. They shut down their desires and dreams. They learn to settle for less. Henry David Thoreau says, "The mass of men lead lives of quiet desperation."

Have you ever witnessed what occurs when you inspire someone with your words? Have you ever seen the look in someone's face when you praise them? When you appreciate their work? When you acknowledge an action (even something as small as doing the dishes)?

An amazing thing happens. First, they light up. Second, the very thing you said they are good at suddenly becomes a thing they do with joy. It's a miracle. If you tell someone they are a good writer, musician, artist, mother, nurse, worker, cook, etc. suddenly they are inspired to be the best they can possibly be in that particular area, and that energy spreads into other areas of their life.

You give someone a little spark of light and the Holy Spirit lights a bonfire.

ALL BECAUSE YOU LOOKED AT THEM AS IF THEY HAD GONE FAR BEYOND THEIR ACTUAL ACCOMPLISHMENTS IN TIME.

Try it.

You'll be amazed by what occurs when you see someone through the eyes of Christ. You see someone's perfection and before long, they are seeing it for themselves. Then suddenly, one unsuspecting day, you catch a glimpse of yourself and realize you have gone far beyond your own accomplishments in time. It's truly astonishing.

Here is a chapter on charity in the bible, Corinthians 13:

Though I speak with the tongues of men and of angels, and have not charity, I am become as sounding brass, or a tinkling cymbal.

And though I have the gift of prophecy, and understand all mysteries, and all knowledge; and though I have all faith, so that I could remove mountains, and have not charity, I am nothing.

And though I bestow all my goods to feed the poor, and though I give my body to be burned, and have not charity, it profiteth me nothing.

Charity suffereth long, and is kind; charity envieth not; charity vaunteth not itself, is not puffed up,

Doth not behave itself unseemly, seeketh not her own, is not easily provoked, thinketh no evil;

Rejoiceth not in iniquity, but rejoiceth in the truth;

Beareth all things, believeth all things, hopeth all things, endureth all things.

Charity never faileth: but whether there be prophecies, they shall fail; whether there be tongues, they shall cease; whether there be knowledge, it shall vanish away.

For we know in part, and we prophesy in part.

But when that which is perfect is come, then that which is in part shall be done away.

When I was a child, I spake as a child, I understood as a child, I thought as a child: but when I became a man, I put away childish things.

For now we see through a glass, darkly; but then face to face: now I know in part; but then shall I know even as also I am known.

And now abideth faith, hope, charity, these three; but the greatest of these is charity.

what is your mission statement?

It's always good to have the END GOAL in sight, and then the means will take care of itself. What is your goal? What is your mission? What is your purpose? What is your function?

It's really helpful to know the general direction you are heading in order to get to your final destination.

If you know that your final goal is happiness, you could just go there now. If you know that your final goal is to be at peace, to forgive, to love, to give, to have no problems, you could simply skip over a whole lot of drama and go directly to the prize.

My own function is: GORGEOUS FOR GOD.

The mission statement of Gorgeous for God is "to inspire and motivate individuals to be as God created them . . . perfect."

Laurie Beth Jones, author of *Jesus in Blue Jeans*, says that a good mission statement should be:

1. easy enough for a 5-year old to remember
2. can be recited at gunpoint.

Today I want you to think about your own mission statement. Write it down. Play around with a few ideas. Find what works for you and which describes perfectly your reason for being in the world. Find something that will make you leap out of bed in the morning with enthusiasm.

Have fun.

let me not forget my function

It's great to do a lesson every day, for the simple reminder it offers.

Today is Lesson 64: *Let me not forget my function.*

The purpose of the world you see is to obscure your function of forgiveness, providing you with a justification for forgetting it.

This is so true. Everything in the world makes you forget about God—until you begin practicing to remember Him in every situation, in every minute. Do you notice that? Do you notice that you usually forget about God until things start going wrong and you need help?

What is your function?

ANSWER: to be the light of the world.

It is a function given to you by God. It does not matter what happens to you during the day. It does not matter if things seem to be falling apart or if things seem to be going well. What the body's eyes look upon is false. It does not matter if what you see is "good" or "bad"—your function is to see beyond all of it, and shine bright.

The world is false. Do not try to fix it. It is what it is. Things happen. People do nasty things. There is war and deception and lies. Don't be bothered by any of it.

Remember: the world doesn't change, YOU CHANGE.

You change your perception and you will see the world differently. You see other people differently. It's quite simple. You will see what a game life is. You wake up in the morning with a purpose and a function. Life is not meant to be a struggle. God's Will for you is perfect happiness. You are not here to suffer.

So how is all this accomplished? SHINE BRIGHT. Give your light away, extend it, help someone, smile, laugh . . . and you will see your world change before your very eyes.

Every decision you make is one of isolation OR extension. There are no other choices to make. Either you are caving in on yourself or you are extending. There is no in-between. Every choice you make leads to happiness or unhappiness. Either you are mulling over your problems OR you are giving yourself away. Look at all your actions and you will see this is true. Either you are contained within yourself OR you are expanding out into the world and the universe. Try it. You'll see.

Do not be confused by this. It does not mean that you be an angel or a saint. It means that you are consciously aware of your thoughts, every moment of the day. It means that in your solitude you are quietly aware that you are being helpful to yourself and others. This is extension. It can take the form of helping others physically or it can take the form of helping others in thought. In extension, you always think good thoughts of other people and you want good things for them. You want everyone to be happy. This is extension.

Isolation is when you have shut the door and put up the walls around you. It is the place where you try to solve your problems all by yourself. It is the place where you weep in quiet desperation. It is the place where you think that other people are doing things to you, and "if only" THEY would change you would be happy. This is isolation. It is a place where you compare yourself to others.

Extension is a state of mind where you have an open-door-policy. Where the door is always open. Where you have placed yourself in a situation where people can find you if they need you. Your heart and mind are open. It is a place where if the phone rings or someone comes to you, your attention immediately goes there. This is what it means to let the day flow. You let everything be revealed to you.

In a place of extension, people know they can come to you even without you saying a single word. In extension, people are drawn toward you.

In *A Course in Miracles* Jesus talks about YOU being a safe haven, a place where the weary ones can come to rest, a garden in the desert. This is what extension means.

Have you ever seen individuals that have isolated themselves, even in an office of 100 people? You can spot these people immediately at a party. They send off a vibe that they do not want to be approached and they are not available. Isolation does not mean you go sit on a mountaintop all by yourself. It means you have erected a wall between you and other people.

So, let us not forget our function today. Our function is extension. Light extends. It cannot be contained. It goes out and shines away the darkness.

And how does it do this?

ANSWER: Simply by being itself.

Light doesn't do anything. Do you notice? It simply IS. Light shines, and everyone feels better. It warms and it makes happy.

TODAY'S ACTION: I WILL SHINE BRIGHT BECAUSE I AM THE LIGHT OF THE WORLD. LET ME NOT FORGET MY FUNCTION. LET ME FORGIVE AND BE HAPPY.

it's impossible to serve two masters

God, help me remember my ONE PURPOSE AND ONE GOAL—that I am here for the salvation of the world, to give of myself as You give, and to be truly helpful.

I understand why constant daily reminders are necessary because there is always a tendency to get sidetracked. It's easy to get distracted. Take it from me, I know. My mind is constantly wandering. That's not the problem. The question is: How long does it take me to realize my mind has wandered and how long till I get it back on track?

I pray for the release of MY plan and MY ideas and MY agenda. I don't know what anything is for and I don't know what is in my best interest. I pray that I remember my purpose for being here today and always. I pray that I be active in God's plan for salvation. I pray for my own peace and happiness, as well as for the world. I pray that I be helpful and useful. I place the past, present and future in the Hands of God. Whatever He wants me to do is what I want to do.

I let go of the outcome.

God, I am Yours.

Help me to remember I am under no laws but Yours. I'll go wherever You want me to go, and do whatever You want me to do. I'm happy to do whatever, go wherever, say what needs to be said.

Use me.

I am your faithful servant. It is impossible to serve two masters. Now I let all worldly laws go, and rest in you, Father. You are my Father and I am Your Son.

You, who read this, are the love of my life.

I am in love with you.

My brothers and sisters, peace and joy I offer you. That I may have God's peace and joy as mine.

My gratitude permits my love to be accepted without fear. And thus am I restored to my reality at last. All that intruded on my holy sight forgiveness takes away. And I draw near the end of senseless journeys, mad careers and artificial values. I accept instead what God establishes as mine, sure that in that alone I will be saved; sure that I go through fear to meet my Love.

You, who read this, are my counselor and savior. In you is God reflected and Christ looks back upon me from my Self.

You cannot even begin to imagine my gratitude for you. This day we enter into Paradise, acknowledging ourselves as One, united in the holy Love of God.

I love you.

shine on, bright thing

So, this is it. Today is the day. There is nothing to figure out. There is nothing to worry about. There is nothing to "get." There's nothing to understand. It's a brand new day. The past is gone. I love you.

YOU ARE THE LIGHT OF THE WORLD.

Who shines and shines forever, in every situation?

You do.

You are reading this book. Your time must be up. You must have asked for help. You must have prayed for something, because you are holding this book in your hand.

I'm so grateful we've come this far together.

We are standing at the edge of the world, with our feet barely touching the ground. And yet we are grateful to stay until every hand is united in love.

Ask yourself the question. Look around. Everyone is shrouded in various degrees of darkness. Just look around and be honest. Everyone's anxious about something. Or scared. Or anticipating. Or complaining. Or just merely existing. Everyone is rolling along or waiting for something to happen. I am simply asking you to LOOK around. Open your eyes. Observe.

What do you see?

Everyone just kind of going along in their routine, with some degree of misery or fear. Be honest. Do you know anyone who is happy all the time?

It is given to you TO BE THAT ONE.

The total savior in every situation. The brightest light in every room you walk in. The pure reflection of God on earth.

YOU.

There is no one to follow, so you can stop waiting for someone to show you how it's done. I am telling you how it's done. Be bright. Let go of everything. Be here only for today. Be helpful.

What have you got to lose? You've been waiting for something to happen, right? THIS IS THE MOMENT. This is the moment when everything starts to be drastically different for you, and the world. YOU BEGIN IT. Don't wait for someone else to take the first step, because everyone else is waiting for someone else to take the first step. It is up to YOU.

What does the sun do? It's all light. It shines and it shines forever. It doesn't analyze problems. It doesn't go dark. It doesn't change based on circumstances. It has one function: TO SHINE.

This is what you are. You are the light of the world.

The clouds may come, but the sun is still there, as bright as always: shining and shining forever. The clouds affect it not at all. The sun doesn't get angry at clouds and darkness. THE SUN DOESN'T EVEN KNOW OF CLOUDS AND DARKNESS. Think about it. It's just shining bright. Doing its thing. Being what it is.

You rise in the morning and you shine and shine forever. Just like the sun. It's very simple. It's not difficult. You become the thing you always were . . . LIGHT.

So, have fun. Nothing can affect you now.

our final happy game on earth

It is certain that as you change your mind your entire world will transform before your very eyes. This will simply be a nice idea in your head until you see it for yourself.

YOU MUST HAVE AN EXPERIENCE.

This is not a game of make-pretend. As you begin to practice these lessons in your daily life, things will change for you. I guarantee it. You will be able to do all that Jesus did . . . and more. But you must do what he asks of you.

The end of the Workbook says:

This course is a beginning, not an end. Your Friend goes with you. You are not alone. No one who calls on Him can call in vain. Whatever troubles you, be certain that He has the answer, and will gladly give it to you, if you simply turn to Him and ask it of Him. He will not withhold all answers that you need for anything that seems to trouble you. He knows the way to solve all problems, and resolve all doubts. His certainty is yours. You need but ask it of Him, and it will be given you.

Lesson 339 says, "*I will receive whatever I request.*"

This is a true statement. You will receive whatever you request.

If this is not your experience, then something has gone wrong ("if miracles are not occurring, then something has gone wrong") God wills you perfect happiness. He will that all your troubles and pains disappear. He wills you have everything you need in time.

I will receive whatever I request.

No one desires pain. But he can think that pain is pleasure. No one would avoid his happiness. Everyone will receive what he requests. But he can be confused indeed about the things he wants; the state he would attain. What can he then request that he would want when he receives it? He has asked for what will frighten him, and bring him suffering. Let us resolve today to ask for what we really want, and only this, that we may spend this day in fearlessness, without confusing pain with joy, or fear with love.

What are you asking for?

Let us resolve today to ask for what we really want, and only this, that we may spend this day in fearlessness, without confusing pain with joy, or fear with love.

What do you want?

You might ask for something in prayer, but maybe you are afraid to receive it. Maybe you want conflicting things? What do you really want? Try not to put spiritual overtones onto your answer. This is between you and God. Don't get all sophisticated or philosophical. Be a little child. Ask for what you want. Really look at it. Don't be afraid.

Come to a place of honesty.

You want to be happy. You want to be at peace. You want to feel safe and loved. Ask for everything. Jesus says, *"You do not ask for too much, you ask for far too little."* Ask for everything your heart desires.

Perfect peace that cannot be disturbed. Perfect health that cannot be altered. Perfect faith that moves mountains. Be a little kid. Jesus in *A Course in Miracles* says this is *"our final happy game on earth."*

Don't be concerned about anything. You are the light of the world. Healed and whole and perfect, shining in the reflection of God's Love. It's accomplished.

I am glad you found me.

If you don't already own *A Course in Miracles*, I highly recommend you buy it and begin practicing. If you already own the book, I say, look at it again.

Every day I find a new jewel in there. This is just beginning, and we have only scratched the tip of the iceberg. We haven't seen anything yet! The adventure is just getting started.

This is a day of special celebration.

Message from Jesus to you from *A Course in Miracles:*

And now in all your doings be you blessed.

God turns to you for help to save the world.

Teacher of God, His thanks He offers you,

And all the world stands silent in the grace

You bring from Him. You are the Son He loves,

And it is given you to be the means

Through which His Voice is heard around the world,

To close all things of time; to end the sight

Of all things visible; and to undo

All things that change. Through you is ushered in

A world unseen, unheard, yet truly there.

Holy are you, and in your light the world

Reflects your holiness, for you are not

Alone and friendless. I give thanks for you,

And join your efforts on behalf of God,

Knowing they are on my behalf as well,

And for all those who walk to God with me.

AMEN

Lightning Source UK Ltd.
Milton Keynes UK
UKOW04f0454040917
308512UK00001B/86/P